React to Python

Creating React Front-End Web Applications with Python

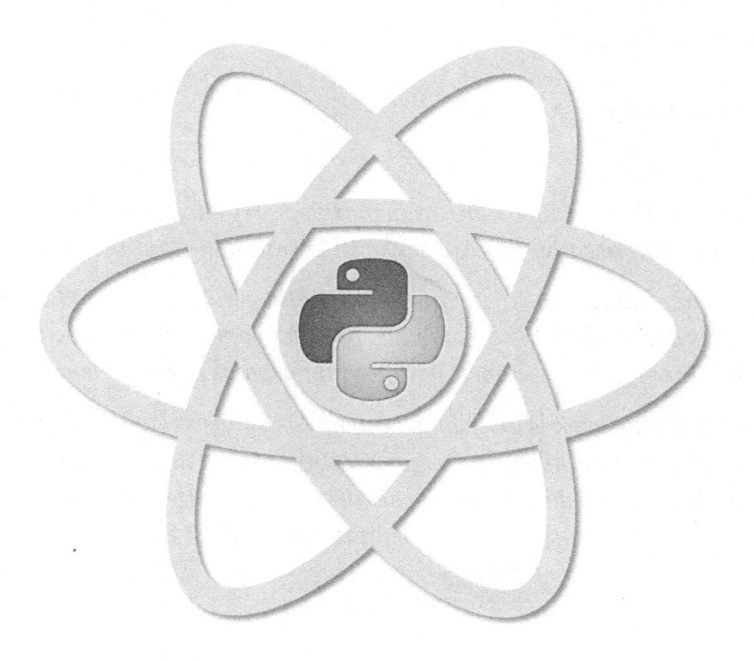

John Sheehan

JennaSys

React to Python
by John Sheehan

Copyright © 2021 by John Sheehan. All rights reserved.

No part of this work may be reproduced or transmitted in any form or by any means, electronic or mechanical, including photocopying, recording, or by any information storage or retrieval system, without the prior written permission of the copyright owner and the publisher.

Technical Reviewer: David Ford
Cover Design: Mike Lugin

May 2021: First Edition

"Python" and the Python logos are trademarks or registered trademarks of the Python Software Foundation, used by the Author with permission from the Foundation.

Trademarked names may appear in this book. Rather than use a trademark symbol with every occurrence of a trademarked name, we use the names only in an editorial fashion and to the benefit of the trademark owner, with no intention of infringement of the trademark.

The information in this book is distributed on an "as is" basis, without warranty. Although every precaution has been taken in the preparation of this work, neither the author(s) nor publisher shall have any liability to any person or entity with respect to any loss or damage caused or alleged to be caused directly or indirectly by the information contained in this work.

To report errors, please e-mail: rtp@jennasys.com

Source code used in this book is available to readers at:

- https://github.com/rtp-book/code
- https://github.com/rtp-book/project

For update notifications, subscribe at : https://pyreact.com

ISBN: 978-1-7365747-0-6
[1346348]

About the Author

John Sheehan graduated with a degree in Computer Science & Engineering from the University of Illinois at Chicago, and has been programming primarily with Python for over a decade. As a freelance software developer, they have developed custom business software for scores of companies throughout the United States. In their free time, John is an avid DIYer, electronics enthusiast, and musician. They are currently based in sunny Southern California, and are the meetup organizer for the local Python and Raspberry Pi user groups.

I would like to thank Dave for introducing me to React and consistently keeping me intellectually honest, and especially Rachel for always being there for me no matter what direction I was heading and for helping to keep me alive in general.

For my Dad, someone who was never afraid to think big.

1940 - 2020

Contents

About the Author	iii
Foreword	xi
Preface	xiv
Why write this book?	xiv
Why use Python for web apps?	xiv
About This Book	xvi
Who this book is for	xvi
What to expect	xvi
Basic requirements	xviii
Conventions used in this book	xviii
Source Code	xx

I Getting Started   1

1	Introduction	2
	1.1 Full-Stack Python	2
	1.2 Transcrypt	3
	1.3 React	4
	1.4 Node Package Manager	5
	1.5 Parcel	5
	1.6 Summary	5
2	First Application	7
	2.1 Transcrypt Installation	7
	2.2 Hello World	8
	2.3 Development Cycle	11
	2.4 Summary	12
3	JavaScript Functions	14
	3.1 Random Numbers	14

	3.2 Summary	16
4	Sourcemaps	18
	4.1 Function Mapping	18
	4.2 Debugging Console	19
	4.3 Summary	21
5	External JavaScript Libraries	22
	5.1 Working with jQuery	22
	5.2 Summary	24
6	Intro to React	26
	6.1 Hello React	26
	6.2 React State	29
	6.3 Summary	30
7	React Concepts	32
	7.1 Document Object Model	32
	7.2 Components and Elements	33
	7.3 Unidirectional Data Flow	34
	7.4 Hooks vs. Classes	35
	7.5 Summary	35
8	Cleaner Code	37
	8.1 Break It Up	37
	8.2 Summary	40
9	Managing JavaScript Packages	41
	9.1 npm	41
	9.2 Using Local JavaScript Libraries	43
	9.3 Summary	46
10	Package Bundler	48
	10.1 Parcel	48
	10.2 Simplified JavaScript Imports	50
	10.3 Build Scripts	54
	10.4 Summary	56
11	Section Summary	58

II	**Building Blocks**	**59**
12	Text Input	60
	12.1 Handling Input	60
	12.2 Generated Elements	65
	12.3 Summary	66

13	Lists		68
	13.1	HTML Lists	68
	13.2	List Component	71
	13.3	Summary	73
14	Forms		75
	14.1	Form Action	75
	14.2	Summary	77
15	React Components		78
	15.1	Adding Functionality	79
	15.2	Adding More Functionality	82
	15.3	Decomposition	86
	15.4	Summary	89
16	JavaScript Examples		91
	16.1	To-Do List	91
	16.2	Class Components to Functions	95
	16.3	Anonymous Functions	99
	16.4	Mapping Functions	99
	16.5	Ternary Statements	101
	16.6	Dictionaries	101
	16.7	Spread Operator	102
	16.8	JSX	103
	16.9	JavaScript Imports	106
	16.10	Using Images	108
	16.11	Putting it Together	108
	16.12	Summary	113
17	CSS		115
	17.1	Stylesheet	115
	17.2	Inline Styles	119
	17.3	Styled Components	122
	17.4	CSS Framework	124
	17.5	Summary	127
18	Material-UI		129
	18.1	Installing Material-UI	129
	18.2	Basic Usage	130
	18.3	Optimized Imports	133
	18.4	Theming	134
	18.5	Styled Components Revisited	140

	18.6 Summary	146
19	**Parcel Web Proxy**	148
	19.1 Flask Web Server	148
	19.2 Proxy Service	150
	19.3 Summary	153
20	**Asynchronous Requests**	155
	20.1 Synchronicity	155
	20.2 Async/Await	162
	20.3 Summary	164
21	**React Context Hook**	166
	21.1 Nested Components	166
	21.2 Context Variables	168
	21.3 Summary	172
22	**Transcrypt Miscellany**	173
	22.1 Standard Library	173
	22.2 Built-in Functions	174
	22.3 Keyword Args	174
	22.4 Immutability	175
	22.5 Truthiness	177
	22.6 Types	178
	22.7 Summary	178
23	**Application Versioning**	180
	23.1 NPM Version	180
	23.2 Application Version	181
	23.3 Summary	182
24	**Google Analytics**	184
	24.1 ReactGA	184
	24.2 Request Timing	189
	24.3 Summary	190
25	**Developer Tools**	192
	25.1 Bundle Visualizer	192
	25.2 React Chrome Extension	193
	25.3 GA Debug Chrome Extension	194
	25.4 Debug CSS Chrome Extension	195
	25.5 Summary	195
26	**Section Summary**	197

III Putting it all Together — 198

- 27 Project Outline 199
  - 27.1 Application Structure 200
  - 27.2 Folder Structure 200
- 28 Environment Setup 203
  - 28.1 Initial Setup 203
  - 28.2 Parcel Setup 205
  - 28.3 Application Entry Point 207
- 29 Landing Page 217
  - 29.1 Material-UI Theme 217
  - 29.2 Starting Point 221
  - 29.3 Versioning 222
- 30 Modal View 225
  - 30.1 Application Data 225
  - 30.2 Modality 226
  - 30.3 About Component 228
  - 30.4 About Link 230
- 31 REST Service 235
  - 31.1 The Database 235
  - 31.2 The REST Server 240
- 32 Books 252
  - 32.1 Proxy Server 252
  - 32.2 Updated Fetch 253
  - 32.3 Book List 255
  - 32.4 View Control 262
- 33 Menus 268
  - 33.1 Landing Page Revisited 268
  - 33.2 View Routing 273
- 34 User Login 277
  - 34.1 Snackbar 277
  - 34.2 Session User 278
  - 34.3 Login Modal 281
  - 34.4 Login Functionality 283
- 35 Lookups 292
  - 35.1 Container View 292
  - 35.2 Table List 294
  - 35.3 Menu Control 297

36	User Context		304
	36.1	Context Definition	304
	36.2	Using the Context	306
37	Editing Lookups		309
	37.1	Saving Data	309
	37.2	Editing Items	312
	37.3	Menu Control	318
38	Filtering Data		321
	38.1	Filter Form	321
	38.2	Lookup Data	325
39	Editing Books		330
	39.1	View Container	330
	39.2	Select Lists	334
	39.3	Data Entry	337
	39.4	Edit Control	343
40	SPA Redirect		351
	40.1	Redirect Functionality	351
	40.2	Page Routing	356
	40.3	Redirecting Pages	359
41	Deploying the Application		373
	41.1	Web Server	374
	41.2	WSGI Container	374
	41.3	Gunicorn	375
	41.4	NGINX	376
	41.5	Flask for Static Content	379
	41.6	Security	381
42	Conclusion		384

Foreword

Some time ago I made a walk, together with a colleague, in one of the rare patches of nature in the vicinity of Rotterdam, the Netherlands. In order to reach the nice and quiet parts, we had to cross a large road construction project, connecting two main highways in order to lessen the traffic through the city. As we stood on the high pedestrian-bridge, I was struck by the professionality and the amount of planning that was demonstrated below me. People moving like ants in parade, machines like large bugs, each seemingly knowing exactly where to go, what to do and when. A best practice for everything. Safety procedures. Second sourcing of materials. Well tested long term behaviour of constructions. Appropriate and well kept tools and machines. Of course, sometimes roads get washed away. But road construction is rarely abandoned after threefold overruns in budget and planning. Whereas for software... Well, that's normal, isn't it. Whether you look at space travel, air transportation or car electronics, software is the Achilles heel. Still.

While the infrastructure supporting the web world features a lot of redundancy by virtue of its distributed nature, this doesn't hold for the software that pumps data through its veins. Under a cloak of ever changing IT-slang, referring to ever changing silver bullets, there's a patchwork of organically grown "technologies", a euphemism for ad-hoc approaches to challenges that are bound to arise if a solution to a very particular problem is pushed far beyond its limits, rather than rethought from scratch. Datastreams coded in ASCII rather than binary, requiring five times more bandwidth than physics dictates, sandboxed interpreters that try to cover up for security challenged operating systems well in their sixties, relational databases serving bulk numerical data from power-hungry server farms, languages designed to add some motion to static webpages, but now used for neural nets and handling big data. And then the XMLHttpRequest, the cat flap through which massive streams of largely redundant data try to convince consumers that they need a new mobile phone since the old one gets so slow. And of course 4GL, or 5GL.

In such a situation of organic growth, a primitive law drives progress: Survival of the fittest. For every JavaScript library that's still alive after three years, at least a handful have been abandoned, leaving a trace of unmaintainable applications. Web development is the art of finding the winners. And wherever I look, one winner seems clear. If one of my students has to do a front end job at some company for her graduation, I routinely ask: React? And of late the answer is: Yes. Without exception. The React paradigm works. Once you master it. Out of many possible choices, React seems to have hit a sweet spot. With its declarative approach to data dependencies and DOM-tree updates it really takes a burden off the shoulders of the developer: How to create a GUI that's truly responsive, not in the superficial sense of adapting it's layout to things like screen size and orientation, but in adapting its contents in response to user actions and data dependencies. It makes a GUI behave intelligently, without the vulnerable micro-management coming with purely imperative coding.

React will probably be with us for quite some time, and that's good. But the same holds for the underlying language, and here tastes differ. Nothing wrong with that, some like ice-creams and others like fruit. But, no matter what your preferences are, languages matter! I've never heard a carpenter argue that her tools are unimportant. But it's quite normal to hear a self-nominated IT expert claim that programming languages don't matter. Developers making such a claim should be convicted to programming in assembly for the rest of their career. With web assembly they might. Unfortunately the browser world doesn't offer much choice. Nothing bad about JavaScript. If you grew up with front end development, it's probably your first language and therefore your frame of reference. Mine was Basic. It was the perfect language, I could do anything in it, using only goto's. Until I discovered Pascal. And then C. And then C++. And then: Python.

Python is growing. The push comes from the world of application scripting, simulation, industrial controls, big data and neural nets. That's also the world I come from. And when I had to develop an occasional (unavoidable) front-end I did so in JavaScript. But we didn't match. And writing 80% of my application in Python and 20% in JavaScript led to an inversion of Pareto's rule: 20% of the result cost me 80% of the effort. That was when Transcrypt was born. I tried out some existing alternatives, but performance was a problem in the computationally heavy applications (even in the front-end) I had to deal with. So I did what I liked to do as a student. I wrote a compiler. As the GitHub repo was public, it drew some attention. And cooperation. That's where it started. But the browser world kept changing rapidly. There were bundlers, npm and: React.

I could not have written the book that lies in front of you. But I am glad that it WAS written. John Sheehan is standing firmly on two legs, one in the front-end world and the other in the Python world. And he has a gift to explain things clearly. This book will teach you a lot. For starters it is THE most clear explanation of the principles behind React I've ever seen. The first few chapters finally got me up

React to Python

Learning Curve Hill. But there's more. Taking the clean function oriented interface of React as a starting point, he takes you on a pure Python trip. Rather than explaining Python code in terms of JavaScript equivalents he introduces Python as the natural way to code React applications, and never looks back.

After explaining the basics the terrain is further prepared for construction by introducing an expandable set of best practices. Code that directly depends on React idiosyncrasies is encapsulated in a small interface module, growing with needs. All other modules are pure Python and indeed, Pythonic: highly readable and concise. With this, the book offers a view in the "divide and conquer" strategies of an experienced developer.

Finally a convincing right-sized example of a single page web application is built. This is where it all comes together. The code is clean, modular and readable. This is how you write applications that you dare to meet again for maintenance after five years. Code that lets you sleep well at night.

So what's the general nature of the landscape beyond Learning Curve Hill? Well, it looks good to me! If the front end of your application isn't WYSIAYG (What You See Is All You Get) but needs to have significant algorithmic and data processing functionality due to scalability considerations, you may find yourself in a good place. A function-oriented GUI, connected seamlessly to a truly object-oriented engine, matching the structure of the application domain, offers scalability and maintainability that until now was reserved for back ends only. Python can do that for you. On the client. With load balancing and code reuse between client and server. The proof of the pudding is the eating. Python wasn't my first language. React wasn't my first GUI library. But the combination has made development of complex, maintainable front ends doable. Not that it makes development easy. But it puts me in control of the process. And that makes ME sleep well...

Jacques de Hooge
Creator of Transcrypt

Preface

Why write this book?

For myself, learning the approach to front-end web development that is presented here was transformative. Prior to this, I had avoided diving too deep into front-end web development in general, because web development frameworks seemed to always be in a state of flux. And the ones that had been evolving over the last few decades always seemed somewhat cumbersome to use, added to the fact that I'd have to use a programming language other than Python on top of it. When I was first introduced to React, I was intrigued because it appeared to be a new way to look at web development that didn't seem to be as tedious to use as other frameworks I'd looked into. But that didn't really do me much good because it *still* required me to commit to the whole JavaScript ecosystem. Then I found Transcrypt. A transpiler that converts your Python code into JavaScript and allows you to make direct calls to JavaScript libraries from Python. And it turns out it works really well with React!

For me, the ability to iteratively build up a web application in an elegant way without ever leaving Python, still to this day feels magical and fun*. It is for this reason I wanted to write this book and share my approach with other Python developers.

CSS layout issues excepted

Why use Python for web apps?

I have on occasion observed that software developers tend to have rather strong opinions about the programming languages they use, and frequently even stronger opinions about the languages they *don't* use. Debates about a particular language's characteristics will live on for as long as there are still software developers coding. And the arguments that ensue will likely continue to end up never actually resolving anything. That said, I *really* enjoy programming with Python. It fits my style, the way I think, I appreciate its versatility, and I like the Python community. I am also of the opinion that curly braces and semicolons are syntactic code cruft, but I digress.

React to Python

One of my main annoyances when programming is to have to mentally switch languages when working on a project. Switching from Python to JavaScript and back again when going from back-end code to front-end code is not a smooth process for me, and tends to give me mental whiplash. It's like I have to reboot my brain into a different operating system every time I make the switch, and it disrupts whatever programming flow I might have had going on. So I went in search of a way to always keep my brain in Python mode when working on a full-stack web project, while minimizing the complexity required in the typical web development toolchain. As a side benefit, using the same language for the back-end and front-end code also opens up opportunities for code reuse.

The result of what I ended up with is what you'll see presented here. While perhaps a bit unorthodox by today's standards, this approach goes beyond just a "because I can" type of exercise. I feel it is a viable and practical option for Python developers to create professional, functional, and beautiful web applications - in Python.

About This Book

Who this book is for

This is, first and foremost, a Python book. While the focus is on front-end web development, the goal here is to do almost all of the coding in Python. To be blunt, this book is primarily intended for Python developers that don't particularly care to write JavaScript code but still want to develop modern front-end web applications.

Note that this book is decidedly NOT an introduction to Python and does assume a fundamental understanding of the Python language by the reader. Additionally, it is not an introduction to web development in general. Basic knowledge of HTML and CSS syntax and function, and perhaps being able to read at least a little bit of plain vanilla JavaScript, is highly recommended.

On the other hand, as the title of the book suggests, the React.js library is the basis for the approach used in this book for developing front-end web applications. While a working knowledge of React would be helpful in understanding some of the concepts presented here, it is not required.

What to expect

What follows is an opinionated guide on one way to approach using Python for creating an application that runs in a web browser. While there are several libraries and frameworks currently available to accomplish this task (Brython, Skulpt, Batavia, Pyodide, etc.), the method outlined in this book uses the Transcrypt transpiler. Via a compilation step, Transcrypt will convert your Python code into JavaScript so that it can be run directly in a web browser, with little if any performance degradation compared to writing native JavaScript.

Because there are many language differences between Python and JavaScript, we will walk you through the fundamental concepts of React, but using the terminology and from the vantage point of a Python developer. At the same time, while this book will give you enough fundamental knowledge of React to create functional and responsive React-based web applications, it is not intended to be a complete and definitive reference for the React library itself.

React to Python

While this book will recommend several software applications related to the development toolchain, it will not go into too much depth on how to install those applications onto your machine. Given the number of variations on each of the popular operating system platforms, it doesn't make sense to fill pages and pages of the book with installation details that wouldn't even apply to most readers. Where appropriate, reference links will be provided for installation information about specific software applications.

The book is broken up into three parts. The first gets the developer environment set up, guides you through the basic concepts, and gives you an idea of how things fit together. Part two then gives you examples of how to accomplish specific tasks and utilize various JavaScript libraries from your Python code. In these first two sections, there will be several small and mostly contrived standalone code examples to illustrate specific points. The last part of the book will walk you through building up a functional sample web application from scratch using the concepts you learned in the previous sections.

In the first half of the book, we primarily focus on functionality and not so much on how things look. As such, we'll avoid getting into CSS layout and making things look nice until the second half. The first half of the book will also have many detailed explanations of every aspect of the code examples. As we get deeper into the book, it will focus more on just the relevant parts of the code as related to the current context.

While many of the code examples in the book seem repetitive, it was done purposely to offer a context to compare different ways of doing things, and to present new concepts within the context of what has already been covered. The third part of the book will make up for some of that repetition with all new code.

I would recommend reading the book in its entirety from start to finish (of course). However, if you are already pretty familiar with typical web development workflows, I would still definitely go through the part of the first section that deals with using Transcrypt. Likewise, if you are already familiar with HTML, you might be able to just skim through the first few chapters of the second section.

This book is intended to be more of a tutorial than a reference, but at the same time offering you code examples to accomplish specific tasks. Later on, if you need to figure out how to implement a certain feature, you can jump right to that section of the book and use the provided example as a point of reference to integrate that feature into your own code. We cover a lot of ground in this book, and while it is a blueprint for developing front-end web applications with Python, it is also intended to be a solid starting point that you can then expand on wherever you need to.

Basic requirements

Since this is 2021, it is assumed that you will be using Python version 3.6 or higher. What is presented in this book will likely not work at all with Python 2, and you may run into incompatibilities with Python 3.5 and older. Also, as there may still be some incompatibilities with Transcrypt when using Python version 3.8 and the recently released version 3.9, I recommend sticking with Python 3.7 on these projects for now. It is also highly recommended that you work from within a Python virtual environment for all exercises.

This book makes no assumptions about the code editor you use, and tries to keep the techniques used here as IDE agnostic as possible. That said, using an IDE like PyCharm or VS Code is highly recommended, especially as your web applications become more complex.

The applications developed using the approach presented here will require an ECMAScript 6 capable web browser to be used. This covers pretty much all current versions of the common web browsers, with the exception of Internet Explorer 11, which does not support ES6. If you do need to support IE11, there are ways to do it, but those techniques will not be covered here.

Conventions used in this book

Anything that is referencing a snippet of code or that is meant to be typed as a command will use a `monospaced font`. Any commands that need to be entered in a terminal window (usually with your virtual environment active!) will be preceded with a $. On the other hand, if it is preceded with a >>> if it should be entered at a Python prompt.

File names will be indicated in **bold font** unless they link to source code.

Code listings that are associated with a file name represent a code module that you should create unless otherwise indicated. A link to an online source code repository for these code listings will be provided at the end of each chapter. Single line snippets of code in the book's body text are usually just there to help with the explanations and don't need to be typed in.

Variable and function naming can be a subjective issue, and what I have adopted for these types of Python projects does deviate from the Python style guide somewhat.

For most function names, I use *camelCase* unless it is a React functional component, in which case I will use *PascalCase*. The reason for this is that React expects component names to start with a capital letter and complains when it isn't. Function names are primarily used in a declarative way with React, and can be thought of like a class even though they are being created as Python functions. For state and property variable names, I will use *camelCase* there as well.

For local variables, I stick with using Python style *snake_case*. This is done to help visually identify variables that are not part of the React state, and to also set them apart from function names.

For string identifiers, I will usually use single quotes because I feel it is less visual clutter in the code. However, for strings that get displayed to the user or for strings used in a data context, double quotes will be used to visually set them apart.

Note that if you see "..." in code examples, that means that some code was left out, but is unchanged from a previous example. This was done so as not to take up excess pages in the book unnecessarily. You will see this more in Part 3 of the book when we are working with longer code modules that get refactored as we progress with adding features to the project. Full code listings are available in the online source code repository.

As far as the overall coding style goes, I try to keep it in the spirit of React design patterns when structuring code, while still keeping the code itself Pythonic. And when I say Pythonic, I don't mean it in a pedantic sense. I look at being Pythonic as more of a stylistic goal and not necessarily an inviolable statute of the language. I mean come on, this isn't Java after all. /s

At the end of each chapter, a summary of the steps taken in that chapter will be provided as a chapter review, and links to chapter code or other information relevant to the chapter will be provided as a list of references.

Source Code

The source code from this book is broken up into two separate code repositories and can be found on GitHub. For the chapters in the first and second sections of the book, the source code is located at:

https://github.com/rtp-book/code

You can clone it to your local PC using:

```
$ git clone https://github.com/rtp-book/code.git
```

The source code for the project in the third section of the book is located at:

https://github.com/rtp-book/project

The project repository can be cloned to your local PC using:

```
$ git clone https://github.com/rtp-book/project.git
```

Note that each chapter of the project has a dedicated repository branch. Use `git checkout` to get the code that represents the current state of the project at the end of a given chapter. For example, to see the state of the project code at the end of the chapter on *User Context*, you can use the following git command:

```
$ git checkout step09
```

To get back to the code for the finished project, use the git command:

```
$ git checkout main
```

References:

- Python
  https://www.python.org/downloads/

- Transcrypt Homepage
  https://www.transcrypt.org

- PyCharm Python IDE
  https://www.jetbrains.com/pycharm/

- Python Extension for VS Code
  https://code.visualstudio.com/docs/languages/python

- ECMAScript 6
  http://www.ecma-international.org/ecma-262/6.0/

- PEP 8 -- Style Guide for Python Code
  https://www.python.org/dev/peps/pep-0008/

– Part I –

Getting Started

This section will provide an overview of the developer tools used in the approach that we will be taking in this book for developing modern front-end web applications using Python. It focuses on getting those tools set up, and discusses some of the reasons we would want to use those particular tools for our development toolchain and how they work. Throughout this section, there will be several examples to help visualize the basic use of those tools.

Chapter 1 – Introduction

There are, and have been, many attempts to shoehorn Python into the web browser over the past decade. Some of those solutions may be useful in very limited cases, but most are not practical in a more general sense.

Some of those tools compile Python to JavaScript so the code can be run directly in a web browser, and others have a way to actually interpret Python code in the web browser itself. At the same time, those tools will either be able to process the Python code on the fly, or they will require the Python code to be pre-processed in some manner. What we will be using here, is one that converts your Python code to JavaScript in a pre-processing step.

For any Python developer who has wanted to do front-end web development without spending most of their time programming in JavaScript or TypeScript, what follows here may be what you have been looking for.

1.1 Full-Stack Python

Obviously, the back-end server code could always be Python running, say a Flask REST API or a Django application. So what we are going to focus mostly on in this book is using Python for creating a front-end web UI. For context, this is what a full-stack toolchain might look like:

- **Python** (because Python, of course)
- **Transcrypt** (for transpiling Python to JavaScript)
- **React** (for building functional reactive front-end web applications)
- **Material-UI** (for theming and stylized React components)
- **npm** (for managing JavaScript libraries)
- **Parcel** (for build automation and bundling)
- **Flask / Gunicorn / Nginx** (for serving up the application in production)

As much as I originally wished to avoid the complexities of the typical JavaScript web development ecosystem that all web developers seem to be saddled with, it wasn't completely avoidable. That said, what we need to utilize here isn't too bad compared to what most JavaScript developers deal with.

1.2 Transcrypt

At the heart of the toolchain that allows the magic to happen is Transcrypt, a pip installed Python-to-JavaScript transpiler. Simply put, it takes Python code that you write, and converts that Python code into a JavaScript file. That file can then be loaded into a web browser and the code run, without any kind of browser plug-in or large JavaScript runtime download required. And because the code is pre-compiled into JavaScript before it is downloaded to the browser, application performance is not compromised.

Transcrypt does include a small (~42kb) runtime module that gets served up to the web browser along with your transpiled code and any other JavaScript libraries that you may end up using. In development mode, your original Python source files along with a source map can be made available in the browser for debugging purposes. However, in production mode, only minified JavaScript is served up to the web browser.

The key to using Transcrypt successfully is understanding that it is primarily intended to allow your Python code to utilize existing JavaScript libraries and frameworks like jQuery, React, Material-UI, and others. Put another way, it is not intended to *replace* existing popular JavaScript libraries, but to instead make them directly callable from your Python code. It acts as a bridge between the Python and JavaScript worlds, keeping a foot on both sides. Be aware that you still need to understand *how* the JavaScript libraries are used, but you don't have to code in JavaScript to use them. It doesn't allow you to ignore web development paradigms in general, but you do get to code using the Python constructs and syntax that you know and love.

That said, it does only work with pure Python code, and most third-party pip installed libraries that have dependencies on C modules will not work with it. In practice, this tends not to be too much of an issue as you end up using JavaScript libraries that are designed to run in a web browser instead.

One important requirement I had in using something like Transcrypt, was that it couldn't get in the way of development. In other words, the solution shouldn't be worse than the problem. If using Transcrypt was more of a hassle than switching back and forth from Python to JavaScript, then it wouldn't be worth using.

Another criteria I had was that the resulting Python code had to be Pythonic. I saw no benefit in writing Python code that ended up looking like JavaScript anyway, or that had other languages interspersed throughout the code. The Python linter had to be happy, and I am a believer that readability counts.

Lastly, the end result had to be reliable. I didn't want to be continually troubleshooting transpiler anomalies or inconsistencies in how it needed to be utilized. This kind of gets back to the first point in that I didn't want the toolchain to get in the way of developing the application itself.

Transcrypt passes all of these tests and allows you to develop functional reactive web application UIs with Python. And you don't have to switch your brain to think in JavaScript. You can code a web UI while staying in your Python happy place the entire time.

1.3 React

There are several front-end web frameworks and libraries that currently dominate the web development landscape. Vue, Angular, Ember, and React are a few of the more popular ones. React uses a component-based architecture and can quickly and efficiently update the UI elements in the web browser as the state of an application changes. It has just a handful of core concepts that need to be learned in order for it to be utilized. While other frameworks can also take advantage of the transpiling capability of Transcrypt, React is the one we will be focused on for this book.

Because React.js is a JavaScript library, Transcrypt by design will allow us to use that library and make calls to it directly from our Python code. From a Python standpoint, if you are used to using a procedural or object-oriented programming style, you will have to shift gears slightly as React does employ paradigms best served by a more functional programming style.

Note that in addition to React being an excellent choice for interactive client-side web applications, it can also be used for static web sites that utilize server-side rendering, and be used in place of a templating framework like Jinja. But what we are focusing on in this book are indeed interactive web applications that benefit greatly from the client-rendered component model that React utilizes.

One important note about how we will be using React, is that we will apply the current best practice of utilizing functional components. React class-based components, on the other hand, will NOT be covered here. While it is certainly possible to use React class-based components with Python, function-based components arguably offer a cleaner and more consistent interface and is what we will be building on.

1.4 Node Package Manager

While you can include remotely hosted JavaScript libraries like React right in your HTML file as a script module, as your application grows this method becomes inefficient and unwieldy. To deal with this issue, you will have to resort to more conventional JavaScript package management and build tools. Npm is one of the de facto package management tools for web development, and is fortunately very similar to, and is as easy to use as, Python's pip.

1.5 Parcel

A web application bundler is a tool that takes all of the JavaScript code that your application requires and packages it up into optimized and more easily downloaded files. Parcel is a web application bundler that advertises "zero" configuration and uses a much simpler approach than the more popular Webpack bundler. While Parcel may not be the perfectly clean solution that most Python developers would want, it is still better than what Webpack requires, and is likely the bundler that many Python developers would be more comfortable with. From my own experience, Parcel was actually pretty easy to get set up, and using it is a breeze.

1.6 Summary

While there are many ways to create a web application, few let you utilize Python for the front-end portion. By way of the Transcrypt transpiler, we can utilize rich JavaScript frameworks and libraries like React to create functional reactive modern web applications using Python instead of JavaScript.

References:

- Transcrypt Homepage
  https://www.transcrypt.org
- The Zen of Python
  https://en.wikipedia.org/wiki/Zen_of_Python

- React.js
  https://reactjs.org
- npm
  https://docs.npmjs.com/about-npm
- Parcel
  https://parceljs.org

Chapter 2 – First Application

Before we get too far ahead of ourselves with the details of a full-stack installation, let's start small with a traditional *Hello World* demo.

2.1 Transcrypt Installation

An important note before getting started... As of this writing, Transcrypt will only work with Python 3.6 or 3.7. There are some differences in the syntax tree of Python 3.8 that currently make it incompatible with Transcrypt. Check the Transcrypt GitHub repository for any updates concerning this issue.

It is highly recommended that you use a virtual environment whenever you start a new project. Create a folder for working in, then using a terminal window in your project folder, just run:

```
$ python -m venv venv
```

If your computer has multiple versions of Python installed, you may have to be specific about which Python version you use to create the virtual environment. This can be done either by specifying a full path to the executable, or by using an appropriate symbolic link or shortcut like `python3` or `python3.7` (or `py -3.7` on Windows) instead of just `python`.

Then to activate the virtual environment use the appropriate command for your operating system:

For Windows:
```
C:\> venv\Scripts\activate
```

For Mac or Linux
```
$ source venv/bin/activate
```

You should then see the name of the virtual environment, in this case (venv), appear in front of the command prompt in the terminal window. To exit the virtual environment when you are in it, just use the `deactivate` command.

Since Transcrypt is a Python application, we can install it while in your virtual environment from the pip repository with:

```
(venv) $ pip install transcrypt
```

2.2 Hello World

To use Transcrypt, you first need to have a Python file to transpile into JavaScript. You also need to have an HTML file that references the generated JavaScript file, which will eventually be opened in a web browser. For our *Hello World* application, we'll use the following two files:

Listing 2-1 File: *hello.py*

```python
def say_hello():
    document.getElementById('destination').innerHTML = "Hello World!"

def clear_it():
    document.getElementById('destination').innerHTML = ""
```

Listing 2-2 File: *hello.html*

```html
<!DOCTYPE html>
<html lang="en">
    <body>
        <script type="module">
            import * as hello from './__target__/hello.js';
            window.hello = hello;
        </script>
        <button type="button" onclick="hello.say_hello()">Click Me!</button>
        <button type="button" onclick="hello.clear_it()">Clear</button>
        <div id="destination"></div>
    </body>
</html>
```

To transpile your Python code into JavaScript, we need to run the `transcrypt` command, passing in the name of the Python file to process as a command-line argument to it. So in a terminal window with your virtual environment activated, use the following command to generate a JavaScript file from your Python code:

(venv) $ `transcrypt hello`

That will process the **hello.py** file and generate a folder named __target__ in your project folder. In that folder, you should find the following generated files:

- **hello.js** (JavaScript generated from your Python file)
- **hello.project** (Transcrypt compiler settings)

- **org.transcrypt.__runtime__.js** (The Transcrypt JS runtime library)

If you are on Windows and get an error during the generation of the minified target code like this:

[WinError 2] The system cannot find the file specified

it probably means that you don't have Java installed, which Transcrypt uses for the JavaScript minification process. If so, you can either install the Java Runtime Environment or tell Transcrypt not to minify the output by adding the --nomin option:

(venv) $ transcrypt --nomin hello

In order to properly serve up these newly generated files to your web browser, we will need to use a web server. For now, we can just use the one that Python has built-in. From your project folder in a terminal window, enter:

(venv) $ python -m http.server

This will start up a development web server that will serve up any files in your project folder on port 8000 of your computer. So if you open your web browser and go to:

http://localhost:8000/hello.html

or

http://127.0.0.1:8000/hello.html

You should see the two buttons rendered from the **hello.html** file. Clicking one will display the text, and clicking the other will clear the text. Try it out!

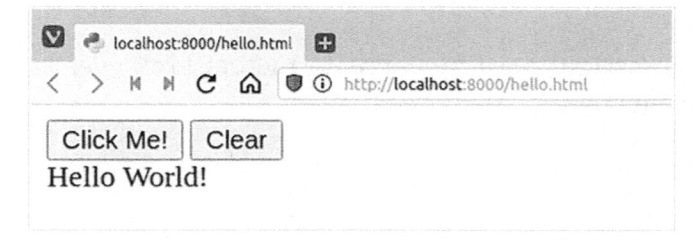

To stop the Python HTTP server, just use *Ctrl-C* in the terminal window to terminate the command.

So let's break down what we just did, starting with the Python file. Our Python module contains two Python function definitions. Both Python functions call methods of the built-in JavaScript document object that allow us to find and manipulate the contents of the DOM (Document Object Model), which is what holds all of the HTML elements in your web page.

Two things should stick out here. The first is that we are calling a method of a *JavaScript* object directly from Python! The second is that we are using *Python* syntax and not JavaScript to do so. Not a curly brace or semicolon in sight! When Transcrypt does its thing, it is able to recognize JavaScript keywords and handles the expression appropriately. The only issue you might run into is with the Python linter, since the keyword document has not been defined in the Python global or local scope, and Python doesn't know what to do with it. Fortunately, Transcrypt gives us a way to quiet the linter in that case, and we'll explore how to do that later on.

Moving on to the HTML file, beyond the standard HTML boilerplate, we are doing two things: pulling our Transcrypt generated function module into the JavaScript namespace, and then calling the functions within that module.

In the `<script>` tag, we tell the web browser where to physically get our function module, and then give it an alias to refer to it as:

```
import * as hello from './__target__/hello.js';
```

Note that we are importing the generated *JavaScript* file and not our original Python file. To make the functions easier to call later on, we then give them a reference in the global `window` namespace:

```
window.hello = hello;
```

After that, we can assign those functions to the `onClick` event attribute of the HTML button elements:

```
onclick="hello.say_hello()"
onclick="hello.clear_it()"
```

One last thing: while it is certainly possible to design your Python modules so that they can be run with the CPython interpreter (the one installed on your computer), in many cases this will not be possible since a lot of your code will actually be making references to JavaScript libraries. If you have an explicit need to run the same Python code both server-side and client-side (after being transpiled), then it is definitely worth the extra effort to design it for that purpose. But if the code is only intended to be transpiled and run in a web browser, don't worry too much about being able to run it on your desktop as well. It will only add unnecessary complications to your code.

2.3 Development Cycle

One thing you will notice as you go through this book is that we never actually run our Python code. *Wait, what?!!* You heard me right. We never actually run the Python code we write in the Python interpreter. It gets transpiled into JavaScript, and *that* is what ultimately runs in the web browser. In fact, since we will be utilizing several JavaScript libraries directly, as mentioned above, our Python code *can't* run using the Python interpreter even if we wanted to since we are making calls to JavaScript functions.

The development cycle we will use generally looks like this:

- Write Python code
- Transpile Python code into JavaScript with Transcrypt
- Run the application in a web browser using the generated JavaScript code
- Test our application in the web browser
- Go back to the Python code and make updates
- Repeat as needed

One tip you may want to use during development, is that it is useful to keep a developer console window open in the web browser whenever you are testing your application. This will allow you to see any unexpected errors and allow you to view the output from your `console` or `print` statements as they happen when you run your application.

What we get out of this workflow is the ability to write code in our favorite programming language. And if we are using a modern IDE, we still get things like code completion, syntax highlighting, and other niceties. While these workflow steps might be a bit more than you are used to when developing with Python, such is the nature of web development itself.

2.4 Summary

What we just did demonstrates the basics of using Transcrypt to generate JavaScript from our Python code, which can then be utilized directly in a web browser. We also saw how we can use JavaScript objects right from our Python code, as well as reference the Transcrypt generated JavaScript objects from an HTML file.

Chapter Review:

1. Make sure Python 3.7 is installed
   https://www.python.org/downloads/release/python-379/

2. Create a Python virtual environment:
   `python -m venv venv`

3. Activate the virtual environment
   `venv\Scripts\activate` (Windows)
   `source venv/bin/activate` (Mac/Linux)

4. Install Transcrypt:
   `pip install transcrypt`

5. Create source files:
   hello.py
   hello.html

6. Transpile source files:
   `transcrypt hello`

7. Run the Python development web server:
   `python -m http.server`

8. Open the application:
   http://localhost:8000/hello.html

References:

- Chapter code
  https://github.com/rtp-book/code/tree/main/ch02

- Transcrypt github repository
  https://github.com/QQuick/Transcrypt
- Java
  https://java.com/en/download/
- Transcrypt on PyPI
  https://pypi.org/project/Transcrypt/

Chapter 3 – JavaScript Functions

At its most basic purpose, Transcrypt allows Python code to call JavaScript functions, and enables JavaScript functions to call Python functions. Let's look at an example that explicitly does both.

3.1 Random Numbers

This simple example is similar to the previous *Hello World* we did:

Listing 3-1 File: *js_function.py*

```python
def get_number():
    new_val = int(window.Math.random() * 10)
    document.getElementById('myval').innerHTML = new_val
```

Listing 3-2 File: *js_function.html*

```html
<!DOCTYPE html>
<html lang="en">
    <body>
        <script type="module">
            import * as getnum from './__target__/js_function.js';
            window.getnum = getnum;
        </script>
        <button type="button" onclick="getnum.get_number()">Click Me!</button>
        <div id="myval">?</div>
    </body>
</html>
```

As before, in a terminal window with your virtual environment activated, use the following command to generate a JavaScript file from your Python code. But this time, let's transpile the Python code with a few options:

(venv) $ `transcrypt --nomin --map js_function`

The options in the Transcrypt command did a few things for us. First, the `--nomin` option causes the resulting JavaScript file to not be minified. This makes it a little easier to see how Transcrypt converts your Python code into JavaScript. The `--map` option causes a sourcemap file to be generated that gets served up to the web browser along with the generated JavaScript file, which can help us with debugging our original Python code right in the browser. Then of course, we specify the entry point to our python code with js_function. So with these command-line options set, we now get several more generated files in our __target__ folder:

- **js_function.js** (JavaScript generated from your Python file)
- **js_function.map** (sourcemap)
- **js_function.project** (Transcrypt compiler settings)
- **js_function.py** (Original Python file)
- **org.transcrypt.runtime.js** (The Transcrypt JS runtime library)
- **org.transcrypt.runtime.map** (sourcemap)
- **org.transcrypt.runtime.py** (The Transcrypt Python runtime)

If it isn't still running, from your project folder, start up the development web server again with:

(venv) $ python -m http.server

Then open the **js_function.html** document with:

http://localhost:8000/js_function.html

Each click of the button should give you a new random number from 0 to 9. While very similar to the previous example, this also demonstrates how we can utilize built-in JavaScript functions from Python:

```
new_val = int(window.Math.random() * 10)
```

As with the JavaScript document object, Python is not aware of the JavaScript window object either. Once again however, Transcrypt is able to provide the correct bridge during the transpilation process in order for us to take advantage of those objects. At the same time, it also modifies the syntax of our code to be valid

JavaScript. For example, compare the line above to what is generated in the **js_function.js** file in the __target__ folder:

```
var new_val = int (window.Math.random () * 10);
```

The differences are subtle but necessary modifications for our code to work properly in a web browser.

One of the limitations you may find with Transcrypt is that there are only a few specific external libraries that have been ported to JavaScript (NumPy in particular), and many of Python's standard libraries are not yet available. While this may seem to be problematic at first, in practice, it is usually just a minor inconvenience since we have full access to equivalent JavaScript libraries to accomplish what we need. For example, rather than importing Python's `random` library, the above example uses the JavaScript `Math.random` function instead. I would expect future updates to Transcrypt to improve on this situation, but that said, almost all of the Python built-in language constructs such as list comprehensions, lambdas, tuples, dictionaries, and more are all supported.

3.2 Summary

The example presented here demonstrates several things:

- We can directly call built-in JavaScript functions from our Python code.
- We can directly reference our Python functions from the HTML document.
- Our Python code has direct access to the `window` and `document` JavaScript objects.

We also saw a basic example of what Transcrypt does to our Python code when transpiling it.

Chapter Review:

1. Create source files:
   js_function.py
   js_function.html

2. Transpile source files:
   `transcrypt --nomin --map js_function`

3. Run the Python development web server:
   `python -m http.server`

4. Open the application:
   http://localhost:8000/js_function.html

References:

- Chapter code
  https://github.com/rtp-book/code/tree/main/ch03

- Numscrypt
  https://transcrypt.org/numscrypt/docs/html/index.html

Chapter 4 – Sourcemaps

Let's look at another simple example and examine how the sourcemap that Transcrypt generates can help us with debugging our Python code in the web browser.

4.1 Function Mapping

Again, we'll use a Python source file that contains a function that we will call from an HTML file that is opened in a web browser:

Listing 4-1 File: *mapping.py*

```python
def print_stuff():
    console.log("Native JS console.log call")
    print("Python print")
    console.invalid_method("This will be an error")
```

Listing 4-2 File: *mapping.html*

```html
<!DOCTYPE html>
<html lang="en">
    <body>
        <script type="module">
            import {print_stuff} from './__target__/mapping.js';
            window.print_stuff = print_stuff
        </script>
        <button type="button" onclick="print_stuff()">Print to Console</button>
        <div id="destination"></div>
    </body>
</html>
```

Since we are in a development mode and not concerned with the size of our generated files, let's transpile the above Python code with the extra options again:

(venv) $ `transcrypt --nomin --map mapping`

Now as before, with the local web server running, open the **mapping.html** document with:

http://localhost:8000/mapping.html

4.2 Debugging Console

Before clicking the button to test it, first open up the debugging console in your browser:

- **Google Chrome** Open the menu in the upper-right corner of the browser window and select *More Tools --> Developer Tools*, then select the *Console* tab.

- **Mozilla Firefox** Click on the menu in the browser's upper-right corner and select *Web Developer --> Web Console*. The *Console* tab should be automatically selected.

- **Apple Safari** First, make sure the Developer Menu is enabled by going into Safari's preferences (*Safari Menu --> Preferences*) and checking it on the *Advanced* tab. Once enabled, you can get to the developer console by clicking on *Develop --> Show JavaScript Console*, and going to the *Console* tab

- **Microsoft Edge** Open the Edge menu in the upper-right corner of the browser window and select *F12 Developer Tools*.

Once you have the developer console view open in the web browser, click the button in the application and see the results in the console.

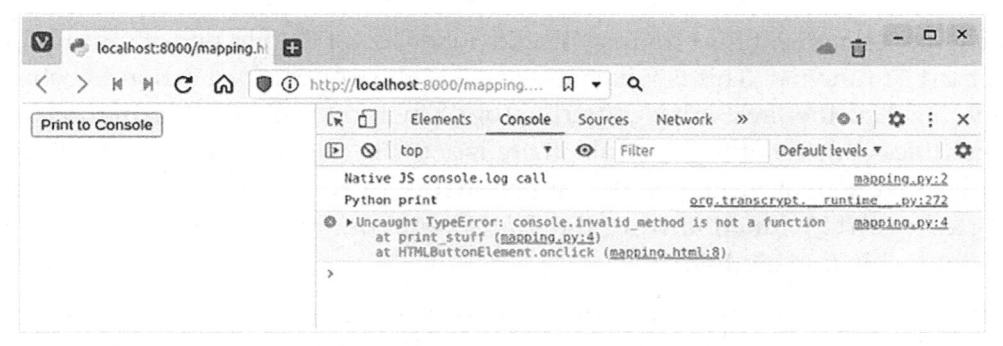

The output of our function demonstrates three things. The first, as we have already seen, is that you can call native JavaScript functions right from Python. In this case, we are calling the JavaScript native `console.log()` function to display some text in the browser console window.

The second thing we see is that the Python `print()` function does the same thing as the JavaScript `console.log()` method. In other words, if you want to output anything to the web browser console window, you can use the Python `print()` function rather than calling the native JavaScript `console.log()` method. Doing this helps keep your Python code looking like Python without having JavaScript commands being interspersed with it.

Note that one exception to using `console.log()` instead of `print()`, is when you want to actually output the contents of a JavaScript object in the console to allow for dynamic inspection of the object instead of just outputting a string representation.

Where Transcrypt does this bridging magic is in its **org.transcrypt.__runtime__.py** module. Let's look at the code that is generated when we run Transcrypt:

Listing 4-3 (Generated code): *mapping.js*

```javascript
// Transcrypt'ed from Python
import {AssertionError, ... print, ...} from './org.transcrypt.__runtime__.js';
var __name__ = '__main__';
export var print_stuff = function () {
  console.log ('Native JS console.log call');
  print ('Python print');
  console.invalid_method ('This will be an error');
};

//# sourceMappingURL=mapping.map
```

In the import statement that Transcrypt adds to the top of the file, one of the imports is a `print()` function. This is what causes the Python `print()` function to behave as if you called the JavaScript `console.log()` method within the namespace of this module. Outside of this module, there is actually a native JavaScript `print()` function that activates the printing functionality of the browser. However, the imported `print()` function from the Transcrypt runtime library overrides this behavior inside this module.

The third thing we see in the web browser console is an error message generated by our third line of code that tries to access a method of the JavaScript console object that doesn't exist:

```
Uncaught TypeError: console.invalid_method is not a function
        at print_stuff (mapping.py:4)
        at HTMLButtonElement.onclick (mapping.html:7)
```

The interesting part of this is that with the sourcemap that Transcrypt generates, instead of telling us where the error occurs in the JavaScript file (which is actually what is currently executing), it gives us a link to where the problem is in our *Python source code!* In this case, it tells us the problem is on line **4** of the **mapping.py** file.

Clicking the provided link will take you right to the offending line in the Python code. So instead of happening upon an error in the generated JavaScript code and then having to figure out what Python code it was generated from ourselves, Transcrypt provides the web browser enough information to do that for you. At the same time, it also conveniently provides a link to jump to the offending line of your Python source code right in the web browser. This feature can speed up the iterative debugging process significantly.

4.3 Summary

What we saw here was how Transcrypt maps Python functions to equivalent JavaScript functionality, and how sourcemaps allow you to debug your Python code in the web browser even though it is the generated JavaScript code that is actually running.

Chapter Review:

1. Create source files:
   mapping.py
   mapping.html

2. Transpile source files:
   ```
   transcrypt --nomin --map mapping
   ```

3. Run the Python development web server:
   ```
   python -m http.server
   ```

4. Open the application:
   http://localhost:8000/mapping.html

References:

- Chapter code
  https://github.com/rtp-book/code/tree/main/ch04

Chapter 5 – External JavaScript Libraries

So far, the only JavaScript functions we have used have been built-in. The next step we want to take is to utilize the functionality of external JavaScript libraries. JavaScript has a vast ecosystem of libraries available for doing web development. As previously mentioned, the philosophy behind Transcrypt is to take advantage of the existence of these libraries that already work in the web browser and use them, rather than try and replace them with a Python equivalent. No sense in reinventing the wheel, right?

There are several ways to accomplish this, the easiest being to import a JavaScript library from a hosted source right from your HTML file. When done this way, we can use the imported objects and call the library's methods from any of our Python modules. This isn't necessarily the best way since it gets added to the global namespace, but it will do for now until we add a few more steps to our workflow.

5.1 Working with jQuery

One of the more common JavaScript libraries that has been in use for some time now is jQuery. While it is not quite as popular as it once was, it still provides a good amount of utility in certain cases.

The following example uses jQuery to dynamically add items to an HTML list element when a button is clicked. Normally with jQuery, to accomplish this task you might do something like this to attach a function to a button onClick event:

```
$(document).ready(function(){
  $("#append_btn").click(function(){
    $("ol").append("<li>List item</li>");
  });
});
```

But let's see if we can use jQuery in a more Pythonic way. As before, we have a Python file that contains our functions, and an HTML file that will load in the web browser.

Listing 5-1 File: *external_jq.py*

```python
# __pragma__ ('alias', 'jq', '$')

def set_click():
    def add_item():
        jq("ol").append("<li>List item</li>")

    jq("#append_btn").click(add_item)

jq(document).ready(set_click)
```

Listing 5-2 File: *external_jq.html*

```html
<!DOCTYPE html>
<html lang="en">
  <head>
    <script src="https://code.jquery.com/jquery-3.5.1.min.js"></script>
    <script type="module" src="./__target__/external_jq.js"></script>
  </head>
  <body>
    <button id="append_btn">Add Item to List</button>
    <ol></ol>
  </body>
</html>
```

Transpile the above Python code with:

(venv) $ `transcrypt --nomin --map external_jq`

And again, with the local web server running, open the **external_jq.html** document with:

http://localhost:8000/external_jq.html

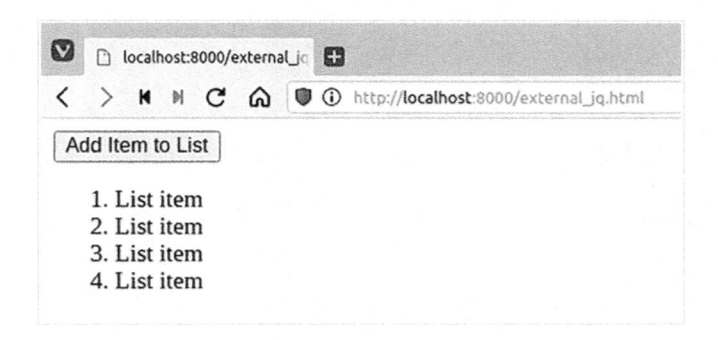

As mentioned earlier, in this case we are loading the jQuery library into the global namespace from an online hosted location with a `<script>` tag in the `<head>` section of the HTML file. When the HTML file loads, our transpiled Python code creates the `set_click()` function and calls the jQuery `$(document).ready()` function, which sets an event handler that will fire when the page is completely loaded. Then, when the document finishes loading, the `set_click()` function is triggered, which will set the `onClick` event property of the button to call the `add_item()` function when it is triggered. Note that simply loading the module from the HTML file as we do here, will run the line of code that ultimately attaches the `onClick` handler to the button after the document finishes loading.

Additionally, while we didn't *have* to do it in this case, we created `add_item()` as an inner function to the `set_click()` function to provide a closure. This pattern will come in handy later when we need to repeat the usage of a function, but have a specific state saved with it for when it is actually called.

One thing you might also notice is the comment at the top of our Python file. It turns out this isn't just any comment but is actually a *pragma*, or compiler directive, for Transcrypt. Since the $ name that jQuery uses is not a valid identifier in Python, we need to provide an alias. In this case, we are telling Transcrypt to replace any occurrence of the identifier jq that it sees at compile time with a $ as it transpiles our Python code into JavaScript. Transcrypt has several different compiler directives available to it, and we'll cover a few more later on in the book.

5.2 Summary

We now know one way to import and utilize third-party JavaScript libraries from our Python code. We were also introduced to using compiler directives for Transcrypt.

Chapter Review:

1. Create source files:
   external_jq.py
   external_jq.html

2. Transpile source files:
   `transcrypt --nomin --map external_jq`

3. Run the Python development web server:
   `python -m http.server`

4. Open the application:
   http://localhost:8000/external_jq.html

References:

- Chapter code
  https://github.com/rtp-book/code/tree/main/ch05
- jQuery
  https://jquery.com/
- Transcrypt Compiler Directives
  https://www.transcrypt.org/docs/html/special_facilities.html#the-pragma-mechanism

Chapter 6 – Intro to React

Now that we understand how to turn our Python code into JavaScript and use external JavaScript libraries, let's use that knowledge to start working with the React library specifically.

6.1 Hello React

Before we dive too deep into how React works its magic, let's once again start with a simple application based on the *Hello World* example we did a few chapters ago. It was just two buttons where one displayed some text, and the other cleared it. But this time, we're going to use the React library to render it. Mimicking the behavior of the previous example will give us some context to reference when learning how React works. Here are the two files we will be referring to:

Listing 6-1 File: *react_hello.py*

```python
def App():
    val, setVal = React.useState("")

    def say_hello():
        setVal("Hello React!")

    def clear_it():
        setVal("")

    return [
        React.createElement('button', {'onClick': say_hello}, "Click Me!"),
        React.createElement('button', {'onClick': clear_it}, "Clear"),
        React.createElement('div', None, val)
    ]

def render():
    ReactDOM.render(
        React.createElement(App, None),
        document.getElementById('root')
    )

document.addEventListener('DOMContentLoaded', render)
```

Listing 6-2 File: *react_hello.html*

```html
<!DOCTYPE html>
<html lang="en">
  <head>
    <script crossorigin
      src="https://unpkg.com/react@16/umd/react.production.min.js">
    </script>
    <script crossorigin
      src="https://unpkg.com/react-dom@16/umd/react-dom.production.min.js">
    </script>
    <script type="module" src="__target__/react_hello.js"></script>
  </head>
  <body>
    <div id="root"></div>
  </body>
</html>
```

Transpile the above Python code with:

(venv) $ `transcrypt --nomin --map react_hello`

Then as before, with the local web server running, open the **react_hello.html** document with:

http://localhost:8000/react_hello.html

In this example, we used three JavaScript objects: the built-in document object, the React object, and the ReactDOM object. In the <head> section of our HTML file, we imported the latter two into our application from a hosted location online, and into the global namespace.

When our generated JavaScript file loads from the HTML file, in addition to defining a few functions, it also adds a document event listener that calls our render function after the document finishes loading. Our render function then in turn uses the `ReactDOM.render()` method to add the two `button` elements and a `div` element to the DOM, as children of the existing hard coded `div` element in the HTML file that has an *id* of "root". If you open the web browser developer console and go to the elements tab, you can see that those elements were in fact added:

```
<body>
    <div id="root">
        <button>Click Me!</button>
        <button>Clear</button>
        <div>Hello React!</div>
    </div>
</body>
```

To add HTML elements to the DOM, the React library has a `createElement()` method that takes a component or tag name and returns a React element. This method generally takes three parameters:

1. The element type as a string or function reference
2. Properties of the element as a Python dictionary
3. Children of the element separated by commas (optional)

The first parameter can be a built-in HTML tag name like `button`, `div`, `input`, etc., and are just specified as lowercase strings. We did this in our App function:

```
React.createElement('button', {'onClick': say_hello}, "Click Me!")
React.createElement('button', {'onClick': clear_it}, "Clear")
React.createElement('div', None, val)
```

The element type can also refer to a user-defined functional component that returns one React element or a list of elements. By convention, the name of user-defined component functions should use PascalCase. Our App function is an example of this:

```
React.createElement(App, None)
```

The second parameter is a Python dictionary that holds properties that apply to the given component. These can be standard properties as defined by the W3C HTML5 specification, CSS style properties, and/or custom properties to be utilized by other user-defined components. If no properties need to be passed in, a value of None is acceptable.

Lastly, any children of the element are supplied, each separated by commas. If there are no child elements, then this parameter can be omitted. This parameter represents the HTML element's `innerHTML` property and can consist of other elements or just a simple string.

6.2 React State

React uses three different ways to store information in the application:

- Properties (or "props" for short)
- State
- Context

We just talked about how properties are passed to a React component, so now let's talk about state and how it differs from properties or "props" for short. While both props and state store data, properties are something that gets passed *in* to a component and is immutable, whereas state is something that is managed and can be updated *inside* of a component. Whenever a component's state changes, the component will be re-rendered based on the values of the new state. One important thing to keep in mind is that changes to a state value are handled by using a setter function instead of being assigned a value directly, and those changes are *asynchronous*. Trying to use the value of a state variable immediately after updating it may result in unintended behaviors because of this asynchronous nature. We will discuss how to deal with this situation later in the book, and also go over the third option of storing information in a context object for later use.

To create a state variable and its corresponding update function that is used to set the value of the state variable, React has a `useState()` method that takes a parameter value that is used to initialize that state variable, and then returns a reference to the new state variable as well as a reference to a companion updater function. Whenever you want to update that variable, you call the update function and pass it the value that you want to update the variable to. In our example, we created a variable `val` and an update function `setVal()` with this statement:

```
val, setVal = React.useState("")
```

To update our state variable, we then called `setVal()` in our two onClick event functions:

```
def say_hello():
    setVal("Hello React!")

def clear_it():
    setVal("")
```

And finally, we used the state variable itself in a `div` element that will display whatever the value of the `val` variable is at the time the App component is rendered:

```
React.createElement('div', None, val)
```

Whenever one of the buttons is clicked and triggers either the `say_hello()` or `clear_it()` functions, the var state variable gets updated and causes the App component to be re-rendered with the new value.

6.3 Summary

In this chapter, we took our basic *Hello World* example and changed it to a reactive application that renders HTML based on state. Here, we just started learning about using React, but we'll dive a little deeper into how it actually works in the next chapter.

Chapter Review:

1. Create source files:
   react_hello.py
   react_hello.html

2. Transpile source files:
   `transcrypt --nomin --map react_hello`

3. Run the Python development web server:
   `python -m http.server`

4. Open the application:
   http://localhost:8000/react_hello.html

References:

- Chapter code
  https://github.com/rtp-book/code/tree/main/ch06
- React
  https://reactjs.org
- W3C HTML5 specification
  https://dev.w3.org/html5/spec/

Chapter 7 – React Concepts

So now that we've seen a simple example of how to use React, let's dig a little more into how React works as well as learn a few architectural concepts. This information isn't critical to know, but it may help you visualize what is happening in your React code a little better.

7.1 Document Object Model

While not an exact comparison, in MVC architecture terms, React is mostly the View layer. It is essentially a function, or collection of functions, that takes the Model as input, and outputs HTML in a tree structure.

As we touched on in the previous chapter, what React gives us is the ability to modify the Document Object Model of a web page dynamically. What this means, is that it allows us to programmatically add and remove HTML elements to and from the DOM based on changes in state as the user interacts with the application.

The main workhorse of React that we'll be using is the `React.createElement()` method. When we use this method along with the `ReactDOM.render()` method, React calculates the changes that need to be made in the DOM and updates it appropriately. We can mimic how it does that update with native JavaScript functions:

1. It first creates the element:
   ```
   el = document.createElement('div')
   ```

2. Then sets properties of the element:
   ```
   el.setAttribute('align', 'right')
   ```

3. Adds children to the element:
   ```
   el.innerHTML = "Hello World!"
   ```

4. And finally, it adds the new element to the DOM tree:
   ```
   document.getElementById('root').append(el)
   ```

In our Python code, the equivalent call to React.createElement() and ReactDOM.render() would look like this:

```
ReactDOM.render(
    React.createElement('div', {'align': 'right'}, "Hello World!"),
    document.getElementById('root')
)
```

By chaining and nesting calls to createElement(), we end up generating an HTML tree structure in the DOM that represents our application user interface. And that element tree ultimately gets inserted into the DOM as a child of the root div hook point that we have in our HTML file, using the JavaScript ReactDOM.render() method. So this:

```
<body>
    <div id="root"></div>
</body>
```

turns into this:

```
<body>
    <div id="root">
        <div align="right">Hello World!</div>
    </div>
</body>
```

7.2 Components and Elements

React is declarative in that we write code that identifies what we want, and then we leave it up to React to take care of performing all of the steps needed to get us to our desired result. To describe what we want, we use functional components. That is, we create a function that returns a React element, or list of elements. These components can change the elements that they return based on the properties that are passed into the component, as well as taking into consideration the current value of any state variables that the component may be managing.

As an example, let's take a view that consists of a title bar, and a form that has three input areas:

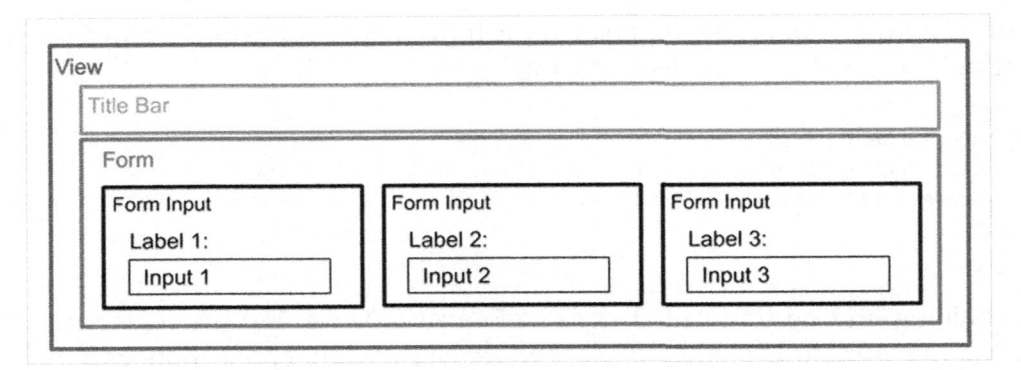

```
┌─View──────────────────────────────────────────────────┐
│ ┌─Title Bar─────────────────────────────────────────┐ │
│ └───────────────────────────────────────────────────┘ │
│ ┌─Form──────────────────────────────────────────────┐ │
│ │ ┌─Form Input──┐ ┌─Form Input──┐ ┌─Form Input──┐   │ │
│ │ │ Label 1:    │ │ Label 2:    │ │ Label 3:    │   │ │
│ │ │ ┌─────────┐ │ │ ┌─────────┐ │ │ ┌─────────┐ │   │ │
│ │ │ │ Input 1 │ │ │ │ Input 2 │ │ │ │ Input 3 │ │   │ │
│ │ │ └─────────┘ │ │ └─────────┘ │ │ └─────────┘ │   │ │
│ │ └─────────────┘ └─────────────┘ └─────────────┘   │ │
│ └───────────────────────────────────────────────────┘ │
└───────────────────────────────────────────────────────┘
```

To turn this view into a component tree, we just have to think of it in terms of which components are a parent of another. In this case, we would probably end up with a component tree that looks something like this:

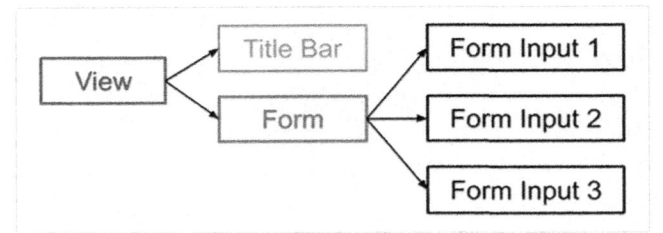

```
                    ┌─Title Bar─┐   ┌─Form Input 1─┐
         ┌─View─┐  ↗└───────────┘ ↗ └──────────────┘
         └──────┘                   ┌─Form Input 2─┐
                  ↘ ┌─Form─┐ ──────→└──────────────┘
                    └──────┘ ↘
                               ┌─Form Input 3─┐
                               └──────────────┘
```

Components can return a single element or an entire tree full of elements that end up getting added to the main element tree structure. And again, by adding components to a list (chaining) and adding child components (nesting), we build up a tree structure that forms our desired UI. It is also valid for a function component to return a value of None, in which case it has no effect on the resulting tree structure.

7.3 Unidirectional Data Flow

Property values generally get created at one level of our component tree, and get passed downward as far as they need to go to get to where they are needed. These properties or props, are frequently the value of a state variable that gets passed down to a lower level component, or it might be a function pointer that acts upon state at one level, but needs to get called by a lower-level component.

If you find that you need to use a state value in a different branch of your tree structure, then you will likely need to move management of that state up to a component that is common between those two branches, and then pass the value back down to both places it is needed as a property. This is a common development pattern in React, and the process is referred to as "Lifting State".

7.4 Hooks vs. Classes

In this book, we will only be using functional components and "hooks" in React parlance. When React was first released, React components were all class-based. Since the addition of functional hooks to the library, the preferred method of creating components is now as pure functions. By using functions instead of classes, and composition with plain functions instead of inheritance, code becomes much simpler, and coding patterns for managing state become much more consistent. Another reason to use React hooks over classes is that managing lifecycle events of components also becomes much cleaner.

That said, functional components and class-based components *can* be mixed in the same tree. And it is definitely possible to use class-based React components with Transcrypted Python. While class-based components will not be covered in this book, if this is something you still wish to do, you can create a Python class that inherits from `React.Component.prototype`. If you want to get a quick start on it, there is a GitHub repository (though now inactive) that has already done the work for you:

https://github.com/doconix/pyreact

Since we are creating our tree of HTML elements based on React functional components, our Python code will naturally take on a functional coding style. But Python being what it is, handles mixing functional, procedural, and OO easily. You just need to be aware of when it is appropriate to use which style.

7.5 Summary

Here we learned the basics of what React does behind the scenes to create HTML elements. Additionally, we now understand that the elements that React creates are put together in a tree structure by chaining and nesting React components. We also learned that data flow in the generated tree is top to bottom, and that data generally flows downward by passing props to child components. And lastly, we covered why we are focusing on the functional components that React now supports, over the original class-based components.

References:

- PyReact - Python React class components
  htttps://github.com/doconix/pyreact

- React Docs - Components and Props
  https://reactjs.org/docs/components-and-props.html

Chapter 8 – Cleaner Code

Now that we have a better understanding of how React works, let's take a look at our previous *react_hello* example and see if we can make our Python code a little more Pythonic by breaking out the JavaScript calls from the Python code and putting them into their own module.

8.1 Break It Up

Let's create a python module specifically for mapping the JavaScript objects to Python objects. This will allow us to isolate the JavaScript portion from the rest of our code, and to just use standard Python imports whenever we need to call those JavaScript functions. This time we have three files we'll be using:

Listing 8-1 File: *pyreact2.py*

```
# __pragma__('skip')
# These are here to quiet the Python linter and are ignored by Transcrypt
React = None
ReactDOM = None
document = None
# __pragma__('noskip')

# Map React javaScript objects to Python identifiers
createElement = React.createElement
useState = React.useState

def render(root_component, props, container):
    """Loads main react component into DOM"""
    def main():
        ReactDOM.render(
            React.createElement(root_component, props),
            document.getElementById(container)
        )

    document.addEventListener('DOMContentLoaded', main)
```

Listing 8-2 File: *react_hello2.py*

```python
from pyreact2 import useState, render, createElement as el

def App():
    val, setVal = useState("")

    def say_hello():
        setVal("Hello React!")

    def clear_it():
        setVal("")

    return [
        el('button', {'onClick': say_hello}, "Click Me!"),
        el('button', {'onClick': clear_it}, "Clear"),
        el('div', None, val)
    ]

render(App, None, 'root')
```

Listing 8-3 File: *react_hello2.html*

```html
<!DOCTYPE html>
<html lang="en">
  <head>
    <script crossorigin
      src="https://unpkg.com/react@16/umd/react.production.min.js">
    </script>
    <script crossorigin
      src="https://unpkg.com/react-dom@16/umd/react-dom.production.min.js">
    </script>
    <script type="module" src="__target__/react_hello2.js"></script>
  </head>
  <body>
    <div id="root"></div>
  </body>
</html>
```

Transpile the above Python code with:

(venv) $ `transcrypt --nomin --map react_hello2`

One thing to note here is that we only need to give Transcrypt the name of our entry point file. It will walk the dependency tree of our Python modules to then transpile any other modules that are referenced in them via Python import statements.

With the local web server running again, open the **react_hello2.html** document with:

http://localhost:8000/react_hello2.html

So we have a few things to break down here. We'll start with the **pyreact2.py** module that now acts as our bridge to the JavaScript libraries we are using. Our `render()` function encapsulates the entry point of our React application, and adds the event listener that waits for the initial document to finish loading before React inserts the dynamically created elements into the DOM. We also map the Python variables `createElement` and `useState` to their JavaScript counterparts. This allows us to directly import these functions into other Python modules without having to worry about how we import the JavaScript libraries.

Finally, at the top of the file we see another pragma, or compiler directive. The compiler directive `__pragma__('skip')` tells the Transcrypt compiler to ignore the lines that follow. Likewise, `__pragma__('noskip')` tells the compiler to once again start processing the lines that follow. What we put in-between those two pragmas, are some stub variables to keep the Python linter from giving us errors due to not knowing what to do with the JavaScript objects. Doing this is not necessary from a functional standpoint, but it keeps your programming IDE from redlining the code. That said, even with this step, you might still get linter warnings. The good thing is that by moving our JavaScript-to-Python mappings into a single module, these non-Python anomalies will be contained in one place rather than being scattered throughout the rest of our application.

Moving on to our new **react_hello2.py** module, you can see that the result of moving the JavaScript portions out of the file is much cleaner Python-looking code. From the standard Python import statement to the function calls, there is nothing here that is *not* Python. To make it easier to use and reduce code clutter a bit, we also gave the createElement import the alias el.

In this case, the only change we made to our HTML file was the name of the imported JavaScript file, so there is really nothing new here.

8.2 Summary

In this chapter, we saw how to make our code more Pythonic by moving the JavaScript mappings to their own file and creating Python convenience methods for using them. This new JavaScript-to-Python mapping module is something we can reuse down the road. We also saw some new compiler directives that allow us to put in lines of code that will be ignored by the Transcrypt transpiler, but to help keep the Python linter happy.

Chapter Review:

1. Create source files:
   pyreact2.py
   react_hello2.py
   react_hello2.html

2. Transpile source files:
   transcrypt --nomin --map react_hello2

3. Run the Python development web server:
   python -m http.server

4. Open the application:
   http://localhost:8000/react_hello2.html

References:

- Chapter code
  https://github.com/rtp-book/code/tree/main/ch08

- Transcrypt Skip/NoSkip Compiler Directive
  https://www.transcrypt.org/docs/html/special_facilities.html#skipping-fragments-while-generating-code-pragma-skip-and-pragma-noskip

Chapter 9 – Managing JavaScript Packages

While using a global import in the HTML file for third-party JavaScript libraries like we have been doing is convenient, it is generally not considered a best practice. And as your applications start getting more complex and using more JavaScript libraries, managing them becomes much more difficult and even unwieldy. Many popular JavaScript libraries may not even be available from a hosted site, so we need to have a better method of utilizing these libraries.

9.1 npm

So that we don't have to rely on third-party hosting of critical components of our applications, we should host these libraries ourselves as part of our application. To manage these locally, we will want to use a JavaScript package manager. One of the most popular ones in use today is npm (Node Package Manager). Like pip for Python, you can use npm to download and install JavaScript libraries that can be found at the npm registry, which is similar to PyPI (Python Package Index) for Python libraries.

The npm package manager application is installed along with Node.js, which is a JavaScript runtime that allows you to run JavaScript programs outside of a web browser. To check and see if you have Node.js installed, you can run this command in a terminal window:

```
$ node -v
```

And to confirm that you have npm installed, you can also run this command in the terminal window:

```
$ npm -v
```

If Node.js and/or npm is not installed, you can download the Node.js installation that is appropriate for your operating system from the Node.js website at:

https://nodejs.org

Installation packages and binaries are available there for Windows, Mac, and Linux. To ensure the best stability, make sure you get an LTS (Long Term Support) version. Since it is an open-source project, the source code is available there as well.

Once Node.js and npm are installed, you can download JavaScript libraries from the npm registry using the CLI (Command Line Interface). In a terminal window from your project folder, enter the following command to initialize the repository for your project:

```
$ npm init -y
```

This creates a file called **package.json**, which is an npm configuration file that is specific to your current project. It contains a project name and version, information about installed JavaScript packages, details about project compilation commands for development and production builds, code repository information, and licensing information about your project.

After that is complete, use this command to download and add React and React-DOM to your project files:

```
$ npm install react@16 react-dom@16
```

This will create a folder in your project called **node_modules/**, where it will store the files for any JavaScript libraries you decide to add to your project. Be advised that you should not venture into this folder unless absolutely necessary. For it is the land of JavaScript, and many a coder has been lost for days in this jungle of ill repute... Anyhow, it automatically updates the **package.json** file and adds the name of the library and version to the list of your project's library dependencies. Like a **requirements.txt** file for Python, the **package.json** file can be used to keep track of and automatically install library dependencies.

By using the @16 after the `react` package name when we installed it, we controlled which major version of the library was installed. If not specified, npm will just install the latest version of a given package. While this may be fine for small projects, you will always want to consider how newer versions of the libraries you use may impact existing code bases.

If you are saving your source code to a code repository like GitHub or BitBucket, you would usually not commit the JavaScript library files with your project. As long as the JavaScript library dependency information is saved in the **package.json** file, and you commit that file to your project repository, we can use it later on to automatically install all of our JavaScript dependencies in case the project ever needs to be rebuilt from scratch.

When you install a JavaScript library with npm, it also takes care of installing any dependencies of that library as well if they don't already exist. So if you look in the **node_modules/** folder now, you will see much more than just the two React libraries that we installed directly:

```
node_modules/
        ├── .bin
        ├── js-tokens
        ├── loose-envify
        ├── object-assign
        ├── prop-types
        ├── react
        ├── react-dom
        ├── react-is
        └── scheduler
```

9.2 Using Local JavaScript Libraries

So now that we have the React and ReactDOM libraries installed locally, we can modify our *react_hello2* files to utilize those locally installed libraries. Then, as a housekeeping step, we can programmatically remove the global references for those libraries that are created when importing them from the HTML file:

Listing 9-1 File: *pyreact3.py*

```python
# __pragma__('skip')
# These are here to quiet the Python linter and are ignored by Transcrypt
window = None
document = None
# __pragma__('noskip')

# Create local references to the React and ReactDOM JavaScript libraries
React = window.React
ReactDOM = window.ReactDOM

# Remove the React and ReactDOM JavaScript libraries from the global namespace
# __pragma__('js', 'delete window.React;')
# __pragma__('js', 'delete window.ReactDOM;')

# Map React javaScript objects to Python identifiers
createElement = React.createElement
useState = React.useState


def render(root_component, props, container):
```

```python
"""Loads main react component into DOM"""

def main():
    ReactDOM.render(
        React.createElement(root_component, props),
        document.getElementById(container)
    )

document.addEventListener('DOMContentLoaded', main)
```

Listing 9-2 File: *react_hello3.py*

```python
from pyreact3 import useState, render, createElement as el

def App():
    val, setVal = useState("")

    def say_hello():
        setVal("Hello React!")

    def clear_it():
        setVal("")

    return [
        el('button', {'onClick': say_hello}, "Click Me!"),
        el('button', {'onClick': clear_it}, "Clear"),
        el('div', None, val)
    ]

render(App, None, 'root')
```

Listing 9-3 File: *react_hello3.html*

```html
<!DOCTYPE html>
<html lang="en">
  <head>
    <script src="./node_modules/react/umd/react.production.min.js"></script>
    <script src="./node_modules/react-dom/umd/react-dom.production.min.js">
    </script>
    <script type="module" src="__target__/react_hello3.js"></script>
  </head>
  <body>
    <div id="root"></div>
```

```
        </body>
</html>
```

Transpile the above Python code with:

(venv) $ `transcrypt --nomin --map react_hello3`

And open the **react_hello3.html** document with:

http://localhost:8000/react_hello3.html

While there were only a few subtle changes to the **pyreact3.py** module, we now have more control over where the libraries get loaded, and we no longer pollute the global namespace unnecessarily.

To break down this code, at the top of the file we once again use the `__pragma__('skip')` and `__pragma__('noskip')` compiler directives to tell Transcrypt to ignore the lines in-between that contain some stub variables that keep the Python linter from giving us errors due to unknown identifiers in the module.

After that, we assign the `React` and `ReactDOM` global objects to local variables that will make them explicitly available to be used in our Python code. One of our design goals here is to isolate the interface to the JavaScript libraries we are calling so that our other code modules can remain as simple and Pythonic as possible.

The next two lines are Transcrypt compiler directives that allow us to directly insert unmodified JavaScript code into the generated JavaScript file. JavaScript statements provided to this compiler directive will get added to the transpiled JavaScript file verbatim:

```
# __pragma__('js', 'delete window.React;')
# __pragma__('js', 'delete window.ReactDOM;')
```

The "delete window.React;" JavaScript statement in the `__pragma__('js')` directive removes the `React` object from the global `window` namespace, which we no longer need since we now have a local reference to it. The same then goes for the global `ReactDOM` object, which we remove as well. After this, the only remaining React library references are then just local to this module. More information about the `__pragma__('js')` directive can be found in the Transcrypt documentation.

The rest of the **pyreact3.py** file is the same as before, and the other two files don't change much. We just updated the import statement in the **react_hello3.py** module to reflect the new *pyreact3* module name, and we modified the import paths for the React libraries in the HTML file to utilize the locally installed copies instead of pulling them in from an online host.

9.3 Summary

This chapter showed us how to use a JavaScript package manager to download and keep track of any third-party JavaScript libraries that we may end up using in a project. We also learned how to include raw JavaScript statements in our code, and to programmatically manage JavaScript libraries to keep them scoped within a module namespace instead of leaving them loaded globally.

Chapter Review:

1. Install Node.js if it isn't already installed:
   https://nodejs.org/en/download/

2. Initialize the project with npm:
   `npm init -y`

3. Install React libraries:
   `npm install react@16 react-dom@16`

4. Create source files:
   pyreact3.py
   react_hello3.py
   react_hello3.html

5. Transpile source files:
   `transcrypt --nomin --map react_hello3`

6. Run the Python development web server:
   `python -m http.server`

7. Open the application:
   http://localhost:8000/react_hello3.html

References:

- Chapter code
  https://github.com/rtp-book/code/tree/main/ch09

- npm Registry
  https://www.npmjs.com/

- Python Package Index (PyPI)
  https://pypi.org/

- Node.js
  https://nodejs.org/

- Transcrypt JavaScript Compiler Directive
  https://www.transcrypt.org/docs/html/special_facilities.html#inserting-literal-javascript-pragma-js-and-include

Chapter 10 – Package Bundler

We have one more piece to add to our development toolchain that will make our lives a little easier by enabling us to integrate several of our development steps. As a bonus, it also gives us a much simpler way to import our JavaScript libraries.

10.1 Parcel

As mentioned earlier, a web application bundler is a program that takes all of the JavaScript code that your application requires, and packages it up into optimized files that are more easily downloaded to a web browser. This includes your Python code that has been transpiled into JavaScript, as well as any JavaScript libraries that your application may use. While webpack is probably the most widely used web application bundler, it has a reputation for being rather configuration heavy. Since our needs are a bit simpler and we don't need quite as much customization, we will be using Parcel instead, which is advertised as a "zero-configuration" bundler. One of our goals here is to keep the development toolchain as unobtrusive as possible. The relative simplicity of Parcel helps us meet that goal.

Parcel is a JavaScript package itself, and as such, can be installed with npm using this command:

```
$ npm install parcel-bundler --save-dev
```

To test the Parcel bundler and make sure it installed properly, run the following command in the terminal window to make sure that there are no errors:

```
$ npx parcel --help
```

In order for Parcel to automatically transpile our Python code, we will also need to install a Parcel plug-in for Transcrypt with this npm command:

```
(venv) $ npm install parcel-plugin-transcrypt --save-dev
```

The `--save-dev` option in the npm command tells it to add the package being installed as a development dependency in the **package.json** file (as opposed to an application dependency like react).

The Transcrypt plug-in for Parcel adds Transcrypt as one of the steps that the Parcel bundler takes when bundling your application so that you no longer have to run it manually. By default, it will run Transcrypt with the `--nomin`, `--map`, and `--verbose` options. If necessary, these can be overridden by adding additional configuration information to the **package.json** file, but the default configuration is sufficient for our needs.

As of this writing, the Transcrypt plug-in is coded to an older version of Parcel that causes it to break when used with the current Parcel version. While this will hopefully be fixed in a future update, for now we will need to manually update one of the plug-in's JavaScript files before we can use the Transcrypt plug-in.

The file in question is:

./node_modules/parcel-plugin-transcrypt/asset.js

In that file, change line 2 that loads the Parcel Logger module from this:

```
const logger = require('parcel-bundler/src/Logger');
```

to this:

```
const logger = require('@parcel/logger/src/Logger');
```

Once this modification is made to change the location of the Parcel Logger module, the Transcrypt plug-in for Parcel should be working.

NOTE FOR WINDOWS USERS:

For those of you using Windows, there are two more changes that need to be made to the **asset.js** file for it to work in Windows environments. The first is to modify the default Transcrypt build configuration to just use the version of Python that you set your virtual environment up with.

To do that, change line 14 that defines the Transcrypt command to simply use python instead of python3, changing it from this:

```
"command": "python3 -m transcrypt",
```

to this:

```
"command": "python -m transcrypt",
```

The second change has to do with modifying an import file path so that it uses Windows-style back-slashes instead of the Linux/Mac style forward-slashes. For this modification, we can use a string `replace()` method on line 143 to make an inline correction to the file path for Windows environments. So change this line:

```
this.content = `export * from "${this.importPath}";`;
```

to this:

```
this.content = `export * from "${this.importPath.replace(/\\/g, '/')}";`;
```

At some point, I would expect that a modification will be incorporated into the parcel-plugin-transcrypt package so that this hack can be avoided in the future.

10.2 Simplified JavaScript Imports

We do need to make one small change to our HTML file. Since our entire application will be compiled and bundled as a single resource, we now want the application entry point to be our HTML file. So rather than directly specifying the entry point as our Python code, the Python files will get pulled in from the HTML file instead. So let's make that small change by indicating our source Python file instead of the generated JavaScript file:

Listing 10-1 File: *react_hello4.html*

```html
<!DOCTYPE html>
<html lang="en">
  <head>
```

```html
    <script src="react_hello4.py"></script>
  </head>
  <body>
    <div id="root"></div>
  </body>
</html>
```

Another change we can now make since we are using the Parcel bundler, is to use the `require()` module loader function built into Node.js instead of having to use JavaScript functions to manually manage our React libraries:

Listing 10-2 File: *pyreact4.py*

```python
# __pragma__('skip')
# These are here to quiet the Python linter and are ignored by Transcrypt
require = None
document = None
# __pragma__('noskip')

# Load the React and ReactDOM JavaScript libraries into the local namespace
React = require('react')
ReactDOM = require('react-dom')

# Map React javaScript objects to Python identifiers
createElement = React.createElement
useState = React.useState


def render(root_component, props, container):
    """Loads main react component into DOM"""

    def main():
        ReactDOM.render(
            React.createElement(root_component, props),
            document.getElementById(container)
        )

    document.addEventListener('DOMContentLoaded', main)
```

And then lastly, we need to update the module import name in our Python application module to use the new **pyreact4.py** file:

Listing 10-3 File: *react_hello4.py*

```python
from pyreact4 import useState, render, createElement as el

def App():
    val, setVal = useState("")

    def say_hello():
        setVal("Hello React!")

    def clear_it():
        setVal("")

    return [
        el('button', {'onClick': say_hello}, "Click Me!"),
        el('button', {'onClick': clear_it}, "Clear"),
        el('div', None, val)
    ]

render(App, None, 'root')
```

If you are still running the built-in Python web server http.server, use *Ctrl-C* to stop it now. When Parcel builds our application in development mode, it will automatically start up a development web server to serve up the files that it generates.

Now we can build our application with:

(venv) $ npx parcel --log-level 4 --no-cache react_hello4.html

Once it finishes running Transcrypt for us and then bundling the generated JavaScript, Parcel starts up a local HTTP server on port 1234 by default, which we can open here:

http://localhost:1234

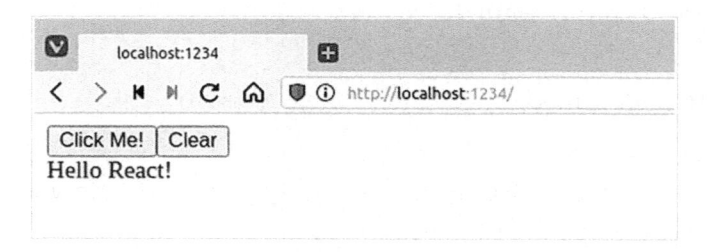

So now, our React web application should work as it did before. But let's take a look at the files that Parcel generated. When Parcel runs, it creates a folder in our project named **dist** where it saves all of the files it generates:

```
dist/
    ├── react_hello4.57fd4402.js
    ├── react_hello4.57fd4402.js.map
    └── react_hello4.html
```

If you look in this folder, one thing you'll notice is that all of our source code has been bundled into a single JavaScript file with the same name as our original Python entry point. This bundle includes all of the JavaScript code from our transpiled Python code, the transpiled Transcrypt runtime module, and any third-party JavaScript libraries that our application utilized, like *react* and *react-dom*.

Also added to the file names, is a hash appended to the end of the name that is based on the file content. The hash value that is appended to the generated JavaScript file makes sure that we are always running the latest version of the generated code and avoids any unwanted file caching that the browser may be doing as we are testing.

You will see the original HTML file in the **dist** folder as well, but if you open it up and look inside, you will see that the Python source file we originally specified in there has been changed to the name of the bundled JavaScript file that was just generated:

Listing 10-4 (Generated code): *dist/react_hello4.html*

```html
<!DOCTYPE html>
<html lang="en">
  <head>
    <script src="/react_hello4.57fd4402.js"></script>
  </head>
  <body>
    <div id="root"></div>
  </body>
</html>
```

When the Parcel development server responds to a request for the HTML file, it will serve up the generated file in the **dist** folder that references the generated JavaScript bundle instead of our original HTML source file that references our Python source code.

If we have the `--map` option specified for Transcrypt, then a sourcemap file will also be in the **dist** folder.

While Parcel is running the development web server, it also looks for changes to the main entry point files, either the HTML file or our Python entry point file. If either of these files changes, it will automatically trigger a recompilation of the application, updating the generated files based on any of our source files that have changed. This update is usually much quicker than the initial build since it does not have to recompile any files that did *not* change, including the Transcrypt runtime in particular.

When serving up our application, the HTML entry point file, regardless of whether it is named **index.html** or not, is assumed to be the default page that is sent as a response to the browser when no other document is specified in the HTTP request. This is why with the Parcel web server, we don't have to explicitly add the name of the HTML file in the URL of our request in the web browser. We can just specify the host and port.

10.3 Build Scripts

To make it easier to build our application for both development and production use, we can add some build instructions to the npm **package.json** file. You will usually want to specify different build options depending on which environment you are building for. For example, while it is nice to have readable non-minified generated JavaScript code and have sourcemaps available for debugging purposes, you would usually not want to do this for production since you want the file sizes sent to the browser to be as small as possible in that case.

We can add named scripts to the **package.json** file that we can call whenever we want to build our application for a specific environment. In the scripts section of the **package.json** file, add these two lines right *before* the existing test script that is there (when adding these lines, note that line breaks are not allowed in JSON strings):

```
"start": "NODE_ENV=development parcel --log-level 4 react_hello4.html
    ↪ --out-dir dist/dev",
"build": "NODE_ENV=production parcel --log-level 4 build react_hello4.html
    ↪ --no-source-maps --out-dir dist/prod",
```

NOTE FOR WINDOWS USERS:

For Windows users, there are a few more steps you may need to take for these scripts to work properly, especially if you are not using an IDE. Because the npm scripts in the **package.json** file will not run correctly using the built-in windows cmd shell, we will need to use the Bash shell that is included with Git. The first step is it make sure that Git is installed with the Git Bash option included. If not installed already, you can find the Git installation for Windows here:

https://git-scm.com/download/win

The second step is to configure Node to utilize the Git Bash shell for running scripts by executing this npm command in a terminal window:

npm config set script-shell "C:\\Program Files\\git\\bin\\bash.exe"

If the Parcel web server is still running, stop it with *Ctrl-C*. Then to make sure we are starting with a clean slate, also delete the existing **dist** folder. We will let Parcel regenerate the content from scratch. Next, go ahead and run the following command in the terminal window:

(venv) $ npm start

This should execute the same Parcel command we used previously, non-minified, and with a generated sourcemap. The only difference is that the generated files will be placed in a sub-folder of **dist** named **dev** this time due to how we specified the output directory in our start script. Note that start is a special script name for development purposes, and the npm run directive is not required for that specific script. To stop the development web server from running, as before, use *Ctrl-C*.

When you have verified the application is still working in the browser, once again stop the Parcel web server. Now try the production build with:

(venv) $ npm run build

This time the generated files should be in the **prod** sub-folder of **dist**, and will be minified without having a sourcemap file being generated. Check and make sure the application still works.

React to Python

With the way our build scripts have now been set up, we will have a generated folder tree that looks like this:

```
dist/
    ├── dev/
    │   ├── react_hello4.57fd4402.js
    │   ├── react_hello4.57fd4402.js.map
    │   └── react_hello4.html
    └── prod/
        ├── react_hello4.67197438.js
        └── react_hello4.html
```

By setting the NODE_ENV environment variable for the different environments in our build scripts, we give the bundler a clue as to what optimizations to perform when bundling the generated code so that the result is appropriate for the specified environment.

10.4 Summary

With Parcel, we now have a reasonably complete development toolchain to turn our Python code into a fully deployable front-end web application. We also now have an easy and effective way of loading JavaScript modules in a way that our Python code can access them.

Chapter Review:

1. Install the Parcel bundler package from npm:
   `npm install parcel-bundler --save-dev`

2. Install the Transcrypt plug-in for Parcel from npm:
   `npm install parcel-plugin-transcrypt --save-dev`

3. Fix the logger library location in the Transcrypt plug-in file:
   ./node_modules/parcel-plugin-transcrypt/asset.js
   `const logger = require('@parcel/logger/src/Logger');`

4. Create source files:
   react_hello4.html
   pyreact4.py
   react_hello4.py

5. Build the application:
   `npx parcel --log-level 4 --no-cache react_hello4.html`

6. Open the application:
   http://localhost:1234

7. Add build scripts to **package.json**:

```
"start": "NODE_ENV=development parcel --log-level 4 react_hello4.html
↪ --out-dir dist/dev",
"build": "NODE_ENV=production parcel --log-level 4 build react_hello4.html
↪ --no-source-maps --out-dir dist/prod",
```

8. Build the application for development with:
   `npm start`

9. Build the application for production with:
   `npm run build`

References:

- Chapter code
  https://github.com/rtp-book/code/tree/main/ch10

- webpack Bundler
  https://webpack.js.org/

- Parcel Bundler
  https://parceljs.org/

- Parcel JavaScript Package
  https://www.npmjs.com/package/parcel-bundler

- Parcel Plug-in for Transcrypt
  https://www.npmjs.com/package/parcel-plugin-transcrypt

- Git for Windows
  https://git-scm.com/download/win

Chapter 11 – Section Summary

Whew! Well that was a long way to go, but we finally have our development environment set up to efficiently create our front-end web applications in Python. To review, we now have the following pieces in place:

- **Python** - *Obviously*
- **Transcrypt** - *To convert our Python code into JavaScript*
- **Npm** - *To download and manage the JavaScript libraries we use*
- **Parcel** - *To process our source files and output something that we can use in a web browser*

In addition to using these tools, we covered how we use a very basic HTML file as the entry point to our application. Then, React is used to dynamically add the actual DOM content for our application by using components that return React elements. We also saw that by putting all of the code that maps Python objects to JavaScript objects into their own file, it lets us use pure Python throughout the rest of our application, keeping it simple, readable, and Pythonic.

In the next section, we'll dig more into the React library and learn some techniques and building blocks we can use to develop professional-looking web applications with Python.

– Part II –

Building Blocks

This section will walk through several stand-alone examples that demonstrate core concepts and features used to build web applications with React in Python. Some parts will be specific to the fact we are using Python to make calls to functions in JavaScript libraries, and some will be more related to web development techniques in general. We will start covering some UI styling options, and also go over how to communicate with some back-end services.

Chapter 12 – Text Input

One of the most fundamental elements used in most web applications is the lowly text box, or more specifically, an HTML `input` element. By default, the `input` element allows the user to enter any text value. By specifying the element's type attribute, you can also get it to be a checkbox or to render specifically formatted data like passwords or dates. Let's look at a basic text input for now and see how we work with it in React.

Remember that React re-renders the page or view whenever there is a change in state. This state change could be triggered by internal events of the application itself, such as data arriving from a network call, or it could be the result of an action by the user. This includes typing a new character into a text box, where the value (or *state*) of the input element changes every time a character is entered. To make sure that React stays in-sync with what the user is doing, we need to make sure we capture and respond to the user updating the contents of a text box. We accomplish that by doing the following:

1. Create a state variable in our code to hold the current contents, or value, of an `input` box.
2. Set the `value` attribute of that `input` box to that variable.
3. Add an `onChange` event handler to the `input` box that updates the state variable anytime the user changes the contents of the `input` box in the UI.

With those steps in place, anytime the value of the React state variable is updated, whether by the user or by your program, React will update the UI to reflect the current state.

12.1 Handling Input

Let's look at the following code example that pops up an alert in the web browser and displays the text that was entered when the *Submit* button is clicked:

Listing 12-1 File: *index.html*

```
<!DOCTYPE html>
<html lang="en">
  <head>
```

```html
    <script src="app.py"></script>
  </head>
  <body>
    <div id="root"></div>
  </body>
</html>
```

Listing 12-2 File: *pyreact.py*

```python
# Load React and ReactDOM JavaScript libraries into local namespace
React = require('react')
ReactDOM = require('react-dom')

# Map React javaScript objects to Python identifiers
createElement = React.createElement
useState = React.useState


def render(root_component, props, container):
    def main():
        ReactDOM.render(
            React.createElement(root_component, props),
            document.getElementById(container)
        )

    document.addEventListener('DOMContentLoaded', main)


# JavaScript function mappings
alert = window.alert
```

Listing 12-3 File: *app.py*

```python
from pyreact import alert, useState, render, createElement as el

def App():
    newItem, setNewItem = useState("")

    def handleSubmit():
        alert(f"Item is : {newItem}")
        setNewItem("")

    def handleChange(event):
```

```
        target = event['target']
        setNewItem(target['value'])

    return el('div', None,
              el('label', {'htmlFor': 'editBox'}, "New Item: "),
              el('input', {'id': 'editBox',
                           'onChange': handleChange,
                           'value': newItem
                          }
                ),
              el('button', {'onClick': handleSubmit}, "Submit"),
             )

render(App, None, 'root')
```

Next, we need to update the two build scripts that we previously added to **package.json** to use the new **index.html** file as the application entry point, which is what we will use moving forward:

```
"start": "NODE_ENV=development parcel --log-level 4 index.html --out-dir
    ↪   dist/dev",
"build": "NODE_ENV=production parcel --log-level 4 build index.html
    ↪   --no-source-maps --out-dir dist/prod",
```

And now we can build the development version of our application with:

(venv) $ npm start

Once it finishes, Parcel will start up a local HTTP server on port 1234 by default, which we can open here:

http://localhost:1234

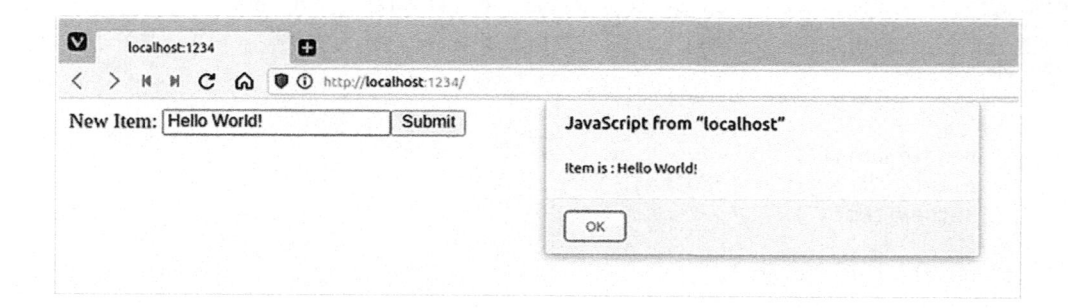

Other than renaming a few things, the HTML file and our **pyreact.py** JavaScript wrapper module haven't really changed much from what we had in the previous section. We did add a JavaScript function mapping for `window.alert()` to the **pyreact.py** module just for convenience and to keep all of the JavaScript calls in one Python module.

Breaking down our **app.py** module, we start with a few imports from the module where we did our mapping of JavaScript functions to Python objects. Using this pattern, we keep the bulk of our application written completely in Python and avoid mixing programming languages that make the Python linter complain.

As in previous examples, we have one React component named App that is the entry point for the `render()` function that inserts our dynamically created elements into the DOM. The important part of the App function, and what makes it a React component, is that the return value is a React element type. In this case, we are returning a `div` element that has an HTML `label`, text `input`, and a `button`, as its children.

You will notice that because the return value is actually one big `createElement()` function call and not actually procedural code, that the typical four-space Python indentation that you are familiar with is not used. It is still valid Python syntax in that we are really just breaking up long lines of code. But it is structured in a way that enhances readability by using the nested function calls as indented code blocks instead of what we would normally see in procedural code. The functional coding style in the return expressions of our React component functions will become more evident as our React UI examples get more sophisticated.

Starting with the `label` element, it has one prop being passed to it that is the `for` attribute that links it to an `input` element by its `id` attribute. This has the effect of allowing the user to click on the `label` and have the focus jump to the linked `input` element. The only child of the label is the text of the label itself. One note is that because "for" is a reserved word in JavaScript, React aliases the "*for*" attribute as "*htmlFor*", and changes it back to "*for*" when it is rendered in the browser.

Next is the `input` element that allows the user to enter a text value. For this element, we are passing three props into it. The first is just the `id` property that the `label` element `for` attribute refers to. The next is the `onChange` property that specifies the event handler that fires every time the value in the `input` box changes. The last is the value that the input box should display. For this one, we are using a React state variable that was previously defined along with the corresponding setter function to update it. So whenever we update the `newItem` state variable using the `setNewItem()` update function, React will re-render the `App` component and use the value of the `newItem` variable to populate the input box.

The function `handleChange()` that we are using to handle the `onChange` event of the `input` box is triggered any time the user modifies the `input` box's value. This happens on every keystroke while the input box has the focus in the web browser. The only thing this function does is make our `newItem` state variable match whatever the user has entered into the input box. This change in state of the `App` component causes React to re-render the page with the new value. Since we use the `newItem` variable for the `input` box's value, React will update the contents of the `input` box to reflect what the user typed in.

When we have this two-way binding between the React state variable and the `input` box, it is referred to as a *controlled component*. This method is generally preferred over using uncontrolled inputs, where you would need to manage transfer of the input state manually.

In the `handleChange()` function, we are using the `event` parameter that is automatically passed to any function that handles an HTML event. The `target` property of the JavaScript generated `event` object contains information about the source of the event. In this case, it would be a reference to the `input` box. From that, we can extract the `value` property of the input box to store in our `newItem` state variable. In JavaScript, we would normally use object dot notation to refer to the value like this:

```
event.target.value
```

While this would usually work in our Python code because Transcrypt is able to translate it properly, there are some cases where it could potentially cause a problem if the key conflicts with a reserved word. In Python, we can treat the event object as a dictionary and use standard Python dictionary syntax instead, which also keeps our code looking like Python:

```
event['target']['value']
```

We treat `event['target']` as a dictionary as well, so we also use `value` as a dictionary key to extract the actual value.

The last element is our *Submit* button that is passed just one prop, and that is the onClick property that calls our handleSubmit() function when the onClick event is fired. The handleSubmit() function calls the JavaScript alert() function from our **pyreact.py** module to display the current value of the newItem state variable, which is also the value of the input box. Because the JavaScript alert() function is blocking, our code will stop executing while the alert is open. When the alert is closed in the web browser, the code continues execution and we reset the value of newItem to an empty string using the setNewItem() update function.

12.2 Generated Elements

If you go into the developer console of the web browser and look at the *Element* tab, you should see an element tree that looks something like this:

```html
<html lang="en">
  <head>
    <script src="/app.12cad815.js"></script>
  </head>
  <body>
    <div id="root">
      <div>
        <label for="newItem">New Item: </label>
        <input id="newItem" value="">
        <button>Submit</button>
      </div>
    </div>
  </body>
</html>
```

Here you can see the content from the original HTML file along with the generated elements from our React App component added into the DOM as children of the original "root" div. One thing you'll notice is that our script file was originally specified as **app.py**, but the Parcel bundler has changed it to use the generated JavaScript bundle instead. This generated file has our transpiled Python code, all of the JavaScript libraries we utilize like React and all of its dependencies, and the Transcrypt runtime library, all bundled into one JavaScript file. The bundled JavaScript file retains the original root name, but has a hash value appended to it which gives it a unique file signature. Whenever your code changes, a new hash value will be generated to ensure you are always using the latest version of your code and not a version that is cached by the web browser.

12.3 Summary

We reviewed the core architecture of a React application, and we also now know how to work with text input boxes in React, as well as how to handle button clicks. The key takeaway here, is that any time you have a value that changes in the UI, you should have a corresponding state variable in your code that stores that value. React uses changes to that state variable in determining when the UI needs to be re-rendered.

Chapter Review:

1. Create source files:
   index.html
   pyreact.py
   app.py

2. Update the build scripts in **package.json**:

```
"start": "NODE_ENV=development parcel --log-level 4 index.html --out-dir
    dist/dev",
"build": "NODE_ENV=production parcel --log-level 4 build index.html
    --no-source-maps --out-dir dist/prod",
```

3. Build the application for development with:
   `npm start`

4. Open the application:
   http://localhost:1234

References:

- Chapter code
  https://github.com/rtp-book/code/tree/main/ch12

- Input element
  https://html.spec.whatwg.org/multipage/input.html

- Label element
  https://html.spec.whatwg.org/multipage/forms.html#the-label-element

- Button element
  https://html.spec.whatwg.org/multipage/form-elements.html#the-button-element

Chapter 13 – Lists

In this chapter, we will build upon what we did previously and give an example of how we can dynamically add and remove elements in our application.

13.1 HTML Lists

For this example, we are going to take the application code from the previous chapter, and instead of just displaying an `alert` when we click the *Submit* button, we will add the value in the input box to a list of displayed items. This time around, we are going to keep the HTML file and **pyreact.py** module the same as last time and just update the **app.py** file as shown here:

Listing 13-1 File: *app.py*

```
from pyreact import useState, render, createElement as el

def App():
    newItem, setNewItem = useState("")
    listItems, setListItems = useState([])

    def handleSubmit():
        new_list = list(listItems)   # Make a copy
        new_list.append(newItem)     # Add the new item
        setListItems(new_list)       # Update our state
        setNewItem("")               # Clear the new item value

    def handleChange(event):
        target = event['target']
        setNewItem(target['value'])

    def getListItems():
        items = []
        for item in listItems:
            element = el('li', {'key': item}, item)
            items.append(element)

        return items

    return el('div', None,
            el('label', {'htmlFor': 'editBox'}, "New Item: "),
```

```
            el('input', {'id': 'editBox',
                         'onChange': handleChange,
                         'value': newItem
                        }
               ),
            el('button', {'onClick': handleSubmit}, "Submit"),
            el('ol', None, getListItems()),
            )

render(App, None, 'root')
```

Most of our core React App component is the same, but we added a few things to support the list we want to build. The first thing we need is a way to store our list items, so using the `React.useState()` method, we added a new state variable to our code called `listItems`. This also gives us the `setListItems()` method to use when we want to update the value of the `listItems` variable.

In the function `handleSubmit()` that handles the `onClick` event of the `button`, we change its behavior by removing the `alert` we had there previously, and add code that will update our `listItems` state variable. Because React uses changes in the value of state and prop variables to know when the UI needs to be re-rendered, we need to use setter functions to update them in a controlled manner and never modify them directly. As such, state and prop variables are immutable, so we need to first make a copy of the current `listItems` state and store it in a local variable called `new_list`. After that, we can add the `newItem` value to the local copy of the list, which is then passed to the `setListItems()` update method to actually update the state of our App component.

Lastly, we reset the value of the `newItem` state variable to an empty string by using the `setNewItem()` update method. Whenever we call `setNewItem()` or `setListItems()` to update our state, React will automatically re-render the UI to reflect the current state of the App component when the current event completes.

In the return statement of our App component, we added a standard HTML ordered list element (`ol`) after the existing `button` element. This will create a list with sequentially numbered list items. To generate the children of the `ol` element, we created the `getListItems()` function that loops through the items in our `listItems` state variable. Then for every item in `listItems`, it appends a new list item (`li`) element to a regular Python list. We then return that list from the function to be used as the children of the `ol` element.

Whenever you have a repeating list of React elements, you should add a "key" property to each element that uniquely identifies that particular element in the list. The value can be anything as long as it does not change between renders, and it is not repeated anywhere else in that list. React uses this key to keep track of which elements have changed between renders to help it be as efficient as possible in determining which components need to be updated when there is a change in state.

One last detail is that we also removed the import for the `alert` function since we are no longer using it here.

If the Parcel development web server is already running, the code we modified should automatically rebuild, though it sometimes requires making the running Parcel web server the active window. If it is not running, then start it back up and build our application again with:

(venv) $ `npm start`

Once it finishes, Parcel will again start up a local HTTP server on port 1234 which we can open here:

http://localhost:1234

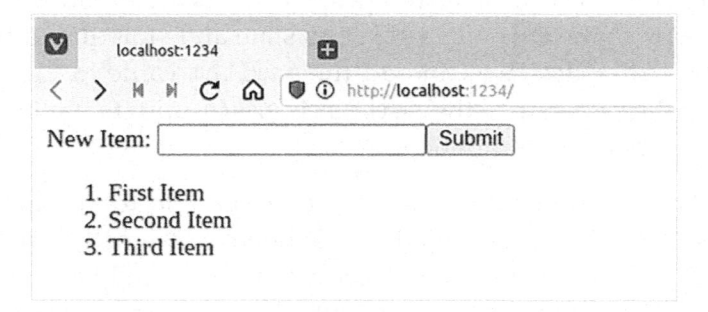

If we now enter a text value into the input box and click the *Submit* button, the item should be added to a list below the `input` box. Repeating this a few times will continue to add to the list, incrementing the numbered value of each added item as it goes.

Looking at the generated HTML in the Elements tab of the web browser development console, we can see an `li` element added to the DOM for every entry that we made and clicked the Submit button for:

```
<html lang="en">
  <head>
      <script src="/app.12cad815.js"></script>
  </head>
  <body>
    <div id="root">
      <div>
        <label for="newItem">New Item: </label>
        <input id="newItem" value="">
        <button>Submit</button>
        <ol>
          <li>First Item</li>
          <li>Second Item</li>
          <li>Third Item</li>
        </ol>
      </div>
    </div>
  </body>
</html>
```

So once again, the key to React is to use state variables to hold any data in your application that can change and affect how the UI is rendered. The HTML elements that you want to add to the DOM are what get returned from the React functional components. The data that you pass in as variables during the creation of these elements determines how React renders the UI.

13.2 List Component

One last change we'll make to our code before moving on to the next topic, is to make what we have a little more React-like. The way we implemented the generation of our list elements works, but it is not a best-practice React design pattern. Since we are already returning a list of React elements anyway, let's change our generic function to be an actual React component instead.

Listing 13-2 File: *app.py*

```
from pyreact import useState, render, createElement as el

def App():
    newItem, setNewItem = useState("")
    listItems, setListItems = useState([])
```

```python
    def handleSubmit():
        new_list = list(listItems)  # Make a copy
        new_list.append(newItem)    # Add the new item
        setListItems(new_list)      # Update our state
        setNewItem("")   # Clear the new item value

    def handleChange(event):
        target = event['target']
        setNewItem(target['value'])

    def ListItems():
        items = []
        for item in listItems:
            element = el('li', {'key': item}, item)
            items.append(element)

        return items

    return el('div', None,
            el('label', {'htmlFor': 'editBox'}, "New Item: "),
            el('input', {'id': 'editBox',
                        'onChange': handleChange,
                        'value': newItem
                        }
            ),
            el('button', {'onClick': handleSubmit}, "Submit"),
            el('ol', None,
                el(ListItems, None)
              ),
        )

render(App, None, 'root')
```

Because the existing function already returns a list of React elements, by just changing the name of our `getListItems()` function to `ListItems()` using the React PascalCase naming convention, it becomes a valid React component itself and can be used by the `React.createElement()` method to create the list elements in a more consistent way. So instead of calling an imperative generic function to get the children of the ordered list, we treat it like any other React component and use the more declarative `createElement()` method that lets React insert the list items into the DOM. In addition to changing the name of the function itself to be recognized by React as a component, we also change how we use it and go from a regular function call like this:

```
el('ol', None, getListItems()),
```

to using it as a React component like this:

```
el('ol', None,
    el(ListItems, None)
),
```

This is an important pattern to use because React can manage the rendering of components more efficiently when they are comprised of other React components, rather than just arbitrary functions. This also helps your code to be more structurally consistent, and can help when debugging components in the web browser.

An important point to note is that we are passing a function reference into `createElement()` in this case and not a string like we have been using for the built-in HTML elements. Also, we are just specifying the function name and not actually calling the function as would happen if we had parentheses at the end of it. To be more specific, we are passing `ListItems` as a callback function to the `createElement()` method, and not calling it directly ourselves.

13.3 Summary

Now we know how to store user-entered data in our application and then present it back to the user by way of an HTML list. We also saw how to update more complex data types, in this case a Python list, by making a copy of a state variable, updating the copy, and then using the associated update method for the state variable to actually change the value of it. State and prop variables should always be treated as immutable, and should never be updated directly by assignment (in other words, don't use an equal sign to update them).

We also learned that directly calling functions to generate elements is not ideal. Instead, it is better to turn those functions into React components, which helps React manage the rendering of your applications more efficiently.

Chapter Review:

1. Update source file (List):
   app.py

2. Build the application for development with:
   `npm start`

3. Open the application:
   http://localhost:1234

4. Update source file (List Component):
   app.py

References:

- Chapter code
  https://github.com/rtp-book/code/tree/main/ch13

- Ordered List element
  https://html.spec.whatwg.org/multipage/grouping-content.html#the-ol-element

Chapter 14 – Forms

Whenever you have text input boxes and buttons to act on the values entered in those boxes, it is common practice to utilize the HTML form element to tie everything together.

14.1 Form Action

Once again, we will build upon what we have been working on in the last few chapters and add the features of an HTML form element to our **app.py** file:

Listing 14-1 File: *app.py*

```
from pyreact import useState, render, createElement as el

def App():
    newItem, setNewItem = useState("")
    listItems, setListItems = useState([])

    def handleSubmit(event):
        event.preventDefault()
        new_list = list(listItems)   # Make a copy
        new_list.append(newItem)     # Add the new item
        setListItems(new_list)       # Update our state
        setNewItem("")               # Clear the new item value

    def handleChange(event):
        target = event['target']
        setNewItem(target['value'])

    def ListItems():
        items = []
        for item in listItems:
            element = el('li', {'key': item}, item)
            items.append(element)

        return items

    return el('form', {'onSubmit': handleSubmit},
              el('label', {'htmlFor': 'editBox'}, "New Item: "),
              el('input', {'id': 'editBox',
                           'onChange': handleChange,
```

```
                            'value': newItem
                        }
                    ),
                el('input', {'type': 'submit'}),
                el('ol', None,
                    el(ListItems, None)
                ),
            )

render(App, None, 'root')
```

With these changes, if the Parcel development web server is already running, it will automatically build just by making the running Parcel web server the active window. If it is not running, then start it back up with npm start to build the application. Once it's done building, refresh the web browser at:

   http://localhost:1234

This time, to convert our little application to be a more conventional HTML form, we just had to modify a few lines of code to get the result we are looking for. While the UI hasn't visibly changed, the behavior reflects the use of the form element.

Most of the changes here are in the type of elements we are returning from our React component. Instead of wrapping everything in a plain div element, we change this to a form, passing in a prop containing the onSubmit event value set to call our handleSubmit() function.

```
el('form', {'onSubmit': handleSubmit},
```

Because our form will now dictate what action gets taken on submit, we don't need our submit button anymore, but we do provide an input element that has a prop passed to it that sets type=submit, which ends up getting rendered as a button that has the built-in action of causing the form to be submitted.

```
el('input', {'type': 'submit'}),
```

Normally when an HTML form gets submitted, it makes a request back to the web server that returns a response to the web browser, which re-renders the entire page with a possibly updated URL. In this case, we don't want that to happen since all of the logic we need to process the submit action is already contained in our application and is already loaded in the web browser. To get around this behavior, we add a statement to our `handleSubmit()` function that tells the web browser to not do what it normally does by default:

```
def handleSubmit(event):
    event.preventDefault()
```

Since we are now utilizing the event object that is passed to HTML event handlers by default, we also need to add it to our Python function as a parameter that is passed in. We were able to omit it previously since we weren't using it.

One of the side benefits of using a formal HTML `form` element is that instead of having to explicitly click the submit button, we now have a default action available that will submit the form when we enter a value into our input box and press [Enter] on the keyboard.

14.2 Summary

Using an HTML form gives us a little more control over how form data is processed, and it only required minor changes to how we structured our React component.

Chapter Review:

1. Update source file:
   app.py
2. Build the application for development with:
   `npm start`
3. Open the application:
   http://localhost:1234

References:

- Chapter code
  https://github.com/rtp-book/code/tree/main/ch14
- Form element
  https://html.spec.whatwg.org/multipage/forms.html#the-form-element

Chapter 15 – React Components

As we mentioned earlier, components are functions that return elements created with the `React.createElement()` method. While it would be certainly possible to have your entire application be built within one component function, most applications of any complexity would benefit from using multiple components, where the application is broken up into logical blocks of functionality.

For example, in creating a tree structure for a simple form application that has a filterable list with a header and footer, you might end up with components chained together like this:

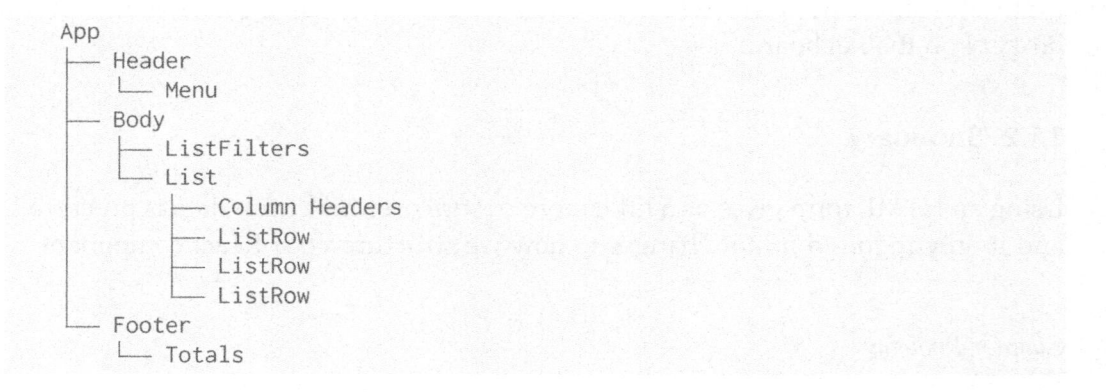

```
App
 ├── Header
 │    └── Menu
 ├── Body
 │    ├── ListFilters
 │    └── List
 │         ├── Column Headers
 │         ├── ListRow
 │         ├── ListRow
 │         └── ListRow
 └── Footer
      └── Totals
```

Each of those listed items could be a separate functional component that generates the elements required for one section of the form. In the case of ListRow, it would also be a reusable component that displays different values based on the props that are passed into it.

In practice, you might start building your application as one component. As you add more and more elements to it to build the UI, it will eventually become unwieldy. To keep it manageable, it should be broken up into smaller parts, or more specifically, components. The concept of composing components is really no different than you would do with any computer program. By taking a large complex problem and breaking it up into smaller, easier to understand modules, the task of creating each of those smaller modules becomes much simpler. By convention, you would typically have one component per Python file, but if you have several small related components, there is nothing wrong with keeping them in a single module. It just comes down to a matter of personal preference at that point.

Fortunately, React makes it very easy to create components. Knowing when and how to break up an application into multiple components is somewhat subjective, but will typically fall on clean lines between function, UI arrangement, or both. Taking the simple list example we did previously, let's look at how we might break that up into logical components, separating the user input section from the list section.

15.1 Adding Functionality

Right now, we have a list that we can add items to, but what if we want to delete items? Let's add that functionality now:

Listing 15-1 File: *app.py*

```python
from pyreact import useState, render, createElement as el

def App():
    newItem, setNewItem = useState("")
    listItems, setListItems = useState([])

    def handleSubmit(event):
        event.preventDefault()
        new_list = list(listItems)    # Make a copy
        new_list.append(newItem)      # Add the new item
        setListItems(new_list)        # Update our state
        setNewItem("")                # Clear the new item value

    def handleChange(event):
        target = event['target']
        setNewItem(target['value'])

    def handleDelete(item):
        new_list = list(listItems)    # Make a copy
        new_list.remove(item)         # Remove the specified item
        setListItems(new_list)        # Update our state

    def ListItem(props):
        return el('li', None,
            props['item'] + " ",
            el('button', {'type': 'button',
```

```python
                        'onClick': lambda: handleDelete(props['item'])
                        }, "Delete"),
                )

    def ListItems():
        items = []
        for item in listItems:
            items.append(el(ListItem, {'key': item, 'item': item}))
        return items

    return el('form', {'onSubmit': handleSubmit},
            el('label', {'htmlFor': 'editBox'}, "New Item: "),
            el('input', {'id': 'editBox',
                        'onChange': handleChange,
                        'value': newItem
                        }
              ),
            el('input', {'type': 'submit'}),
            el('ol', None,
              el(ListItems, None)
              ),
          )

render(App, None, 'root')
```

With those changes in place, refresh the application in the web browser at:

http://localhost:1234

If for some reason the application doesn't refresh and show the *Delete* button that we just added, stop the Parcel development web server with *Ctrl-C*, and delete the generated content in your project folder. These include the **dist**, **__target__** and **.cache** folders. Then, restart the Parcel web server with `npm start`, which will proceed to do a full rebuild of your application.

To delete an item from the list, we created the function handleDelete() that takes the name of the item to delete as a passed in parameter. We then follow the pattern we used when we added the item, starting by making a copy of our listItems state variable. Remember that we want to treat our state variables as immutable, and we should never modify them directly. Next, we remove the item of interest from the local copy of the Python list based on the name that was passed in, and call the setListItems() update function, passing in the local copy of our list that now has the specified item removed. This updates the overall state of the App component and triggers React to re-render the UI.

Since our list will have a "Delete" button for every item in the list, we'll want to make each one specific to that particular item in the list. By using a Python lambda function instead of calling the handleDelete() function directly, we can actually save the value of the current list item inside the function that we attach to the onClick event handler at the time the list element gets created.

To do that, rather than creating all of the list elements in one function, we break out the creation of a *single* list item element into its own React component:

```python
def ListItem(props):
    return el('li', None,
              props['item'] + " ",
              el('button', {'type': 'button',
                 'onClick': lambda: handleDelete(props['item'])
                 }, "Delete"),
        )
```

The props parameter that we pass into the ListItem component is a Python dictionary that has a key named *item*. For the onClick event handler of the button element that we supply to each of the li elements, we use the handleDelete() function. But here, we also include the value of the *item* prop that was passed into the ListItem function as a parameter. This creates a problem though, because we are now *calling* the handleDelete() function when we really only want to provide a reference to the function itself. To get around this, we wrap the call to the parameterized handleDelete() function inside of a Python lambda function. This way, we end up using a reference to the generated lambda function for the onClick event handler instead of the handleDelete() function itself. This has the end effect where every "Delete" button in our list has a unique function pointer for their respective onClick events.

One thing to be careful of when parameterizing your function calls, is to make sure that you have closure on the creation of the function by either wrapping it in a Python `lambda` or by redefining the function every time you use it. If you don't do this, you will end up using the same function reference each time, and the parameters will not change, resulting in unexpected behavior. In fact, it will just use whatever the last values were that were supplied to it, and not be unique for each item in the list.

Now that we have a way of creating an individual `ListItem`, we also modified the existing `ListItems()` (plural) function to generate the list using the new `ListItem` (singular) component:

```python
def ListItems():
    items = []
    for item in listItems:
        items.append(el(ListItem, {'key': item, 'item': item}))
    return items
```

So while we are still looping through the `listItems` state variable, we are now adding slightly more complex `ListItem` components instead of simple built-in HTML `li` elements. Two things to take note of, the first being that since our *list* of elements is still being generated here, this is where we use the key prop that uniquely identifies each item in the list for React to use when rendering. The key prop does *not* need to be used in the `ListItem` (singular) component where we are only generating one individual list item and not a series of list items. The second prop we are passing to the `ListItem` component is the *item* value that we use to parameterize to the `handleDelete()` function as discussed above.

15.2 Adding More Functionality

Now that we can add and remove items from our list, let's also add the ability to edit items in the list. Here's the updated code to do so:

Listing 15-2 File: *app.py*

```python
from pyreact import useState, render, createElement as el

def App():
    newItem, setNewItem = useState("")
```

```python
    editItem, setEditItem = useState("")
    listItems, setListItems = useState([])

    def handleSubmit(event):
        event.preventDefault()
        new_list = list(listItems)  # Make a copy
        if len(editItem) > 0:  # In edit mode
            new_list[new_list.index(editItem)] = newItem
        else:  # In add mode
            new_list.append(newItem)  # Add the new item
        setListItems(new_list)  # Update our state
        setNewItem("")  # Clear the new item value
        setEditItem("")  # Clear the edit item value

    def handleChange(event):
        target = event['target']
        setNewItem(target['value'])

    def handleDelete(item):
        new_list = list(listItems)  # Make a copy
        new_list.remove(item)  # Remove the specified item
        setListItems(new_list)  # Update our state

    def handleEdit(item):
        setNewItem(item)  # Set the new item value
        setEditItem(item)  # Set the edit item value

    def ListItem(props):
        return el('li', None,
                  props['item'] + " ",
                  el('button', {'type': 'button',
                                'onClick': lambda: handleDelete(props['item'])
                                }, "Delete"
                  ),
                  el('button', {'type': 'button',
                                'onClick': lambda: handleEdit(props['item'])
                                }, "Edit"
                  ),
        )

    def ListItems():
        return [el(ListItem, {'key': item, 'item': item}) for item in listItems]

    return el('form', {'onSubmit': handleSubmit},
              el('label', {'htmlFor': 'editBox'},
```

```
            "Add Item: " if len(editItem) == 0 else "Edit Item: "
        ),
        el('input', {'id': 'editBox',
                     'onChange': handleChange,
                     'value': newItem
                    }
        ),
        el('input', {'type': 'submit'}),
        el('ol', None,
            el(ListItems, None)
          ),
    )

render(App, None, 'root')
```

Once you refresh the application in the web browser, you should see the Edit button that we just added:

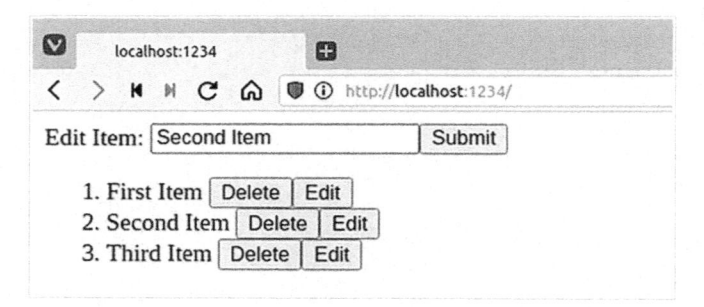

To handle edits, we reuse the text input box we already have, but we need a way of knowing whether we are adding a new value to the list or editing an existing value. To accomplish this, we created a new state variable `editItem` that is either an empty string when not editing or it holds the original value of the item being edited. This allows us to do two things. The first being that when we submit the form, if the value is an empty string then we know we need to add a value instead of edit one. The second is that if there is a non-empty value, we use that original value to look up which list item needs to be changed.

We also use the new `editItem` state variable to determine if the label for the text input box should indicate if we are adding or editing the content in the input box. We did this logic inline by using a Python ternary expression as the child parameter of the `createElement()` method.

```
el('label', {'htmlFor': 'editBox'},
    "Add Item: " if len(editItem) == 0 else "Edit Item: "
),
```

Ternary expressions are frequently used for doing conditional rendering, where what elements get rendered is determined by the current state of the component. This can be something as simple as changing a text value as we did here, or as complex as turning an entire branch of your component tree off and on.

In the case when you want to show a component or not, you can use a ternary expression to either return the component, or if you don't want anything to display, then just return the value None. For example, if we wanted to have our ListItems component be conditionally displayed only if there were items in our list, we could do something like this:

```
el('ol', None,
    el(ListItems, None) if len(listItems) > 0 else None
),
```

Another place a ternary expression is useful, is to substitute a default value when a variable has a value of None. For example, if you are expecting a string value and a variable is nullable, you can do this to ensure the value is a string when you go to use it:

```
myvar_string = myvar if myvar else ""
```

This expression relies on the truthiness of the value of None. That is, None always evaluates to False, and anything that is not None evaluates to True. This is a place you have to be careful because there is a difference in truthiness between Python and JavaScript when it comes to empty lists, dictionaries, and sets. In Python, an empty list evaluates to False, whereas in JavaScript it evaluates to True. If you try to test this value in an expression, you may not get the result you intended. To work around this transpilation anomaly, the most straightforward and recommended way is to just check if your list has a length of zero. For example, the expression len([]) > 0 will always evaluate to False in both Python and JavaScript.

To initiate the edit mode, we set the onClick event handler for the "Edit" button the same way we did for the "Delete" button. We once again used a lambda to create a unique function reference that had the value of the specific item saved as a fixed parameter of the handleEdit() function.

In the handleEdit() function itself, all we do is populate the text input box, and save the original value of the item being edited in our editItem state variable so we can find the right item to update later on when the form gets submitted.

The last bit we snuck in to this update to our code was a change to our ListItems functional component. Instead of creating a local list variable and appending elements to it in a for loop, we changed it to use a Python list comprehension instead. While functionally the same, it accomplishes the same thing with fewer lines of code, but still remains subjectively readable. If you are not used to using list comprehensions, using a for loop is fine. But the pattern of generating lists of elements in React is quite common, and list comprehensions are a very direct and Pythonic way of accomplishing that task.

15.3 Decomposition

Up to this point, we have been using one module, and for that matter one React component, to hold our entire application. Even the ListItem and ListItems components we currently have are inner functions of our main App component. While there is nothing technically wrong with this, and it affords some conveniences from a scoping standpoint, as your application grows it will get more and more unwieldy the more functionality you add to it.

As a simple example of how to physically break up a component once it grows too much, let's extract the ListItems component from the App component and move it into its own module.

Listing 15-3 File: *listItems.py*

```python
from pyreact import createElement as el

def ListItem(props):
    item = props['item']
    handleDelete = props['handleDelete']
    handleEdit = props['handleEdit']

    return el('li', None,
            props['item'] + " ",
            el('button', {'type': 'button',
```

```
                        'onClick': lambda: handleDelete(item)
                    }, "Delete"
                ),
                el('button', {'type': 'button',
                        'onClick': lambda: handleEdit(item)
                    }, "Edit"
                ),
            )

def ListItems(props):
    return [el(ListItem, {'key': item,
                    'item': item,
                    'handleDelete': props['handleDelete'],
                    'handleEdit': props['handleEdit']
                }
            ) for item in props['listItems']]
```

The first thing we did when spitting off the ListItems component was to adjust the import statements to match just what we need. In the **listItems.py** module, the only import we need is the React.createElement() method. In our **app.py** module, we import the ListItems component from the newly created listItems module.

Listing 15-4 File: *app.py*

```
from pyreact import useState, render, createElement as el
from listItems import ListItems

def App():
    newItem, setNewItem = useState("")
    editItem, setEditItem = useState("")
    listItems, setListItems = useState([])

    def handleSubmit(event):
        event.preventDefault()
        new_list = list(listItems)  # Make a copy
        if len(editItem) > 0:  # In edit mode
            new_list[new_list.index(editItem)] = newItem
        else:  # In add mode
            new_list.append(newItem)  # Add the new item
        setListItems(new_list)  # Update our state
        setNewItem("")  # Clear the new item value
        setEditItem("")  # Clear the edit item value
```

```python
    def handleChange(event):
        target = event['target']
        setNewItem(target['value'])

    def handleDelete(item):
        new_list = list(listItems)   # Make a copy
        new_list.remove(item)  # Remove the specified item
        setListItems(new_list)  # Update our state

    def handleEdit(item):
        setNewItem(item)   # Set the new item value
        setEditItem(item)  # Set the edit item value

    return el('form', {'onSubmit': handleSubmit},
            el('label', {'htmlFor': 'editBox'},
              "Add Item: " if len(editItem) == 0 else "Edit Item: "
            ),
            el('input', {'id': 'editBox',
                         'onChange': handleChange,
                         'value': newItem
                        }
            ),
            el('input', {'type': 'submit'}),
            el('ol', None,
              el(ListItems, {'listItems': listItems,
                             'handleDelete': handleDelete,
                             'handleEdit': handleEdit}
              )
            ),
        )

render(App, None, 'root')
```

When we move a component into its own module, we also need to make sure it has access to the state variables and functions that it utilizes. In some cases, these can be moved along with the component itself. But many times, as in this case, we need to keep the state variables where they are because they are also needed at that higher level of the component tree we are building. When that happens, we need to pass the value of those state variables and references to the functions that use them, down to the lower-level components as properties of the component. These props can then be utilized by the lower-level components they were passed into. If you need to change the value of a state variable whose value was passed in as a prop, then you will need to pass that state variable's update function as well.

Prop variables are immutable just like state variables, but unlike state variables, there is no way to update them directly. If the value of a state variable is passed into a lower-level component as a prop, that prop is immutable. To update that prop indirectly, you would use the update function for the state variable (also passed in as a prop) to update the state variable in the parent component. That update in component state will cause React to re-render the UI, and once again pass the value of that same state variable into the lower-level component as a prop, but this time with the updated value.

Sometimes you will need to pass props from a higher level component down through several levels to the component where it is actually needed. We did that here with the `handleDelete()` and `handleEdit()` functions that are used in the `ListItem` component. Even though the `ListItems` component didn't use them directly, those two functions were passed through it as props to get to the `ListItem` component where they are actually used. This is what we were referring to in the first section of the book when we discussed how data flows downward through the tree structure in React.

In the `ListItem` component, we assigned the props that were passed into it to local variables just to make the code a bit clearer.

Note that because Parcel is watching the transpiled files in the __target__ folder for changes, it may not automatically detect changes in your Python files other than the entry point (in this case **app.py**). If you want to force it to do an incremental rebuild without restarting the whole thing, you can just touch the **app.py** file by making a minor change, like adding a space at the end of the file.

15.4 Summary

One thing you've hopefully noticed throughout this whole section of creating front-end web elements and handling web events, is that we haven't had to even *think* about JavaScript! Three things that you may end up using more in Python React applications than you are used to, especially if you don't currently do much functional programming, are ternary expressions, list comprehensions, and lambda expressions.

When developing React applications, your programming mindset should have a focus on data management, that is, the storing and manipulation of data that controls state. Because React is declarative, once you have the structure of the element tree specified, the only moving parts of your application are a function (literally) of changes in state. As long as you manage your state variables properly, React will ensure that the UI is rendered correctly. What this means is that you should avoid manipulating the DOM directly and always let React handle that part. You just tell react *what* to render, not when or how.

Chapter Review:

1. Update source file (Delete Button):
   app.py
2. Build the application for development with:
   `npm start`
3. Open the application:
   http://localhost:1234
4. Update source file (Edit Button):
   app.py
5. Add source file:
   listItems.py
6. Update source file (Decomposed Component):
   app.py

References:

- Chapter code
  https://github.com/rtp-book/code/tree/main/ch15
- Thinking in React
  https://reactjs.org/docs/thinking-in-react.html

Chapter 16 – JavaScript Examples

In this chapter, we'll look at how to convert React examples you might find online into a Python equivalent. Being that React is a JavaScript library, it makes sense that most if not all of the examples you might find to accomplish a specific task will be written in JavaScript. As you start doing this, you will find several patterns that will emerge in performing the manual translation from JavaScript to Python. We'll cover a number of those patterns here.

We will continue to use our existing **pyreact.py** module to bridge JavaScript libraries to Python, but we'll need to add a few simple mappings to it later on.

16.1 To-Do List

The example we are going to use to practice converting JavaScript into a Python equivalent, is a simple *To-Do List* application that uses some of the logic we saw being used in previous chapters. Here is the JavaScript file in its entirety (Note: You do NOT need to create this file!):

Listing 16-1 File: *todo.jsx*

```
import React from 'react';
import ReactDOM from 'react-dom';

class App extends React.Component {
  constructor(props) {
    super(props);
    this.state = {
      newTask: "",
      editTask: null,
      taskList: Array(),
      taskCount: 0,
      taskFilter: "all"
    };
  }

  handleSubmit = (event) => {
    event.preventDefault();
    const taskList = this.state.taskList.slice();
    if (this.state.editTask) {
      const taskIndex = taskList.findIndex(
```

```js
      (task => task.name === this.state.editTask.name)
    );
    taskList[taskIndex].name = this.state.newTask;
  } else {
    taskList.push({name: this.state.newTask, status: false});
  }
  this.setState({newTask: "", editTask: null, taskList: taskList});
}

handleEdit = (task) => {
  this.setState({newTask: task.name, editTask: task});
}

handleDelete = (task) => {
  const taskList = this.state.taskList.filter(function (item) {
    return item.name !== task.name;
  });
  this.setState({taskList: taskList});
}

handleChange = (event) => {
  if (event.target.name === "taskFilter") {
    this.setState({taskFilter: event.target.value});
  } else {
    this.setState({newTask: event.target.value});
  }
}

handleChangeStatus = (event, task) => {
  const taskList = this.state.taskList.slice();
  const taskIndex = taskList.findIndex((item => item.name === task.name));
  taskList[taskIndex].status = event.target.checked;
  this.setState({taskList: taskList});
}

renderTask = (task) => {
  const taskFilter = this.state.taskFilter
  if (taskFilter === "all" ||
      (taskFilter === "open" && !task.status) ||
      (taskFilter === "closed" && task.status)
  ) {
    return (
        <li key={task.name}>{task.name}
          <button
```

```jsx
                    type="button"
                    onClick={() => this.handleDelete(task)}
                >Delete
                </button>
                <button
                    type="button"
                    onClick={() => this.handleEdit(task)}
                >Edit
                </button>
                <label htmlFor="status"> Completed:</label>
                <input type="checkbox"
                    id="status"
                    onChange={(event) => this.handleChangeStatus(event, task)}
                    checked={task.status}
                />
            </li>
        );
    } else {
        return null
    }

}

updateCount() {
    let taskList
    switch (this.state.taskFilter) {
        case "open":
            taskList = this.state.taskList.filter((task => !task.status));
            break;
        case "closed":
            taskList = this.state.taskList.filter((task => task.status));
            break;
        default:
            taskList = this.state.taskList.slice();
    }

    const taskCount = taskList.length;
    this.setState({taskCount: taskCount})
}

componentDidMount() {
    document.title = "ToDo List";
}

componentDidUpdate(prevProps, prevState) {
```

```jsx
    if (prevState.taskList !== this.state.taskList ||
       prevState.taskFilter !== this.state.taskFilter
  ) {
    this.updateCount();
  }
}

render() {
  const taskFilter = this.state.taskFilter;
  return (
      <form onSubmit={this.handleSubmit}>
        <div>Number of Tasks: {this.state.taskCount}</div>
        <div>
          <label htmlFor="all">All Tasks:</label>
          <input type="radio"
                 name="taskFilter"
                 id="all"
                 value="all"
                 onChange={this.handleChange}
                 checked={taskFilter === "all"}
          />
          <label htmlFor="open"> Active:</label>
          <input type="radio"
                 name="taskFilter"
                 id="open"
                 value="open"
                 onChange={this.handleChange}
                 checked={taskFilter === "open"}
          />
          <label htmlFor="closed"> Completed:</label>
          <input type="radio"
                 name="taskFilter"
                 id="closed"
                 value="closed"
                 onChange={this.handleChange}
                 checked={taskFilter === "closed"}
          />
        </div>
        <label htmlFor="newTask">
          {this.state.editTask ? "Edit Task: " : "Add Task: "}
        </label>
        <input id="newTask"
               onChange={this.handleChange}
               value={this.state.newTask}
        />
```

```
        <input type="submit"/>
        <ol>
          {this.state.taskList.map(this.renderTask)}
        </ol>
      </form>
    );
  }
}

ReactDOM.render(<App/>, document.getElementById('root'));
```

Let's break down each piece of this single component React application and convert it to Python, starting with changing the React class component to a React functional component.

16.2 Class Components to Functions

Many examples you might find for React components will be class-based instead of using functional components and React hooks. There are four things in the code structure you'll need to modify to convert from a class component to a functional component:

1. The class declaration (of course)
2. The class constructor
3. Any component lifecycle functions
4. The `render()` method

Starting with the easy part, the class declaration of the App component, we have this:

```
class App extends React.Component {
```

Here, we can just change the class declaration to a simple Python def:

```
def App():
```

Next, we move on to the class constructor. The important part of incorporating this is that it is usually where state variables are created and initialized. If a component doesn't have any state that it's managing, then it may not have a constructor. The App component has five state variables that it uses to keep track of data that can affect the UI.

```
constructor(props) {
  super(props);
  this.state = {
    newTask: "",
    editTask: null,
    taskList: Array(),
    taskCount: 0,
    taskFilter: "all"
  };
}
```

To convert this, we create each of the state variables individually along with their respective state update functions using the React.useState() hook function and pass in the value that we want to initialize the variable to:

```
newTask, setNewTask = useState("")
editTask, setEditTask = useState(None)
taskList, setTaskList = useState([])
taskCount, setTaskCount = useState(0)
taskFilter, setTaskFilter = useState("all")
```

Since we are using functions instead of classes, there is no base class that needs to be initialized.

The third thing to look for are component lifecycle functions. These functions run at specific times in the React components life: at creation, when updated, and when removed. This allows the developer to perform things like connecting to outside services, or updating other parts of the application when these lifecycle functions are triggered by React. This example has two component lifecycle functions to convert:

```
componentDidMount() {
  document.title = "ToDo List";
}

componentDidUpdate(prevProps, prevState) {
  if (prevState.taskList !== this.state.taskList ||
```

```
        prevState.taskFilter !== this.state.taskFilter
    ) {
        this.updateCount();
    }
}
```

In general, the React class component lifecycle methods have been replaced in functional components with the `React.useEffect()` function hook. This function takes two parameters: a function reference to run, and an optional list of variables to monitor for changes. Whenever any of the variables in the list change, the specified function will be executed. This behavior replaces the `componentDidUpdate()` function of a class component. If an empty variable list is provided, the function will run once when the component is mounted in the DOM, and is a substitute for the `componentDidMount()` function. So to replace these two lifecycle functions, we can do something like this:

```
useEffect(lambda: setTitle("ToDo List"), [])
useEffect(updateCount, [taskList, taskFilter])
```

For this to work we will also need to add the JavaScript mappings for `document.title` and `React.useEffect()` to our **pyreact.py** file. In the first `useEffect()` hook, The `setTitle()` function just sets the JavaScript `document.title` property. In this case, since we provided an empty list for our watch conditions, it will just run once when the component is loaded. Note that if you use a value of `None` instead of an empty list, the function will be run *every time* the component is re-rendered. This can cause some performance issues and have undesirable side effects, so don't do that unless you are sure that's what you want.

The second `useEffect()` hook will watch for changes to our `taskList` and `taskFilter` state variables. Any time either one of those changes, the taskCount state variable will be recalculated with the `updateCount()` function, and be based on the number of tasks in our list and how they are specified to be filtered in the UI.

One class component lifecycle function you may come across that we don't have an example of here is the `componentWillUnmount()` function. This is normally used to do things like disconnect from remote services right before a component is being removed from the component tree. Normally, the function you supply as the first parameter to the useEffect() hook should *not* return a value. However, if you need to perform some action when the component is going to be removed, you can provide a function reference as the return value. Then, when the component is about to be removed, React will run the function that you supplied. For example, it might look something like this:

```
def cleanUp():
    def _cleanUp():
        print("Good Bye!")

    return _cleanUp

useEffect(cleanUp, [])
```

Since we provided an empty list as the watch parameter, this useEffect() function will run only once when the component is created. Because we supplied a *function* as a return value from the cleanUp() function that was called, the inner function _cleanUp() that we returned to useEffect() will be called at the time the component is going to be removed and will print the specified text to the web browser console.

The last item in our JavaScript class component conversion to Python is the class render() function. Since we are already in a function that returns React elements, we just need to use the return value of the existing render() function. If there is any other code in the original function, like local variables, it can just be added to the body of our functional component. So Starting with this JavaScript function:

```
render() {
const taskFilter = this.state.taskFilter;
    return (
        ...
    );
}
```

we make the render() function of the class component be the return expression of our new function component:

```
return ...
```

If the JavaScript component you are converting to Python is already a functional component, then you won't have to perform any of these steps. But the other conversion patterns that follow may still apply.

16.3 Anonymous Functions

Using inline anonymous functions in JavaScript React applications is a very common practice. In Python, the PEP 8 style guide suggests using anonymous functions or lambdas sparingly, and there are more limitations to Python lambdas compared to JavaScript's anonymous functions. The main restriction is that Python lambdas can only be a single-line statement. On the other hand, JavaScript anonymous functions can be many lines of code. In this case, the only option is to break out the function and create a named Python function to replace it. If the anonymous function is one line, then substituting it with a Python lambda is certainly an option. For example, take this `onClick` event property that uses an anonymous function to freeze the `task` parameter into the function call:

```
onClick={() => this.handleEdit(task)}
```

This can be directly converted to Python by using a lambda function:

```
'onClick': lambda: handleEdit(task)
```

If the anonymous JavaScript function is too complex for a one-line Python lambda, just create a named Python function, and use that function name in place of where the anonymous function used to be. In general, this is a good thing to do anyway as it usually makes the code easier to read.

16.4 Mapping Functions

Like anonymous functions, the JavaScript `map()` function is also regularly used in JavaScript React applications. It takes an iterable like a JavaScript Array and applies each element in the Array to a supplied function. Python also has a `map()` function, and while that certainly can be used, the Python preference is to use a list comprehension instead. And like the `map()` function that gets heavy use in

React to Python

JavaScript React projects, list comprehensions will become equally useful in Python React projects.

In our JavaScript example, a `map()` function is used to generate the list of task items:

```
{this.state.taskList.map(this.renderTask)}
```

If we were to use the Python map() function, we would turn it into this:

```
map(lambda task: el(ListItem, {'key': task['name'], 'task': task}), taskList)
```

However, it is considered more Pythonic to use a list comprehension, so let's use one of those instead. If you are not familiar with or are uncomfortable with list comprehensions, it is a Python construct that is worth learning. It's basically a one-line `for` loop that creates a new list based on a function.

With list comprehensions, sometimes it's hard to remember which pieces go where, so the way I think of them when creating one, is to start with the for loop part:

```
for task in taskList
```

Then, based on the loop variable (in this case `task`), figure out what the expression should be to create an item in the new list. In this case, we are creating a list of `ListItem` components so our function to create one element looks like this:

```
el(ListItem, {'key': task['name'], 'task': task})
```

Finally, since a list comprehension is creating a new list, we wrap those two things together in square brackets to represent the list:

```
[el(ListItem, {'key': task['name'], 'task': task}) for task in taskList]
```

You can also filter the items that are included in the final list by using an `if` clause after the `for` clause, but we'll leave that for another time.

16.5 Ternary Statements

With functional programming like we are doing with React, it's frequently convenient to create inline logical branching expressions for simple True/False type of conditions. JavaScript has a ternary operator that does just that. It takes a boolean expression that will either evaluate to True or False, followed by a question mark (?), then a value to return if the expression is True, and a value to return if the expression evaluates to False, separated by a colon (:). So in our example, there is a ternary expression that determines what text shows in the UI based on the value of editTask:

```
{this.state.editTask ? "Edit Task: " : "Add Task: "}
```

Python has the same thing, though it is not quite as terse as the JavaScript ternary operator. It is essentially an inline if-else statement:

```
"Edit Task: " if editTask is not None else "Add Task: "
```

The first clause is the result if the expression is True. The clause after the if keyword is the boolean expression to evaluate. The clause after the else keyword is the value to return if the expression evaluates to False.

16.6 Dictionaries

JavaScript has a generic object data type that can behave like a Python dictionary in terms of being able to store key/value pairs. When Transcrypt converts your Python code to JavaScript, it converts Python dictionaries into these standard JavaScript objects. But then, it also adds some methods and attributes to the bare JavaScript object that allows it to behave like a Python dictionary.

That last point is important to remember, because if you create a Python dictionary in Python, it can be utilized in JavaScript as a dictionary. If you get an object back from JavaScript (like a React component prop that is passed in) that happens to have key/value pairs, it might *not* be a dictionary and will just be a plain JavaScript object. If you're not careful, you may find this out the hard way when you try to use a dictionary method like update() on it and it gives you an error saying that it doesn't have an update() method. If you don't need any special dictionary methods then you can use it as-is as a key/value lookup, but if you *do* need those methods, you'll need to make it an actual dictionary again. Usually, just doing something like this will do the trick:

```
python_dict = dict(js_object)
```

This will take the bare JavaScript object and create a proper Python dictionary out of it, adding in the attributes and methods that make it a Python dictionary.

It should be noted that because JavaScript is more limited than Python in the data types that can be used as dictionary keys, I would recommend you stick with just using strings. In JavaScript, numbers as keys will get coerced into strings, and more complex objects like tuples are not allowed at all.

Regarding dictionary syntax, in Python you access dictionary elements using the string value of the key for the element you wish to reference:

```
task['status']
```

However, in JavaScript it is also permissible to access elements of a JavaScript object by using a dotted value syntax like this:

```
task.status
```

Because of how Transcrypt works, it is actually possible to get away with using the dot syntax for referencing dictionary keys in your Python code that gets transpiled into JavaScript. However, be aware that if any of the dictionary keys happen to be reserved words in Python, your application may not behave the way you expect it to.

Personally, I feel that when you're in Python land you should do it the Python way. While it may be a bit more inconvenient to use the Python dictionary syntax, your code will be more consistent, your brain will always be thinking in Python, and you'll run into fewer bugs down the road.

16.7 Spread Operator

In JavaScript, you may see a parameter notation that looks like this:

React to Python

```
var myObject = { foo: 'bar', bar: 123, baz: false };
var newObject = { ...myObject, bar: 42};
//newObject { foo: 'bar', bar: 42, baz: false }
```

The "..." notation is the JavaScript *Spread* operator which performs a function similar to what a dictionary `update()` method would be used for. It expands a list of parameters and merges or replaces values based on the keys of the parameters that follow. So to get similar behavior in Python you could do this:

```
myObject = { foo: 'bar', bar: 123, baz: false }
newObject = {}
# newObject { }
newObject.update(myObject)
# newObject { foo: 'bar', bar: 123, baz: false }
newObject.update({bar: 42})
# newObject { foo: 'bar', bar: 42, baz: false }
```

Because we are frequently working with immutable objects in React, we first start with an empty dictionary and use `update()` to populate it with the original values to get a new copy before updating the target value. Note that if the dictionary value is a complex object, you may need to use a `deepcopy()` function to make sure you are getting new values and not just copying object pointers. After that, you can use the `update()` method again to apply the new values.

You may also see the "..." notation in a JavaScript function definition, in which case it is a *Rest* parameter, which in Python is the same as using `*args` to refer to an arbitrary number of arguments.

16.8 JSX

It is common practice when using JavaScript to create React applications to utilize JSX, or JavaScript XML. Every example of a React component you find will almost always use JSX syntax for specifying the elements to be rendered. JSX is a syntax extension to JavaScript that looks like HTML but is actually just a cleaner way to create a `React.createElement()` statement. When transpiled from JSX to pure JavaScript, it basically just turns a JSX expression like this:

```
<button onClick={handleClick}>Click Me</button>
```

into this JavaScript expression:

```
React.createElement("button", {onClick: handleClick}, "Click Me")
```

When using JSX in JavaScript, it uses a somewhat familiar syntax and perhaps provides a better visualization of the React component tree that you are building. But since we are programming in Python, there are a few issues that it causes. The first being that the angle brace syntax is not valid Python, and Transcrypt would not be able to process our Python code properly if we had JSX embedded in our **.py** files. The second reason is more subjective, but one of the reasons we are using Transcrypt is to Program in Python, and introducing a pseudo XML syntax into our code kind of moves us away from that goal.

While Transcrypt *does* have a compiler directive that provides a mechanism for utilizing JSX, the restrictions placed on using it generally defeats the purpose of using JSX in the first place. The Transcrypt *xtrans* `pragma` allows us to shell out to another external translator application during Transcrypt's own transpile process. In other words, our transpiler would call another transpiler to process the JSX code in our application.

Personally, I prefer not to use JSX for several reasons.

1. It's not Python
2. It adds additional complexity to the developer toolchain
3. It is somewhat non-intuitive to have a transpiler shelling out to another transpiler
4. It's a bit kludgy to use with the Transcrypt pragma mechanism
5. It's not Python

So that said, the steps to convert JSX to Python code are pretty straightforward. We will basically be manually doing what a JSX transpiler does for JavaScript code, which is turning JSX code into calls to `React.createElement()`. For example, consider a JSX expression in JavaScript like this that would render a built-in HTML `div` tag:

```
<div>Number of Tasks: {this.state.taskCount}</div>
```

We would convert it to Python like this:

```
el('div', None, f"Number of Tasks: {taskCount}")
```

Assuming we imported `createElement` from **pyreact.py** and aliased it as `el`, the first step is to turn it into an `el()` function call. Next, if it is a built-in HTML tag, we put the tag in quotes and get rid of the angle braces. If there are tag attributes, we would put those in as a Python dictionary for the second parameter of the function. The last step is to take the inner part of the HTML tag and put it in as the third parameter of the function, converting it to Python syntax as necessary.

Here is another JSX example that has tag attributes including an inline anonymous function:

```
<button type="button" onClick={() => this.handleEdit(task)}>
  Edit
</button>
```

In this one we have a bit more work to do, but it's the same process: convert it to a `createElement()` function, turn the tag attributes into a dictionary, and make the inner text the third parameter:

```
el('button', {'type': 'button', 'onClick': lambda: handleEdit(task)},
  "Edit"
  )
```

If there is no inner text for the tag, then the third parameter of the `createElement()` function can be omitted. On the other hand, if there are no tag attributes, the second parameter of `createElement()` must still be supplied as None. If the tag is a React component instead of a built-in HTML tag, the process is the same. The only difference is that the tag name (in PascalCase) does *not* get quoted. Take this JSX expression for example:

```
<ListItems
   listItems={listItems}
   handleDelete={handleDelete}
   handleEdit={handleEdit}
/>
```

The above gets converted to Python like this:

```
el(ListItems, {'listItems': listItems,
            'handleDelete': handleDelete,
            'handleEdit': handleEdit}
)
```

While JSX may subjectively have some readability advantages, it is somewhat problematic to use with Python. As such, converting JSX to simple Python function calls eliminates those problems.

16.9 JavaScript Imports

We covered a few different ways of importing JavaScript libraries into the scope of our Python projects early on in the book. Moving forward, we'll assume that you are using the Parcel web application bundler, and using npm to locally store copies of the JavaScript libraries that you will be using in your project. So that said, the basic import of a JavaScript library will use the Node.js `require()` function like this:

```
React = require('react')
```

This ES5 style statement will cause the application bundler to import the JavaScript library into the current namespace and assign it to the Python variable on the left of the statement. Once we do that, we can import the library into another Python module as if it were a native Python object.

By comparison, you might come across the same JavaScript import with ES6 syntax, which would look like this:

```
import React from 'react';
```

For the React library, we are importing the top-level default object. For other JavaScript libraries, we may want to just import one named function from the library. This applies especially if the libraries are large and you only need one small function out of it. For example, consider a JavaScript ES6 import that looks like this:

```
import { FixedSizeList } from 'react-window';
```

If we were to look at the source code for that library, we'd see that the function is exported in the JavaScript file using a named export as:

```
exports.FixedSizeList = FixedSizeList;
```

So based on that, we can import it into our Python file like this:

```
FixedSizeList = require('react-window')['FixedSizeList']
```

Note that in the Python version of the import, we are essentially doing a dictionary lookup of the function that we wish to import. Other times, the library might have a default export function set. So let's say we have a JavaScript import that looks like this:

```
import Button from '@material-ui/core/Button';
```

If the JavaScript library assigns the exported function to the `exports.default` property as it does for this one, we will need to structure that import in our Python file in a way similar to how we just handled the named JavaScript export, like this:

```
Button = require('@material-ui/core/Button')['default']
```

The reason for this has to do with the fact we are using an ES5 style import, and the library we are using does not directly support that import style. In this case, the workaround is just to use a dictionary lookup on the import with the key `['default']` instead of the actual function name.

Unfortunately, JavaScript libraries use several different ways of exporting their function names. You should always check the documentation for the JavaScript library to see if they have an ES5 style import indicated that uses the `require()` function. If not, there may be a little extra sleuthing required on your part to get it to work.

Sometimes it's straightforward, but other times you have to actually go into the source code of the JavaScript library (in the **node_modules/** folder where npm installs the libraries locally) to find the function export itself, so that we can then understand how to properly import it into our Python namespace. The *"main"* key in the **package.json** file of the JavaScript library will give you a starting point for where to look for clues as to how the JavaScript library is structured. The good news is that you only need to figure it out once for any given JavaScript library, then you can reuse the import definition moving forward.

16.10 Using Images

Another handy thing you can do with the `require()` function is to bring a static image into the Python namespace to be displayed in an HTML `img` tag. So if we import an image with this:

```
applogo = require("../static/app_logo.png")
```

Then we can import `applogo` into another module as a standard Python object and use it in the creation of a React `img` element:

```
el('img', {'src': applogo, 'width': '40%'})
```

Besides the convenience, loading images this way lets the Parcel bundler help you identify any missing images, and can also result in more compact file sizes when the images get bundled with your application.

The importing of JavaScript libraries into your Python namespace is one of the key aspects of utilizing Transcrypt. While it can be a little messy bridging that gap sometimes, it works pretty seamlessly once connected. We will see more examples of importing JavaScript libraries later in the book.

16.11 Putting it Together

Taking all the above into account, here is the final Python file converted from JSX:

Listing 16-2 File: *app.py*

```python
from pyreact import setTitle, useEffect, useState, render, createElement as el

def App():
    newTask, setNewTask = useState("")
    editTask, setEditTask = useState(None)
    taskList, setTaskList = useState([])
    taskCount, setTaskCount = useState(0)
    taskFilter, setTaskFilter = useState("all")

    def handleSubmit(event):
        event.preventDefault()
        new_list = list(taskList)  # Make a copy
        if editTask is not None:  # In edit mode
            taskIndex = new_list.index(editTask)  # Get list position
            new_list[taskIndex].update({'name': newTask})  # Update name
        else:  # In add mode
            new_list.append({'name': newTask, 'status': False})  # Add new item
        setTaskList(new_list)  # Update our state
        setNewTask("")  # Clear the new item value
        setEditTask(None)  # Clear the edit item value

    def handleEdit(task):
        setNewTask(task['name'])  # Set the new item value
        setEditTask(task)  # Set the edit item value

    def handleDelete(task):
        new_list = list(taskList)  # Make a copy
        new_list.remove(task)  # Remove the specified item
        setTaskList(new_list)  # Update our state

    def handleChange(event):
        target = event['target']
        if target['name'] == 'taskFilter':
            setTaskFilter(target['value'])
        else:
            setNewTask(target['value'])

    def handleChangeStatus(event, task):
        target = event['target']
        new_list = list(taskList)  # Make a copy
        taskIndex = new_list.index(task)  # Get list position
        new_list[taskIndex].update({'status': target['checked']})  # Update
```

```python
        setTaskList(new_list)  # Update our state

def ListItem(props):
    task = props['task']
    if taskFilter == "all" or \
            (taskFilter == "open" and not task['status']) or \
            (taskFilter == "closed" and task['status']):
        return el('li', None,
                  task['name'] + " ",
                  el('button',
                     {'type': 'button',
                      'onClick': lambda: handleDelete(task)
                     }, "Delete"
                  ),
                  el('button',
                     {'type': 'button',
                      'onClick': lambda: handleEdit(task)
                     }, "Edit"
                  ),
                  el('label', {'htmlFor': 'status'}, " Completed:"),
                  el('input',
                     {'type': 'checkbox',
                      'id': 'status',
                      'onChange': lambda e: handleChangeStatus(e, task),
                      'checked': task['status']
                     }
                  ),
               )
    else:
        return None

def ListItems():
    return [el(ListItem, {'key': task['name'], 'task': task}) for task in
    ↪ taskList]

def updateCount():
    if taskFilter == 'open':
        new_list = [task for task in taskList if not task['status']]
    elif taskFilter == 'closed':
        new_list = [task for task in taskList if task['status']]
    else:
        new_list = [task for task in taskList]

    setTaskCount(len(new_list))
```

React to Python

```python
useEffect(lambda: setTitle("ToDo List"), [])
useEffect(updateCount, [taskList, taskFilter])

return el('form', {'onSubmit': handleSubmit},
        el('div', None, f"Number of Tasks: {taskCount}"),
        el('div', None,
            el('label', {'htmlFor': 'all'}, "All Tasks:"),
            el('input', {'type': 'radio',
                         'name': 'taskFilter',
                         'id': 'all',
                         'value': 'all',
                         'onChange': handleChange,
                         'checked': taskFilter == 'all'
                        }
            ),
            el('label', {'htmlFor': 'open'}, " Active:"),
            el('input', {'type': 'radio',
                         'name': 'taskFilter',
                         'id': 'open',
                         'value': 'open',
                         'onChange': handleChange,
                         'checked': taskFilter == 'open'
                        }
            ),
            el('label', {'htmlFor': 'closed'}, " Completed:"),
            el('input', {'type': 'radio',
                         'name': 'taskFilter',
                         'id': 'closed',
                         'value': 'closed',
                         'onChange': handleChange,
                         'checked': taskFilter == 'closed'
                        }
            ),
        ),
        el('label', {'htmlFor': 'editBox'},
            "Edit Task: " if editTask is not None else "Add Task: "
        ),
        el('input', {'id': 'editBox',
                     'onChange': handleChange,
                     'value': newTask
                    }
        ),
        el('input', {'type': 'submit'}),
        el('ol', None,
           el(ListItems, None)
```

```
        ),
    )
render(App, None, 'root')
```

As we mentioned earlier, to keep all of the Python to JavaScript mapping in one place, we'll add the `React.useEffect()` function with a simple mapping as we did for the other React functions. However, since `document.title` is just a property, we'll make a simple setting function to make it more clear what is happening when we use it in our Python code.

Listing 16-3 File: *pyreact.py*

```
# Load React and ReactDOM JavaScript libraries into local namespace
React = require('react')
ReactDOM = require('react-dom')

# Map React javaScript objects to Python identifiers
createElement = React.createElement
useState = React.useState
useEffect = React.useEffect


def render(root_component, props, container):
    def main():
        ReactDOM.render(
            React.createElement(root_component, props),
            document.getElementById(container)
        )

    document.addEventListener('DOMContentLoaded', main)


# JavaScript function mappings
alert = window.alert


def setTitle(title):
    document.title = title
```

For this chapter, we utilize the same HTML file entry point that we have been using, but here it is again just for reference:

Listing 16-4 File: *index.html*

```html
<!DOCTYPE html>
<html lang="en">
  <head>
    <script src="app.py"></script>
  </head>
  <body>
    <div id="root"></div>
  </body>
</html>
```

With all of this in place, once you fire up Parcel with `npm start` and build it, you should now have a working React application. Later on, we'll revisit this mini-application and use it as a basis for working with CSS and another React UI framework to make it look a little nicer.

http://localhost:1234

16.12 Summary

We covered quite a bit in this chapter. Because there are repeating patterns for converting React components from JavaScript to Python, it will become second nature after a bit of practice. But it will help to know what these patterns are as you dive deeper into learning new features of the React library. Most code examples you find, official or otherwise, are probably going to be written in JavaScript and use JSX. The good news is that Transcrypt does a great job of mapping Python to JavaScript, and you'll find that the code that is converted to Python will generally be much easier to work with.

Chapter Review:

1. Update source files:
   app.py
   pyreact.py
2. Build the application for development with:
   `npm start`
3. Open the application:
   http://localhost:1234

References:

- Chapter code
  https://github.com/rtp-book/code/tree/main/ch16
- React State and Lifecycle
  https://reactjs.org/docs/state-and-lifecycle.html
- React Conditional Rendering
  https://reactjs.org/docs/conditional-rendering.html
- React Components and Props
  https://reactjs.org/docs/components-and-props.html
- React JSX
  https://reactjs.org/docs/introducing-jsx.html
- React Without JSX
  https://reactjs.org/docs/react-without-jsx.html
- Transcrypt External Translator Compiler Directive
  https://www.transcrypt.org/docs/html/special_facilities.html#using-an-external-transpiler-pragma-xtrans-translator-cwd-workingdirectory

Chapter 17 – CSS

I admit, I have no love of CSS. I frequently spend more time fighting CSS layout issues than I do actually coding application logic. But it is an unavoidable reality of front-end web application development, so here we are.

We're not going to go into any specifics of how CSS itself works, as there are plenty of other resources for that out there. What we *will* talk about is how to directly utilize CSS in your Python React applications.

17.1 Stylesheet

We'll start with using a simple stylesheet as you would for any other static web site. For that, we first need a CSS file:

Listing 17-1 File: *app.css*

```css
body{
    font-family: Arial, sans-serif;
}
.submitBtn {
    margin: 10px;
    color: darkgreen;
    width: 60px;
}
.deleteBtn {
    color: darkred;
}
.editBtn {
    color: blue;
}
button {
    margin-right: 5px;
    width: 60px;
}
.editing {
    color: blue;
}
.adding {
    color: darkgreen;
}
```

Some of the selectors in our CSS file apply directly to an HTML element type, and some use a named CSS class selector. The style attributes for the native element selectors will automatically be applied to the referenced element, like the button selector:

```
button {
    margin-right: 5px;
    width: 60px;
}
```

For these, we don't need to do anything to our React elements for them to inherit the specified CSS style properties. For the class specifiers like `.submitBtn`:

```
.submitBtn {
    margin: 10px;
    color: darkgreen;
    width: 60px;
}
```

We will need to add the referenced class name to the React element it is intended for. Because the word `class` is a reserved word in JavaScript, React aliases this word with `className` instead. So when we add this attribute to our element, it looks like this:

```
el('input', {'type': 'submit', 'className': 'submitBtn'})
```

When React renders the element in the web browser, it will change the `className` keyword to `class` during the render process. If you inspect the element tree in the web browser, you'll see that it ends up looking like this:

```
<input type="submit" class="submitBtn">
```

In order for the selectors in the stylesheet to be available to our application, we'll need to add a link to it in our HTML file:

Listing 17-2 File: *index.html*

```html
<!DOCTYPE html>
<html lang="en">
  <head>
    <script src="app.py"></script>
    <link rel="stylesheet" href="app.css" />
  </head>
  <body>
    <div id="root"></div>
  </body>
</html>
```

Now let's take a previous code example and strategically add in our CSS class names in four places, to make it look like this:

Listing 17-3 File: *app.py*

```python
from pyreact import useState, render, createElement as el

def App():
    newItem, setNewItem = useState("")
    editItem, setEditItem = useState("")
    listItems, setListItems = useState([])

    def handleSubmit(event):
        event.preventDefault()
        new_list = list(listItems)  # Make a copy
        if len(editItem) > 0:  # In edit mode
            new_list[new_list.index(editItem)] = newItem
        else:  # In add mode
            new_list.append(newItem)  # Add the new item
        setListItems(new_list)  # Update our state
        setNewItem("")  # Clear the new item value
        setEditItem("")  # Clear the edit item value

    def handleChange(event):
        target = event['target']
        setNewItem(target['value'])

    def handleDelete(item):
        new_list = list(listItems)  # Make a copy
        new_list.remove(item)  # Remove the specified item
```

```python
            setListItems(new_list)  # Update our state

    def handleEdit(item):
        setNewItem(item)   # Set the new item value
        setEditItem(item)  # Set the edit item value

    def ListItem(props):
        return el('li', None,
                  el('button', {'type': 'button',
                                'onClick': lambda: handleDelete(props['item']),
                                'className': 'deleteBtn'
                                }, "Delete"
                  ),
                  el('button', {'type': 'button',
                                'onClick': lambda: handleEdit(props['item']),
                                'className': 'editBtn'
                                }, "Edit"
                  ),
                  props['item'],
               )

    def ListItems():
        return [el(ListItem, {'key': item, 'item': item}) for item in listItems]

    return el('form', {'onSubmit': handleSubmit},
              el('label',
                 {'htmlFor': 'editBox',
                  'className': 'adding' if len(editItem) == 0 else 'editing'
                 },
                 "Add Item: " if len(editItem) == 0 else "Edit Item: "
              ),
              el('input', {'id': 'editBox',
                           'onChange': handleChange,
                           'value': newItem
                          }
              ),
              el('input', {'type': 'submit', 'className': 'submitBtn'}),
              el('ol', None,
                 el(ListItems, None)
              ),
           )

render(App, None, 'root')
```

If we build this version and open it up in the web browser, you'll see that in addition to adding some layout spacing and having the sans-serif font being applied, our buttons (and input submit) along with the input label are all color-coded. For the input label, we used a ternary expression that will cause the CSS class being used to change based on if the `editItem` variable has a value or not:

```
'className': 'adding' if len(editItem) == 0 else 'editing'
```

So if we are in edit mode, it will be blue, otherwise it will stay green.

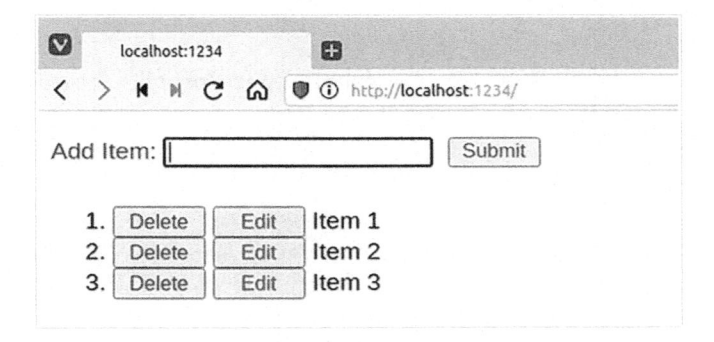

17.2 Inline Styles

Using inline CSS is the most direct way to apply style attributes to your React elements. Let's remove the stylesheet reference in the HTML file and then move the CSS styles into our application, adding them directly to the elements as a `style` prop:

Listing 17-4 File: *index.html*

```
<!DOCTYPE html>
<html lang="en">
  <head>
    <script src="app.py"></script>
  </head>
  <body>
    <div id="root"></div>
  </body>
</html>
```

Listing 17-5 File: *app.py*

```python
from pyreact import useState, render, createElement as el

def App():

    ...

    def ListItem(props):
        return el('li', None,
                    el('button', {
                        'type': 'button',
                        'onClick': lambda: handleDelete(props['item']),
                        'style': {'color': 'darkred',
                                  'marginRight': '5px',
                                  'width': '60px'
                                 }
                       }, "Delete"
                    ),
                    el('button', {
                        'type': 'button',
                        'onClick': lambda: handleEdit(props['item']),
                        'style': {'color': 'blue',
                                  'marginRight': '5px',
                                  'width': '60px'
                                 }
                       }, "Edit"
                    ),
                    props['item'],
                 )

    def ListItems():
        return [el(ListItem, {'key': item, 'item': item}) for item in listItems]

    if len(editItem) == 0:
        editStyle = {'color': 'darkgreen'}
    else:
        editStyle = {'color': 'blue'}

    return el('form', {'onSubmit': handleSubmit,
                       'style': {'fontFamily': 'Arial, sans-serif'}
                      },
                el('label',
                    {'htmlFor': 'editBox', 'style': editStyle},
```

```
                "Add Item: " if len(editItem) == 0 else "Edit Item: "
            ),
            el('input', {'id': 'editBox',
                         'onChange': handleChange,
                         'value': newItem
                        }
            ),
            el('input', {'type': 'submit',
                         'style': {'margin': '10px',
                                   'color': 'darkgreen',
                                   'width': '60px'
                                  }
                        }
            ),
            el('ol', None,
                el(ListItems, None)
            ),
        )
render(App, None, 'root')
```

The basic change we made here was to trade the className prop that referenced a style in an external stylesheet, for a style prop with all of the style attributes provided directly. When doing this, we provide a dictionary as the value for the style prop that has the style attributes that we wish to assign to the element. One thing to note is that React needs the attribute names to be modified if they contain a dash. If they do, they should be converted to camelCase format, removing the dash from the name. So in this case, font-family becomes fontFamily and margin-right becomes marginRight.

Another thing we did here, was to move the style logic for the input label text color to an external variable. Moving the logic outside of the element rendering can help to declutter your code and make it easier to visualize the structure of the element tree that you are building. In general, if the inline CSS you are applying to an element gets to be too unwieldy or you need to apply the same CSS to multiple elements, moving the style attributes to a variable can be a good way to keep your code clean.

17.3 Styled Components

If you have a situation where you want the style for a particular element to be consistent everywhere you use it, another option is to create a *styled* component. This is where you create a new reusable React component for the sole purpose of giving it a fixed style. For example, if you want all of your button elements to have a default set of style attributes applied to them, rather than have to apply a `className` attribute to the element each time you use it, you would instead use your custom styled component that has the style you want already applied to it. Here we do that for our Edit and Delete buttons by creating a styled component called `Button` (with a capital "B"):

Listing 17-6 File: *app.py*

```
from pyreact import useState, render, createElement as el

def App():

    ...

    def Button(props):
        new_props = {'type': 'button'}
        new_props.update(props)
        new_style = new_props.pop('style', {})
        new_style.update({'marginRight': '5px', 'width': '60px'})
        new_props.update({'style': new_style})
        return el('button', new_props)

    def ListItem(props):
        return el('li', None,
                el(Button,
                    {'onClick': lambda: handleDelete(props['item']),
                     'style': {'color': 'darkred'}
                    },
                    "Delete"
                ),
                el(Button,
                    {'onClick': lambda: handleEdit(props['item']),
                     'style': {'color': 'blue'}
                    },
                    "Edit"
                ),
                props['item'],
            )
```

```
...

render(App, None, 'root')
```

So here we created a new React functional component called Button that takes props as a parameter and is based on the built-in HTML button element. What we want to do here, is to have the new Button component use preset style attributes, but then also incorporate any style attributes that are passed into it, as we are doing with the color attribute in this case. There are four things we need to consider to make this work right:

1. We need to merge our styled component props with the props that are passed into it.
2. The props value passed into our Button component is immutable. Because it is read-only, we can't update it directly, so we need to make a copy of it.
3. The props value passed in is a JavaScript object and not a dictionary, so it doesn't have the expected Python dictionary methods available to it.
4. The value style attribute is a JavaScript object that is nested within props, so we'll have to extract that on its own in order to manipulate it.

In our Button component, we start by creating a Python dictionary containing props that are going to be defaults for this component. If there didn't happen to be any, we would just use an empty dictionary {}. Next, we add the props that were passed into our component to the new dictionary. By creating the Python dictionary first and then adding the passed in props, we don't have to worry about the fact that the passed in props value is actually a plain JavaScript object. The values will just get put into the existing Python dictionary, and will then behave as we would expect a Python dictionary to behave.

Now that we have all of the props in a proper Python dictionary, we can extract the style property, giving it a default of an empty dictionary in case there wasn't a style prop that was passed in, and then add our component-specific style attributes to it. Note that because of the order we are updating the style prop in, the marginRight and width attributes we are providing will override these values if they are also being passed in. The last step is to add the combined style attribute back into the props dictionary, since we had previously removed it with the dictionary pop() method.

With all of our props and styles combined together, we can finally return a new built-in HTML button element that uses all of them. The purpose of making all this extra effort becomes clear when we use the `Button` component in the `ListItem` component. We now only need to specify the button `color` in the `style` attribute instead of the entire button style that we originally had. This technique helps to keep the element tree portion of our code a lot cleaner and easy to understand.

17.4 CSS Framework

There are many CSS frameworks available that make styling your application a little easier, especially if you are graphic design challenged like me. We'll take a quick look at *Bootstrap*, a popular CSS framework that has a number of predefined CSS classes that can help maintain the consistency of the visual aspects of your application. Bootstrap has more features than we can get into here, so for now, we'll just focus on a few of the CSS classes it has, and give you an idea of how to incorporate them into your Python web application.

Bootstrap generally relies on a grid system for layout, and uses classes to represent `style` attributes. To apply any mix of styles to a given element, you just need to add each of the style classes that represent the attributes that you want to apply. First, we need to add the Bootstrap stylesheet from the online hosted location to our `index.html` file:

Listing 17-7 File: *index.html*

```html
<!DOCTYPE html>
<html lang="en">
  <head>
    <script src="app.py"></script>
    <link rel="stylesheet"
   href="https://maxcdn.bootstrapcdn.com/bootstrap/4.0.0/css/bootstrap.min.css"
    >
  </head>
  <body>
    <div id="root"></div>
  </body>
</html>
```

We can then apply the Bootstrap classes to our Python file:

Listing 17-8 File: *app.py*

```python
from pyreact import useState, render, createElement as el

def App():

...

    def ListItem(props):
        return el('li', {'className': 'list-group-item p-1'},
                    el('button',
                        {'onClick': lambda: handleDelete(props['item']),
                         'className': 'btn btn-danger btn-sm mr-2'
                        },
                        "Delete"
                    ),
                    el('button',
                        {'onClick': lambda: handleEdit(props['item']),
                         'className': 'btn btn-primary btn-sm mr-2'
                        },
                        "Edit"
                    ),
                    props['item'],
                )

    def ListItems():
        return [el(ListItem, {'key': item, 'item': item}) for item in listItems]

    if len(editItem) == 0:
        editClass = 'text-success'
    else:
        editClass = 'text-primary'

    return el('div', {'className': 'container m-1'},
                el('form', {'onSubmit': handleSubmit,
                            'className': 'form-inline col-10 my-2'
                        },
                    el('label',
                        {'htmlFor': 'editBox', 'className': editClass},
                        "Add Item: " if len(editItem) == 0 else "Edit Item: "
                    ),
                    el('input', {'id': 'editBox',
                                 'onChange': handleChange,
                                 'value': newItem,
```

```
                        'className': 'form-control ml-2'
                    }
                ),
                el('input', {'type': 'submit',
                        'className': 'btn btn-success ml-2'
                    }
                ),
            ),
            el('ul', {'className': 'list-group col-10 ml-2'},
                el(ListItems, None)
            ),
    )

render(App, None, 'root')
```

This time, our application takes on a whole new look since we are using the style theming of the Bootstrap framework:

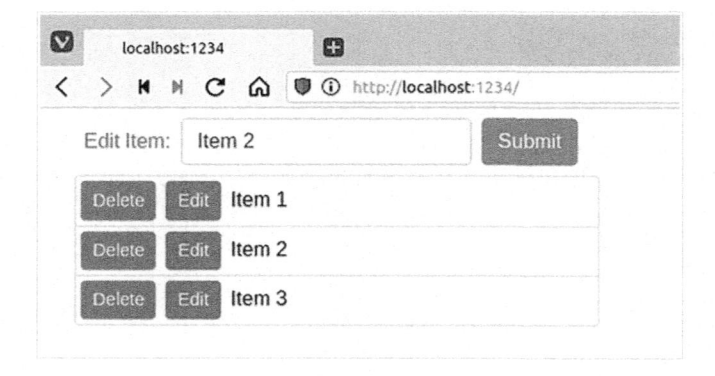

You will notice that we no longer have any CSS `style` properties in our code. All styling is now done by applying the Bootstrap `class` names to the elements. In some ways, the classes are just shorter and easier to read versions of the `style` attributes we were using before, and we just stack the classes as needed to achieve the desired effect.

Looking at our Edit button as an example, we can break down what each class is doing:

```
'className': 'btn btn-primary btn-sm mr-2'
```

- `btn` - Formats the element as a button
- `btn-primary` - Uses the Bootstrap primary color for the button (blue)
- `btn-sm` - Uses the smaller version of a button
- `mr-2` - Adds in a level 2 margin on the right side of the button

In Bootstrap, there are classes that apply to specific types of elements, like the ones that start with `btn-` for `button` elements. Then there are classes that are universal like the ones for spacing, as in this case `mr` for right margins. The Bootstrap framework has a relatively short learning curve, and you can get highly-styled pages without having to fight as many common CSS issues.

One change we made to the code was instead of using the HTML `form` element as our top-level container, we added an HTML `div` element and assigned the Bootstrap `container` class to it. This allows us to utilize the Bootstrap grid system for controlling the layout, and to move the item list out of the form itself.

One last minor modification we made was to change our list from an ordered list (`ol`) to an unordered list (`ul`). This just removed the numbers on the list items to work better with the Bootstrap layout.

17.5 Summary

We now know several ways we can utilize CSS in our React application to improve the appearance and manage the layout of our components. We also saw a couple of ways to make the applied style conditional on the state of the application. Any of these methods are acceptable to use, and it just depends on whatever you are most comfortable with.

Chapter Review:

1. Add source file (Stylesheet):
   app.css

2. Update source files:
   index.html
   app.py

3. Build the application for development with:
   `npm start`

4. Open the application:
   http://localhost:1234

5. Update source files (Inline Styles):
   index.html
   app.py

6. Update source file (Styled Components):
   app.py

7. Update source files (CSS Framework):
   index.html
   app.py

References:

- Chapter code
  https://github.com/rtp-book/code/tree/main/ch17

- W3C Cascading Style Sheets
  https://www.w3.org/Style/CSS/

- Bootstrap CSS Framework
  https://getbootstrap.com/docs/4.1/getting-started/introduction/

Chapter 18 – Material-UI

If you're like me and struggle with making things look good from an overall style standpoint, using an opinionated CSS framework can have a lot of advantages, since someone else with a richer background in graphic design has already made many style decisions for you. Materialize is one of those CSS frameworks. Based on Google's Material Design specification, it has many predefined themes and components that look good right out of the box. Similar to Bootstrap, it uses predefined style classes that you assign to your elements to apply the styles.

The Material-UI library takes it a step further and provides pre-styled and more customizable React components based on the Material Design specification that you can use to replace the raw built-in HTML elements. So essentially, it's like having a set of React components that have Materialize CSS classes already assigned for you. It also provides cleaner ways to incorporate custom CSS classes into your project as well. While there is a bit of a learning curve to understand the details of the components it provides, the end result you get with the look and feel of your applications is well worth the effort.

18.1 Installing Material-UI

While it is possible to use the online hosted version of the Material-UI JavaScript library, it is not recommended. So let's install it locally and let the Parcel bundler do its magic. In a terminal window for your project run:

(venv) $ `npm install @material-ui/core`

To property utilize the Material-UI library, we need to add a reference to the Google icon and font stylesheets that Material-UI uses to our **index.html** file:

Listing 18-1 File: *index.html*

```
<!DOCTYPE html>
<html lang="en">
  <head>
    <script src="app.py"></script>
    <link rel="stylesheet"
        href="https://fonts.googleapis.com/css?family=Roboto:300,400,500,700&display=swap"
```

```
    />
   <link rel="stylesheet"
         href="https://fonts.googleapis.com/icon?family=Material+Icons"
    />
  </head>
  <body>
    <div id="root"></div>
  </body>
</html>
```

Next, we'll create a module specifically for mapping the Material-UI components to Python objects by importing the Material-UI `core` module and mapping a few of the components:

Listing 18-2 File: *pymui.py*

```
MaterialUI = require('@material-ui/core')

# Basic MUI components
Button = MaterialUI.Button
List = MaterialUI.List
ListItem = MaterialUI.ListItem
Typography = MaterialUI.Typography
Input = MaterialUI.Input
InputLabel = MaterialUI.InputLabel
Box = MaterialUI.Box
```

18.2 Basic Usage

Now that we have access to a selection of the Material-UI JavaScript components from Python, let's take our previous example and put them to use by replacing the plain HTML elements with the Material-UI components:

Listing 18-3 File: *app.py*

```
from pyreact import useState, render, createElement as el
from pymui import Button, List, ListItem, Typography, InputLabel, Input, Box

def App():
    ...
```

```python
def ItemVu(props):
    return el(ListItem, {'dense': True},
            el(Button,
                {'variant': 'contained',
                 'color': 'secondary',
                 'size': 'small',
                 'style': {'marginRight': '0.5rem'},
                 'onClick': lambda: handleDelete(props['item']),
                },
                "Delete"
            ),
            el(Button,
                {'variant': 'contained',
                 'color': 'primary',
                 'size': 'small',
                 'style': {'marginRight': '0.5rem'},
                 'onClick': lambda: handleEdit(props['item']),
                },
                "Edit"
            ),
            el(Typography, {'variant': 'body1'}, props['item'])
        )

def ListItemsVu():
    return [el(ItemVu, {'key': item, 'item': item}) for item in listItems]

if len(editItem) == 0:
    editColor = 'secondary'
    editLabel = "Add Item:"
else:
    editColor = 'primary'
    editLabel = "Edit Item:"

return el(Box, None,
        el('form', {'onSubmit': handleSubmit},
            el(InputLabel,
                {'htmlFor': 'editBox', 'color': editColor},
                editLabel
            ),
            el(Input, {'id': 'editBox',
                       'onChange': handleChange,
                       'value': newItem
                }
            ),
            el(Button, {'type': 'submit',
```

```
                        'variant': 'contained',
                        'style': {'marginLeft': '0.5rem'}
                    }, "Submit"),
                ),
            el(List, None,
                el(ListItemsVu, None)
                ),
            )

render(App, None, 'root')
```

With Material-UI, many of the attributes that were part of the `style` property, like `color`, are now direct properties of the component itself. In addition to those, each Material-UI component has properties that define its look and feel in terms of how it gets rendered, like the `variant` and `size` properties. That said, the `style` property is still available for making inline tweaks to the style attributes. Making adjustments to margins and padding is frequently done here.

One of the things that the Material-UI components do behind the scenes, is to generate and manage custom CSS classes for each element. So if you were to look at the element tab in the web browser developer console, you would see many class names that were automatically generated. It stacks these class names together much as we did earlier ourselves with the Bootstrap CSS framework. So in that sense, you can think of Material-UI components like the styled-components we discussed in the previous chapter on CSS.

Most of the Material-UI components we used are self-explanatory. The Box component is a fancy replacement for an HTML `div` element, and the `Typography` component just gives us more control over how plain text appears.

Because one of the Material-UI components is named `ListItem`, we did rename our own component from `ListItem` to `ItemVu`, since it represents the view of a single item. Then for consistency, we also renamed `ListItems` to `ListItemsVu`, indicating that it is the view representing all of the items in our list.

We also kept the native HTML `form` element here, mostly because it's a bit simpler to use, but it also shows that you can mix and match Material-UI and native HTML elements as needed. To get the most out of Material-UI and understand all of the possible variations for each component, the online documentation for Material-UI is your friend. The official Material-UI documentation has demos of component variations, and clear API documentation for each component in the library.

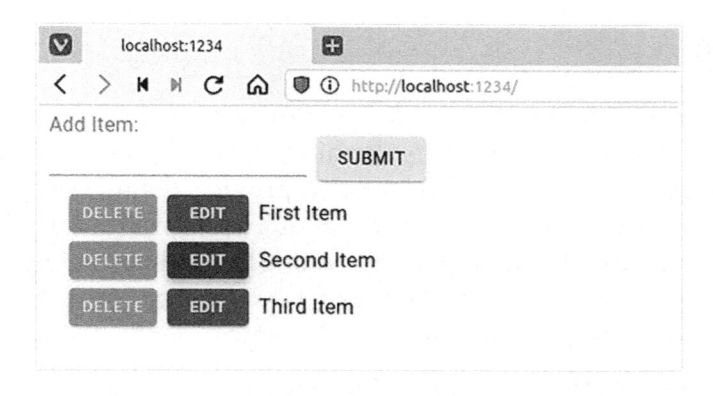

18.3 Optimized Imports

Rather than importing the entire Material-UI library, which is fairly large, we should change the imports in the **pymui.py** module to directly import just the components that we need. This can help to reduce the download times required by the web browser. So making a nuanced change to our **pymui.py** file accomplishes this:

Listing 18-4 File: *pymui.py*

```
# Basic MUI components
Button = require('@material-ui/core/Button')['default']
List = require('@material-ui/core/List')['default']
ListItem = require('@material-ui/core/ListItem')['default']
Typography = require('@material-ui/core/Typography')['default']
Input = require('@material-ui/core/Input')['default']
InputLabel = require('@material-ui/core/InputLabel')['default']
Box = require('@material-ui/core/Box')['default']
```

Here, we employed the technique described in an earlier chapter to get the proper form of the import required for each individual JavaScript function that we wanted to utilize, based on how the respective JavaScript module is structured. After doing this, we no longer need to pull in the entire `@material-ui/core` library, and can remove it from our **pymui.py** module. By structuring our imports this way, the size of the JavaScript bundle file that is generated by the Parcel bundler gets cut in half.

18.4 Theming

In addition to providing slick reusable components, one of the major features that Material-UI brings to the table is theming. This allows you to not only set your color scheme, but is where you can also provide default properties for the Material-UI components that you use throughout your application. Because of its flexibility, understanding the theming and styling mechanisms of Material-UI can be one of the more challenging aspects of using it. But once you find a pattern you like to use, it becomes pretty straightforward to implement.

Let's start by first adding a few more Material-UI components to our **pymui.py** module so we can get a little fancier with our UI:

Listing 18-5 File: *pymui.py*

```
# Basic MUI components
Button = require('@material-ui/core/Button')['default']
List = require('@material-ui/core/List')['default']
ListItem = require('@material-ui/core/ListItem')['default']
Typography = require('@material-ui/core/Typography')['default']
Input = require('@material-ui/core/Input')['default']
InputLabel = require('@material-ui/core/InputLabel')['default']
Box = require('@material-ui/core/Box')['default']
TextField = require('@material-ui/core/TextField')['default']
Paper = require('@material-ui/core/Paper')['default']
AppBar = require('@material-ui/core/AppBar')['default']
Container = require('@material-ui/core/Container')['default']

# Theming
ThemeProvider = require('@material-ui/styles/ThemeProvider')['default']
useTheme = require('@material-ui/styles/useTheme')['default']
createMuiTheme = require('@material-ui/core/styles/createMuiTheme')['default']
colors = require('@material-ui/core/colors')
```

Then let's create a custom theme for our application that, among other things, defines what our primary and secondary base colors are, and also changes the default values for a few component properties:

Listing 18-6 File: *appTheme.py*

```
from pymui import createMuiTheme, colors

theme = createMuiTheme({
```

```
    'palette': {
        'primary': colors['teal'],
        'secondary': colors['pink'],
        'special': {
            'main': colors['deepPurple'][600],
            'contrastText': colors['common']['white'],
        },
    },
    'overrides': {
        'MuiButton': {
            'root': {
                'margin': '0.5rem'
            },
        },
    },
    'props': {
        'MuiButton': {
            'variant': 'contained',
            'size': 'small',
        },
        'MuiTextField': {
            'type': 'text',
            'variant': 'outlined',
            'InputLabelProps': {'shrink': True},
            'InputProps': {'margin': 'dense'},
            'margin': 'dense',
        },
    },
})
```

The `createMuiTheme()` function takes a nested Python dictionary that can set the properties and styles of several different component aspects that affect the look of our application. There are three categories we used here. The first obvious one is the `palette` configuration. In this one, we set the base colors for the built-in `primary` and `secondary` selectors to be `teal` and `pink` respectively, by selecting colors from the `color` object of Material-UI. The `primary` and `secondary` colors are used in most of the Material-UI visual components and set the overall color scheme of your application.

In addition to those, we also created a new color selector called `special`, where we specify the base color as well as the contrasting color that is typically used for text that is placed on top of the `main` color. Material-UI also has `light` and `dark` variations of the `main` color that if not explicitly specified, will be automatically calculated as relative values based on the `main` color.

```
'special': {
  'main': colors['deepPurple'][600],
  'contrastText': colors['common']['white'],
},
```

The next two categories set global style and component properties. The `override` theme category is used to set CSS style defaults for any of Material-UIs components. These global styles are arranged first by the component's stylesheet name, which is often the name of the component preceded by "Mui", and then by the rule that you want to override in the stylesheet. For example, the `Button` component has a stylesheet name of `MuiButton`. To verify the proper name, you will need to look at the API docs for the Material-UI component that you wish to modify. The stylesheet name will be found in the *Component name* section of the documentation, and the rule name will be in the *CSS* section. Most of the time, you will be setting style defaults for the `root` rule name. However, if the component is complex, it will have many additional rules that you can modify at lower levels of the component. In our theme example, we are setting the default `margin` style in the `root` rule of the `MuiButton` stylesheet.

```
'overrides': {
  'MuiButton': {
    'root': {
      'margin': '0.5rem'
    },
  },
},
```

The last theme category we are using is `props`, which is used for setting default Material-UI component properties. Unlike the `override` section that sets CSS style attributes directly, the component `props` affect CSS style rules indirectly, and are specific to individual components. Similar to the `override` section of the theme, the `props` category is arranged by the component stylesheet name. Then within each component name, you can specify default values for the `props` within each component. Like the CSS rules, valid properties for each individual component can be found in the *Props* section of the Material-UI component API documentation.

So in our example, we set default `prop` values for the `MuiButton` and `MuiTextField` names that affect the `Button` and `TextField` components respectively. For the `MuiButton` component, we set the default style to be a contained and small button configuration. The `MuiTextField` is a little more complex. In addition to setting top-level `type`, `variant`, and `margin` props, we also set props related to the underlying `Input` and `InputLabel` components that the `TextField` component is comprised of. This is common for some of the more complex Material-UI components, where the props of underlying components are exposed via props of the main component, that are then passed down to the lower-level component to use. In this case, the `TextField` component has props for `InputProps` and `InputLabelProps` that can be easily set.

Now that we have our Material-UI theme in place, let's use it in the example application we've been working with:

Listing 18-7 File: *app.py*

```
from appTheme import theme
from pyreact import useState, render, createElement as el
from pymui import Button, List, ListItem, Typography, Box, TextField
from pymui import Paper, Container, AppBar, ThemeProvider, useTheme

def App():

...

    def ItemVu(props):
        item = props['item']
        current_theme = useTheme()
        specialColor = current_theme['palette']['special']['main']
        button_style = {'margin': '0 0.5rem 0 0'}

        return el(ListItem, {'dense': True},
                el(Button,
                    {'color': 'secondary',
                     'style': button_style,
                     'onClick': lambda: handleDelete(item)
                    },
                    el('span', {'className': 'material-icons'}, 'delete'),
                    "Delete"
                ),
                el(Button,
                    {'color': 'primary',
                     'style': button_style,
                     'onClick': lambda: handleEdit(item)
                    },
```

```
                    el('span', {'className': 'material-icons'}, 'edit'),
                    "Edit"
                ),
                el(Typography, {'style': {'color': specialColor}}, item)
            )
    def ListItemsVu():
        return [el(ItemVu, {'key': item, 'item': item}) for item in listItems]

    if len(editItem) == 0:
        editColor = 'secondary'
        editLabel = "Add Item:"
    else:
        editColor = 'primary'
        editLabel = "Edit Item:"

    return el(ThemeProvider, {'theme': theme},
            el(Container, {'maxWidth': 'sm'},
                el(AppBar, {'position': 'static',
                            'style': {'marginBottom': '0.5rem'}
                           },
                    el(Box, {'width': '100%', 'marginLeft': '0.5rem'},
                        el(Typography, {'variant': 'h6'}, "React to Python")
                    )
                ),
                el(Paper, {'elevation': 2},
                    el('form', {'onSubmit': handleSubmit,
                                'style': {'marginLeft': '1rem'}
                               },
                        el(TextField, {'InputLabelProps': {'color': editColor},
                                       'label': editLabel,
                                       'value': newItem,
                                       'onChange': handleChange,
                                       'autoFocus': True
                                      }
                        ),
                        el(Button, {'type': 'submit',
                                    'size': 'medium'
                                   }, "Submit"),
                    ),
                    el(List, None,
                        el(ListItemsVu, None)
                    ),
                )
            )
```

```
        )
render(App, None, 'root')
```

We've added several components to our application to improve how it looks, starting with the ThemeProvider that wraps our entire application with the theme we just created. By putting this as our top-level component, the theme becomes available to all components below it in the tree.

Below the ThemeProvider, we added a Container component that we use to set the outer envelope size of our application. Then inside that container, we added an AppBar for displaying a title, and a Paper component that highlights the main portion of the application. Within the AppBar, we use the Typography component to change the size of the title text. We also changed the InputLabel and Input components into a single TextField component that combines them both together for us in a stylistic way.

In our ItemVu component, we retrieved a reference to the outer theme object using the useTheme() hook method of Material-UI. This allows us to drill down and grab the special color identifier we created in our theme, and then use it to set the color of the displayed item text. We also create an inline style for setting the right margin of the item buttons, that we can use in both of the locations it is needed at.

By using a theme in our application, the props that we need to specify in each component get reduced since they are set globally. Additionally, our application maintains a consistent look without having to specify every style and prop detail on every component.

Also, note that even with all of the component changes we just made, the portion of our code that controls the functionality of the application has not changed. We still use the same event handlers and function calls.

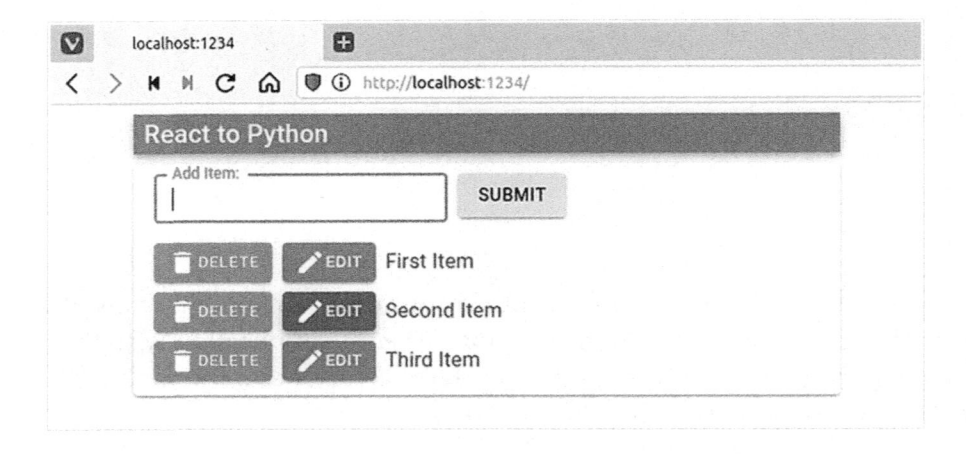

18.5 Styled Components Revisited

In addition to using a theme to set the global default styles and component props, it can be beneficial to do the same thing at a component level. While using a ThemeProvider to wrap a single component in order to change its style and props is possible, nesting themes can be tricky. You run into issues with overriding the outer theme for the application itself unless you provide a merge function to merge the inner theme with the outer theme.

Instead, Material-UI gives us several ways to apply styles to individual components more directly. In addition to using inline styles like we have been, in the chapter on CSS we also used composition to create a new reusable component that had a specific style incorporated into it. If you need to set props of a Material-UI component as opposed to just the CSS style, using composition is the best way to do it.

If you do just need to set the style of a component, or if you need to use CSS pseudo-classes which you can't do with inline styling, you can use the Material-UI styled() function to easily create a styled component. To be specific, the styled() function takes a component as an argument, and returns a function that takes a style dictionary to apply to it. This might sound a little more complicated than it actually is, so here's an example to help clarify it:

```
StyledButton = styled(Button)(
    {
        'minWidth': '6rem',
        'margin': '0 0.5rem 0 0',
        '&:hover': {'backgroundColor': 'yellow'}
    }
)
```

Here, we are creating a new component called `StyledButton` that uses the `styled()` function, having a Material-UI `Button` component as its argument. We then pass in a dictionary of style attributes to what is actually the output of the `styled()` function, to assign the new style options. Now we can use the `StyledButton` component just like we would use the standard `Button` component, and it will retain the style attributes we applied to it. So this is a simpler version of the component composition we did earlier to inject style attributes into an existing component. The restriction is that we can only affect CSS `style` attributes and not component `props` like we can do with a component composition.

If you need to apply styles to several components or need more flexibility in applying styles, Material-UI also provides the `makeStyles()` function that, given a dictionary of style attributes, will return another function that you can then use to generate CSS `style` classes. These classes can then be applied to any component as a `className` prop, as you would for a normal CSS class.

```
useStyle = makeStyles(
    {
        'root': {
            'minWidth': '6rem',
            'margin': '0 0.5rem 0 0',
            '&:hover': {'backgroundColor': 'yellow'}
        }
    }
)
```

Then to utilize it in a component, you call the created function to generate the classes, and then use those classes in the component props. For example:

```
classes = useStyle()

React.createElement(Button,
        {'className': classes.root,
```

```
            'onClick': lambda: handleDelete(item)
        },
        "Delete"
    )
```

In addition to being able to create multiple style classes at once, you can also pass props into the makeStyles() function to make the generated styles context-specific:

```
useStyle = makeStyles(
    {
      'root': {
        'minWidth': '6rem',
        'margin': '0 0.5rem 0 0',
        '&:hover': {'backgroundColor': lambda props: props['bgcolor']}
      }
    }
)
```

Then when you call the function to generate the classes, you can pass in props:

```
classes = useStyle({'bgcolor': 'blue'})
```

Like the Material-UI `styled()` function, you can not set component-specific `props` using `makeStyles()`, but any valid CSS `style` attribute, including using pseudo-classes like `'&:hover'`, are acceptable. If you have a situation where you need to set both component props and pseudo-class style attributes, you will have to use a combination of `styled()` or `makeStyles()` along with component composition to create a new component that incorporates both.

Before we wrap up this chapter on Material-UI, let's use both of these component styling methods in our example application. We'll first need to add the new Material-UI functions to our **pymui.py** module:

Listing 18-8 File: *pymui.py*

```
# Basic MUI components
Button = require('@material-ui/core/Button')['default']
List = require('@material-ui/core/List')['default']
ListItem = require('@material-ui/core/ListItem')['default']
Typography = require('@material-ui/core/Typography')['default']
```

```
Input = require('@material-ui/core/Input')['default']
InputLabel = require('@material-ui/core/InputLabel')['default']
Box = require('@material-ui/core/Box')['default']
TextField = require('@material-ui/core/TextField')['default']
Paper = require('@material-ui/core/Paper')['default']
AppBar = require('@material-ui/core/AppBar')['default']
Container = require('@material-ui/core/Container')['default']

# Theming
ThemeProvider = require('@material-ui/styles/ThemeProvider')['default']
useTheme = require('@material-ui/styles/useTheme')['default']
createMuiTheme = require('@material-ui/core/styles/createMuiTheme')['default']
colors = require('@material-ui/core/colors')
makeStyles = require('@material-ui/styles/makeStyles')['default']
styled = require('@material-ui/styles/styled')['default']
```

Where you put your styles and styled-components is up to you, but in this case, we'll put them in the **appTheme.py** module to keep the global styling and theming all in one place. This makes them easily accessible to any other Python modules that might need them:

Listing 18-9 File: *appTheme.py*

```
from pymui import createMuiTheme, colors, makeStyles, styled, Button
from pyreact import createElement as el

theme = createMuiTheme({
    'palette': {
        'primary': colors['teal'],
        'secondary': colors['pink'],
        'special': {
            'main': colors['deepPurple'][600],
            'contrastText': colors['common']['white'],
        },
    },
    'overrides': {
        'MuiButton': {
            'root': {
                'margin': '0.5rem'
            },
        },
    },
    'props': {
        'MuiButton': {
```

```python
            'variant': 'contained',
            'size': 'small',
        },
        'MuiTextField': {
            'type': 'text',
            'variant': 'outlined',
            'InputLabelProps': {'shrink': True},
            'InputProps': {'margin': 'dense'},
            'margin': 'dense',
        },
    },
})

StyledButton = styled(Button)({
    'minWidth': '6rem',
    'margin': '0 0.5rem 0 0',
    '&:hover': {'backgroundColor': theme['palette']['special']['main']}
})

useStyle = makeStyles({
    'root': {
        'minWidth': '6rem',
        'margin': '0 0.5rem 0 0',
        '&:hover': {'backgroundColor': lambda props: props['bgcolor']}
    }
})

def ListButton(props):
    new_props = {'style': {'minWidth': '6rem', 'margin': '0 0.5rem 0 0'}}
    new_props.update(props)
    return el(Button, new_props)
```

Here we've included examples for styled(), makeStyles(), and component composition that all accomplish the same thing, with the exception that we can't use pseudo-classes in the latter. In the StyledButton component, we pull in a theme color right from the theme object in this module. In the makeStyles() function, we will pass the same color value in via a prop when we call the useStyle() function.

Lastly, because of the way we are composing the ListButton composition component, the style we are applying will get overridden if there is a style prop that is passed into the ListButton component. It is important to consider this if you have a situation where merging styles may be required.

Now let's see how these styling options get used in our application:

Listing 18-10 File: *app.py*

```python
from appTheme import theme, useStyle, ListButton, StyledButton
from pyreact import useState, render, createElement as el
from pymui import Button, List, ListItem, Typography, Box, TextField
from pymui import Paper, Container, AppBar, ThemeProvider, useTheme

def App():

    ...

    def ItemVu(props):
        item = props['item']
        theme = useTheme()
        specialColor = theme['palette']['special']['main']
        classes = useStyle({'bgcolor': specialColor})

        return el(ListItem, {'dense': True},
                el(Button,
                    {'color': 'secondary',
                     'className': classes.root,
                     'onClick': lambda: handleDelete(item)
                    },
                    el('span', {'className': 'material-icons'}, 'delete'),
                    "Delete"
                ),
                el(StyledButton,
                    {'color': 'primary',
                     'onClick': lambda: handleEdit(item)
                    },
                    el('span', {'className': 'material-icons'}, 'edit'),
                    "Edit"
                ),
                el(Typography, {'style': {'color': specialColor}}, item)
            )

    ...

render(App, None, 'root')
```

When you build and run this version, you'll see that with the two different styling options we used, we've preserved the spacing we had before without having to specify it where the components are actually being utilized. We also added in our custom `special` color when hovering over either the *Delete* or *Edit* buttons. We didn't actually use the `ListButton` composition component in this example, but if we did, it would be used just like any other regular component.

18.6 Summary

Material-UI is a powerful React component library that helps you develop attractive applications based on the Google Material Design specification. By using the theming feature of Material-UI, you can ensure that your UI look and feel is consistent across your entire application. Material-UI also provides several mechanisms to specify CSS styles for components that are much more sophisticated than using external stylesheets. We will be exploring more of the Material-UI library when we develop a full application in section three of this book.

Chapter Review:

1. Install Material-UI package:
   `npm install @material-ui/core`
2. Update source files (Material-UI):
   index.html
   app.py
3. Add source file:
   pymui.py

4. Build the application for development with:
   `npm start`

5. Open the application:
   http://localhost:1234

6. Update source files (Optimized Imports):
   pymui.py

7. Update source files (Theming):
   pymui.py
   app.py

8. Add source file:
   appTheme.py

9. Update source files (Styled Components):
   pymui.py
   appTheme.py
   app.py

References:

- Chapter code
  https://github.com/rtp-book/code/tree/main/ch18

- Google Material Design
  https://material.io/

- Materialize CSS framework
  https://materializecss.com

- Material-UI Documentation
  https://material-ui.com/getting-started/usage/

Chapter 19 – Parcel Web Proxy

In our development environment, there will likely be times when we are running our own back-end REST services like Flask, that our application relies on to get its data from. In production, you would conventionally have a public-facing web server that responds to all requests for your application. It would then forward, or proxy, incoming requests for the back-end services on to an application server hosting Flask that is *not* public-facing. Locally, while you could just run the Parcel web server and the Flask web server on two different ports, it's much cleaner if you get one of them to proxy the other as you would in a production setting. This saves you from having to mess around with cross-origin resource sharing, or port mapping. Unfortunately, unlike the Webpack bundler, the current version of Parcel doesn't support using its development web server as a proxy for another web server. But being that this is a highly opinionated book, I'm going to show you a way you can work around that current limitation of Parcel.

19.1 Flask Web Server

The first thing we're going to need to make this work is to have a back-end web server that we can proxy. To meet that requirement, let's install Flask and create a simple web service. While in your virtual environment, install Flask from the pip repository with:

(venv) $ `pip install flask`

With Flask installed, create a simple web service that takes a user ID as part of the URL and returns details about that user in the form of a JSON response:

Listing 19-1 File: *webserver.py*

```
from flask import Flask, jsonify

users = [
    {"ID": 1, "FirstName": "Valeria", "LastName": "Lammerding",
     "Email": "vlammerding0@flickr.com", "JobTitle": "Geologist III",
     "Username": "vlammerding0", "Active": False},
    {"ID": 2, "FirstName": "Bond", "LastName": "Tomczynski",
     "Email": "btomczynski1@ehow.com", "JobTitle": "Environmental Specialist",
     "Username": "btomczynski1", "Active": True},
```

```python
    {"ID": 3, "FirstName": "Nowell", "LastName": "Triplet",
     "Email": "ntriplet2@sciencedirect.com", "JobTitle": "Business Analyst",
     "Username": "ntriplet2", "Active": False},
    {"ID": 4, "FirstName": "Patience", "LastName": "Boulds",
     "Email": "pboulds3@reverbnation.com", "JobTitle": "Assistant Manager",
     "Username": "pboulds3", "Active": True},
    {"ID": 5, "FirstName": "Darelle", "LastName": "Lemonby",
     "Email": "dlemonby4@prweb.com", "JobTitle": "Staff Accountant I",
     "Username": "dlemonby4", "Active": True}
]

app = Flask(__name__)

@app.route('/user/<userid>')
def get_user(userid):
    person = next((user for user in users if str(user['ID']) == userid), {})
    return jsonify(person)

@app.route('/users')
def get_userlist():
    user_list = []
    for user in users:
        user_name = ', '.join([user['LastName'], user['FirstName']])
        user_list.append([user['ID'], user_name])
    return jsonify(user_list)

if __name__ == "__main__":
    app.run(debug=True, port=8000)
```

For brevity, we just have a few user records, but that's enough to do what we need to do for now. If you run this file module with:

(venv) $ python -m webserver

With the Flask web server running, you should be able to surf to it in a web browser with:

http://localhost:8000/user/3

And then get a JSON response like this:

```
{
  "Active": false,
  "Email": "ntriplet2@sciencedirect.com",
  "FirstName": "Nowell",
```

```
"ID": 3,
"JobTitle": "Business Analyst",
"LastName": "Triplet",
"Username": "ntriplet2"
}
```

Using this URL should also get you a list of all of the user IDs and names:

http://localhost:8000/users

Now that we have our perhaps not so resilient web server up and running, let's look at how we're going to proxy it so that we can better test our front-end applications.

19.2 Proxy Service

Since the development web server built into the Parcel bundler does not currently support acting as a proxy for another web service such as Flask on its own, we need to utilize a web server that can support that capability. The Express.js web framework for Node.js fits this requirement nicely and is very lightweight. Along with that, we will also utilize the `http-proxy-middleware` JavaScript library that lets us cleanly integrate with the Parcel web server. This setup has a very small footprint, and we can install both of these with `npm` like any other JavaScript library:

(venv) $ `npm install express http-proxy-middleware --save-dev`

This will install both JavaScript libraries as development dependencies and add them to the **package.json** file.

Most of the time, your back-end web server will have some kind of a RESTful API that accepts a request from a web client and responds by sending back JSON data. One assumption we will make, is that the request URL for the back-end REST service has an endpoint that can be differentiated from requests for the front-end via a regex filter. For example, it is common for a REST API to have a URL that starts with **/api/**, whereas requests going to the front-end web server start with something else besides that. The proxy middleware can use this pattern to know when to respond to the request locally, and when to forward it on to the back-end web server.

Next, we need to have a script to do the routing for the proxy service. Because it runs in Node.js it will have to be a JavaScript file (sorry!), but it's pretty straightforward:

Listing 19-2 File: *dev-server.js*

```
const Bundler = require('parcel-bundler');
const express = require('express');
const { createProxyMiddleware } = require('http-proxy-middleware');

const app = express();

const apiProxy = createProxyMiddleware('/api', {
  target: 'http://localhost:8000',
  pathRewrite: {'^/api': ''}
});
app.use(apiProxy);

// parcel options
const options = {minify: false, cache: false, outDir: 'dist/dev', logLevel: 4};

const bundler = new Bundler('./index.html', options);
app.use(bundler.middleware());

bundler.on('buildEnd', () => {
  console.log('Parcel proxy server has started at: http://localhost:8080');
});

app.listen(8080);
```

This script creates an instance of the Express.js web server, and adds two plug-ins to it. The first is the HTTP proxy middleware that looks at the URL for the incoming request, and if it starts with **/api/** will strip off the **api** part and send it on to the back-end Flask server that we have running on port 8000. If the URL *doesn't* start with **/api/** then it just processes the request normally, sending it to the Parcel development web server. That brings us to the second plug-in, which is for the Parcel bundler. For that one, we specify the entry point file for our application, and then all of the Parcel options that we currently have in the **start** script in the

package.json file. Just to let us know when the server is ready to start accepting HTTP requests, we also added a console message that gets displayed once the Parcel build process is complete.

Unlike some development web servers that have built-in proxying capability, this method actually proxies both the front-end and back-end services on a new port. The new port is specified in the last line of the script, which is 8080 in this case. If you'd like more details about the parameters used for the proxy service, the documentation for the http-proxy-middleware library has more information.

The last bit we want to do is add a script to our **package.json** file that will run our dev proxy server. In the `scripts` section of **package.json**, add in the command to run the **dev-server.js** file using Node.js right after the `start` and `build` scripts that are already there:

```
"start": "NODE_ENV=development parcel --log-level 4 index.html --out-dir
    ↪ dist/dev",
"build": "NODE_ENV=production parcel --log-level 4 build index.html
    ↪ --no-source-maps --out-dir dist/prod",
"dev": "node dev-server.js",
```

With that script in place, instead of starting the Parcel build process and development web server with `npm start` as we have been, we can use the new `dev` script instead:

(venv) $ `npm run dev`

In addition to starting up the HTTP proxy script, it will also start the Parcel build process and development web server. If everything is working correctly, you should be able to get to the React application we've been working with here:

http://localhost:8080/

And, assuming it is running, you can also get to the Flask back-end server here:

http://localhost:8080/api/user/4

Note that even though the route in our Flask application is looking to match requests to **/user/**, we access it via the proxy server with **/api/user/** which the proxy server then forwards to Flask with the **/api** portion removed. On a side note, since we are not doing anything to prevent it, the original URLs for the back-end and front-end servers are still available as well.

19.3 Summary

In order to unify HTTP communication in our development environment between the front-end application and our back-end server, we set up a proxy server so that all communication on the front-end goes through one web server port, and forwards requests to the back-end server as needed. To keep things simple, we used a lightweight web server and JavaScript proxy library that accomplishes just what we need it to do. It integrates cleanly with the existing Parcel framework that we are already using, without adding a lot of additional overhead.

Chapter Review:

1. Install Flask:
   `pip install flask`

2. Add source file:
   webserver.py

3. Start the web server:
   `python -m webserver`

4. Test the web service:
   http://localhost:8000/user/3
   http://localhost:8000/users

5. Install HTTP Proxy package:
   `npm install express http-proxy-middleware --save-dev`

6. Update the build scripts in **package.json**:

   ```
   "dev": "node dev-server.js",
   ```

7. Add source file:
   dev-server.js

8. Build the application and run the proxy server with:
   `npm run dev`

9. Test the proxy server:
   http://localhost:8080/
   http://localhost:8080/api/user/4

References:

- Chapter code
  https://github.com/rtp-book/code/tree/main/ch19
- Sample Data Generator
  https://mockaroo.com
- Cross-Origin Resource Sharing (CORS)
  https://developer.mozilla.org/en-US/docs/Web/HTTP/CORS
- Express Web Framework
  https://expressjs.com
- http-proxy-middleware JavaScript Library
  https://www.npmjs.com/package/http-proxy-middleware

Chapter 20 — Asynchronous Requests

Now that we have a proxy server to host our back-end and front-end web servers, let's talk about how we get data into our front-end application from our back-end server.

20.1 Synchronicity

In front-end web development, a good user experience is key to a successful application. The last thing you want to do is have to display a spinning wait icon while your application sends a query to the back-end web server to pull in data. For this reason, synchronous web service calls have gone out of style in favor of using asynchronous calls. This results in your application not going into a holding pattern while waiting for data to arrive, and instead continues to be responsive to the user's actions. When the data you requested finally arrives from the back-end server, your application processes it at that point asynchronously.

Being a Python developer, your first inclination for making HTTP requests might be to import the `urllib` module or the Python `requests` library, but they won't work with Transcrypt. Fortunately, they are not needed as there are existing JavaScript libraries available that we can utilize in our front-end web applications that can handle the asynchronous communication tasks for us, and they work well in a web browser. The one we'll focus on here is the `window.fetch()` method that is built-in to JavaScript.

In its simplest form, the `fetch()` method takes a URL string as a parameter and returns a *promise*. The promise object that is returned from the `fetch()` method is kind of a placeholder in your code for an asynchronous function call. When the response is received back from the server, the status of the promise object is updated, and it will call a function you provide to process the returned data. If there is an error during the `fetch()` call, then it will call another function that you provide for handling errors. The callback functions you provide to `fetch()` and the order they are processed is referred to as the *promise chain*. To simplify using the `fetch()` method, let's wrap it in a Python convenience function that will make it easier to use in our application, where we can just give it a URL and a callback function to pass the returned data to. Since it's a JavaScript call, let's also put in in a separate module called **jsutils.py** so we don't clutter up any of our pure Python modules:

Listing 20-1 File: *jsutils.py*

```
console = window.console

def fetch(url, callback):
    def check_response(response):
        if response.status != 200:
            console.error('Fetch error - Status Code: ' + response.status)
            return None
        return response.json()

    try:
        promise = window.fetch(url)
        response = promise.then(check_response)
        response.then(callback)
        promise.catch(console.error)
    except object as e:
        console.error(e)
```

Since we now have a module for miscellaneous JavaScript-to-Python mappings, we also added a mapping for the `window.console` object. This will let us use `console.log()` and `console.error()` to display messages in the web browser console window from our other Python modules without getting complaints from the Python linter.

This Python `fetch()` function wraps the JavaScript `window.fetch()` method and hides some of the asynchronous promise noise from your main application. It takes as parameters, a URL string, and a function to call once the data is received from the back-end server. Inside the function, we first call the `window.fetch()` method with the provided URL that returns a promise.

```
promise = window.fetch(url)
```

The first thing we want to do with the eventual response is to check the status of the response to make sure that the server processed it successfully. To do this, we provide a function that does that error check to the `then()` method of the promise, which will get called once the actual response is received.

```
response = promise.then(check_response)
```

We also provide a function to run if some other error occurs with the promise via the `catch()` method.

```
promise.catch(console.error)
```

If the response status is OK, we call the `json()` method that formats the response as a JSON object, but that method also returns another asynchronous promise object. So the callback function that we originally provided is passed into another `then()` method of that promise object, which calls it once the JSON object is finally retrieved.

```
response.then(callback)
```

Since we are actually catching JavaScript errors at runtime and not Python exceptions, the except clause in our `try/except` block will just grab the generic JavaScript `error` object and use the error message out of that if something goes wrong.

The JavaScript `fetch()` method has a somewhat complex behavior if you are not used to it, so our Python wrapper function has a lot going on in it. But fortunately, we've hidden most of that complexity, and we now have a utility function that you can just reuse as needed.

Now that we have that in place, let's create a simple React application that pulls data from the Flask server application that we created in the last chapter. This example will load a list of user IDs and names that will populate a dropdown select box. Then, when a selection from that list is made, it will request the user's first name, last name, and their username from the Flask server and display that information in three other read-only text boxes:

Listing 20-2 File: *app.py*

```
from pyreact import render, useState, useEffect, createElement as el
from pymui import Box, TextField
from jsutils import fetch
```

```python
def StyledTextField(props):
    new_props = {'type': 'text',
                 'fullWidth': True,
                 'variant': 'outlined',
                 'InputLabelProps': {'shrink': True},
                 'InputProps': {'margin': 'dense'},
                 'margin': 'dense',
                 }

    new_props.update(props)
    return el(TextField, new_props)

def UserVu(props):
    users = props['users'] if props['users'] else []

    def userToRow(user):
        return el('option', {'key': user[0], 'value': user[0]}, user[1])

    return [userToRow(user) for user in users]

def App():
    users, setUsers = useState([])
    userID, setUserID = useState("")
    firstName, setFirstName = useState("")
    lastName, setLastName = useState("")
    username, setUsername = useState("")

    def handleChange(event):
        target = event['target']
        setUserID(target['value'])
        setFirstName("")
        setLastName("")
        setUsername("")

    def getUser():
        def _getUser(data):
            user_info = data if data else {}
            if len(user_info) > 0:
                setFirstName(user_info['FirstName'])
                setLastName(user_info['LastName'])
                setUsername(user_info['Username'])
            else:
                setFirstName("")
```

```python
                setLastName("")
                setUsername("")

        if len(userID) > 0:
            fetch(f"/api/user/{userID}", _getUser)

    def getUsers():
        def _getUsers(data):
            user_list = data if data else []
            user_list.sort(key=lambda user: user[1])
            setUsers(user_list)
            setUserID("")

        fetch("/api/users", _getUsers)

    useEffect(getUser, [userID])
    useEffect(getUsers, [])

    return el(Box, {'key': 'App', 'style': {'width': '200px'}},
            el(Box, {'alignItems': 'center'},
                el(StyledTextField, {'label': "Select User",
                                    'value': userID,
                                    'onChange': handleChange,
                                    'select': True,
                                    'SelectProps': {'native': True},
                                    'autoFocus': True,
                                    },
                    el('option', {'key': '', 'value': ''}),  # Blank row
                    el(UserVu, {'users': users}),
                ),
            ),
            el(StyledTextField, {'label': 'First Name',
                                'value': firstName,
                                'disabled': True,
                                }
            ),
            el(StyledTextField, {'label': 'Last Name',
                                'value': lastName,
                                'disabled': True,
                                }
            ),
            el(StyledTextField, {'label': 'Username',
                                'value': username,
                                'disabled': True,
                                }
```

```
            ),
        ),

render(App, None, 'root')
```

In addition to our main App component, there is also a StyledTextField composite component that defaults several component properties so we don't have to repeat them for every TextField we use.

There is also a UserVu component that builds up the option list that will populate our dropdown select box. This takes the list of user IDs and names as a prop that is passed in, and creates a list of option elements, one for each user. To ensure that we have a valid iterator, we use a ternary expression on the incoming prop and supply an empty list if it happens to have a value of None:

```
users = props['users'] if props['users'] else []
```

Moving into the main App component, we create five state variables and their respective update functions with the React.useState() method.

```
users, setUsers = useState([])
userID, setUserID = useState("")
firstName, setFirstName = useState("")
lastName, setLastName = useState("")
username, setUsername = useState("")
```

There is one state variable that holds the list of all of the users, one for the currently selected user, and one each to hold the first name, last name, and username of the selected user.

The handleChange() function is similar to what we've seen before, in that it will update the TextField value whenever a new selection is made from the dropdown list. When that value changes, we also clear out the user's detail values since they would not match the selected value at that point.

Jumping down to the element tree in the return statement, we used our styled component for all four text boxes. What makes the first one special, is that we set the select property to True, turning it into a select box. There are a couple of different variations you can use, but by setting the native prop of SelectProps to

True, it uses the underlying platform for rendering the list. To create the list itself, you just add HTML `option` elements as children of the `TextField` component.

And now we get to the interesting part. Getting the data from the back-end server into our front-end application. Starting with loading the list of user IDs and names into the select box, we created the `getUsers()` function that calls our Python `fetch()` function:

```
fetch("/api/users", _getUsers)
```

Here we pass in the URL for the REST API call to get the list of users as the first argument, and then a reference to the inner function `_getUsers()` as the callback function to pass the received data into. When the callback function is run after the data is received, it updates the `users` state variable, and also clears out the `userID` state variable just to be thorough.

What triggers the outer `getUsers()` function to be run, is the `React.useEffect()` hook function:

```
useEffect(getUsers, [])
```

In the JavaScript chapter, when we covered component lifecycle events, we talked about the `useEffect()` function. With this function, you give it a function to run, and you tell it *when* to run the function. By giving it an empty list, the function will run one time, right after the component loads. So in this case, the request for the data that fills the select list gets made when the App component finishes loading.

Similarly, we also have a `getUser()` function that is used to retrieve the user's first name, last name, and username from the back-end server based on the current value of the `userID` state variable:

```
if len(userID) > 0:
    fetch(f"/api/user/{userID}", _getUser)
```

To not make unnecessary calls to the back-end server if there is no user selected, we make sure that there is one selected by checking that the `userID` state variable has a non-empty value before calling the `fetch()` function.

The callback function we created as inner function _getUser(), handles updating the `firstName`, `lastName` and `username` state variables. If the server doesn't return any data, then those state variables get reset to empty strings. The useEffect() function is again used to trigger the call to the getUser() function:

```
useEffect(getUser, [userID])
```

But this time, we have the `userID` state variable in the watch list, so our getUser() function gets called anytime that `userID` state variable is updated.

If you run the Flask web server with `python -m webserver` as we did in the last chapter, and then have the proxy server running with `npm run dev`, selecting a user from the dropdown list should cause the First Name, Last Name, and Username text boxes to be filled in. Selecting a different user should then update those text boxes. If you open up the developer console in the web browser and go to the *Network* tab, with *All* or *XHR* filters selected, you should be able to see the network calls being made any time you make a new selection. If you then reload the entire page, you should also see the initial call to the REST server that retrieves the initial list of users as well.

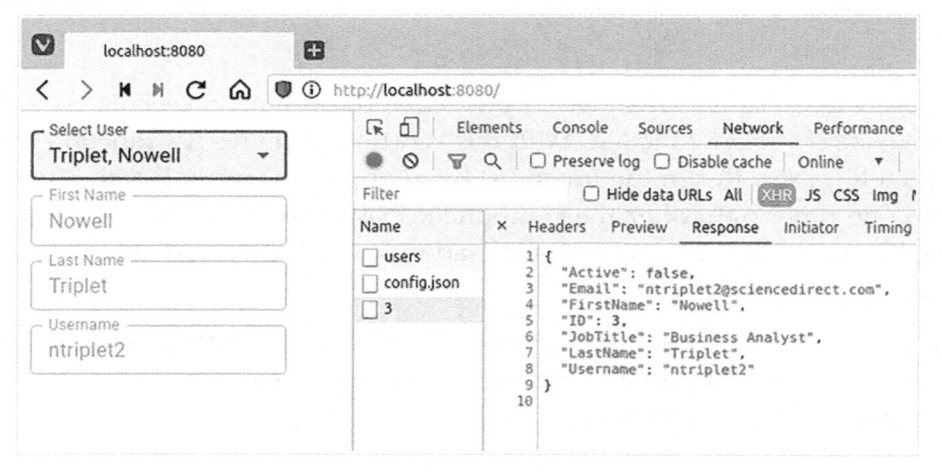

20.2 Async/Await

While the promise model does allow us to make asynchronous calls to our back-end server, the model tends to be a bit clunky. It can be difficult to catch errors, and it can be difficult to debug with all the callbacks and promise objects. For this reason, many people prefer to use the async/await model instead, which wraps the promise model and allows your code to look more like it would if you were using a synchronous approach.

We can change our Python `fetch()` function to use the async/await model instead of the promise model:

Listing 20-3 File: *jsutils.py*

```
console = window.console

polyfill = require("@babel/polyfill")  # required by async/await

async def fetch(url, callback):
    try:
        response = await window.fetch(url)
        if response.status != 200:
            console.error('Fetch error - Status Code: ' + response.status)
        else:
            data = await response.json()
            callback(data)
    except object as e:
        console.error(e)
```

To utilize async/await, some web browsers will require the JavaScript polyfill library, which is an ES6 compatibility layer, so we load that here.

The first thing you may notice in our updated Python `fetch()` function is that our code now looks a bit more like "normal" Python. The second thing you may notice is the `async` keyword in front of our function definition. This tells Python, and JavaScript after it gets transpiled by Transcrypt, that the function runs asynchronously and returns a *promise* object. The good news is that we no longer need to deal with that object directly. Any time an asynchronous function call is made inside a function that has been declared with `async`, we use the `await` keyword to signal that the code should wait:

```
response = await window.fetch(url)
```

So now, we can get the response directly from the call to `window.fetch()`, and the code will wait for the response to be completed in the background. After we get the response, we check the response status code as we did before, to make sure the server responded OK. Then if all is good, we call the `json()` method asynchronously, again using the `await` keyword:

```
data = await response.json()
```

As before, the code will pause while that function call is completed, then finally, we pass the JSON data into our callback function and call it directly:

```
callback(data)
```

Error handling with async/await is also simplified and less ambiguous. We can now just wrap the asynchronous code in a normal `try/except` block just like you would regular synchronous code, without having to worry about where the error actually happens. So errors will be caught whether they happen in our code or in the promise object. This contrasts with what we did before, where we had to utilize the `catch()` method of the promise as well as have a separate `try/except` block to catch other errors.

We did keep the `fetch()` function signature the same, so no changes will be required in our example application. And if you run it now, it will still be working as before. The only difference is that our code is now a bit cleaner.

20.3 Summary

It is important to use asynchronous communication between your front-end application and the back-end web service so that the user experience is not compromised, and your front-end web application can run more efficiently. It also works really well with the React data model since the UI will get re-rendered anytime the state variables are updated, and you don't have to concern yourself with *when* that happens, as React automatically handles it for you. Whether you use the promise asynchronous model or the async/await model is just up to your personal preference. But the async/await model tends to result in cleaner, easier to follow code.

Chapter Review:

1. Add source file (Promise):
   jsutils.py

2. Update source file:
   app.py

3. Build the application for development with:
   `npm run dev`

4. Open the application:
   http://localhost:8080

5. Update source file (Async/Await):
   jsutils.py

References:

- Chapter code
  https://github.com/rtp-book/code/tree/main/ch20

- JavaScript Fetch API
  https://developer.mozilla.org/en-US/docs/Web/API/Fetch_API/Using_Fetch

Chapter 21 – React Context Hook

So far, we have used *state* variables that are managed by a component, and *props* that are explicitly passed down into child components. These two ways to store and pass data normally work well for most situations. Sometimes however, you might need to pass a prop value down through multiple levels of components in order to get the data to the component that actually needs to use it. If your component tree is complex, this can make it difficult to keep track of where the data came from, and also adds to the complexity of each component that is in between the source of the data and where it actually gets used, even if those intermediate components don't use that piece of data themselves.

21.1 Nested Components

Fortunately, React provides a *context* mechanism that allows you to *implicitly* pass data down to child components in a way that will not affect the intermediate components that don't need to use that data. Let's use a contrived example that has several layers of components that pass a state variable from the top component down four levels to another component where it is actually used:

Listing 21-1 File: *app.py*

```
from pyreact import render, useState, createElement as el
from pymui import Box, TextField

def ROTextField(props):
    new_props = {'fullWidth': True,
                 'variant': 'outlined',
                 'InputLabelProps': {'shrink': True},
                 'InputProps': {'margin': 'dense'},
                 'margin': 'dense',
                 'disabled': True
                 }

    new_props.update(props)
    return el(TextField, new_props)

def Component2(props):
    return el(Box, None,
              el(ROTextField, {'label': 'Row 2', 'value': 'Row Two'}),
```

```
                    el(Component3, {'testVal2': props['testVal1']})
                )

def Component3(props):
    return el(Box, None,
                el(ROTextField, {'label': 'Row 3', 'value': 'Row Three'}),
                el(Component4, {'testVal3': props['testVal2']})
            )

def Component4(props):
    return el(Box, None,
                el(ROTextField, {'label': 'Row 4', 'value': 'Row Four'}),
                el(Component5, {'testVal4': props['testVal3']})
            )

def Component5(props):
    return el(Box, None,
                el(ROTextField, {'label': 'Copy From Row 1',
                                 'value': props['testVal4']}
                ),
            )

def App():
    testVal, setTestVal = useState("")

    def handleChange(event):
        target = event['target']
        setTestVal(target['value'])

    return el(Box, {'key': 'App', 'style': {'width': '200px'}},
                el(TextField, {'label': 'Row 1',
                               'value': testVal,
                               'onChange': handleChange}
                ),
                el(Component2, {'testVal1': testVal})
            )

render(App, None, 'root')
```

In this example, we created the composition component ROTextField as a read-only version of the Material-UI TextField component just to make things look nice. Then we have several components that we daisy-chain together, passing the testVal state value down through each component layer as a prop. In the last component in the tree, we finally use the testVal prop and display the value in the text box. None of the other intermediate components use the testVal prop. It's just passed through each component, down to where it is needed.

If you build and run this, the value that is typed into the first text box and stored in a state variable of the main App component, will be reflected in the last text box as well, being passed down as props through the component tree.

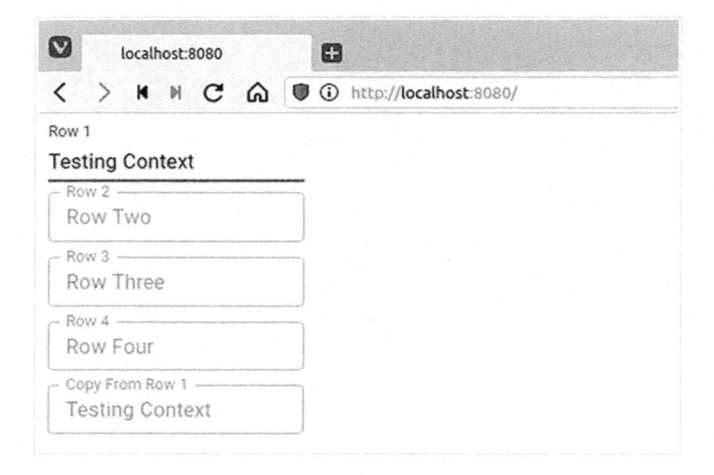

21.2 Context Variables

When passing props down multiple levels to where they are needed, it can involve a lot of repetitious code, and it can be tedious to keep track of them. To help in this situation, React has a set of methods that can be used to create the equivalent of what would be component-scoped global props. That is, a context variable that works just like component props, but can be accessed anywhere in the component tree below where it is created. Using this mechanism, a prop doesn't need to be passed down explicitly through any intermediate components in order to be utilized at a lower level in the component tree.

The first thing we need to do is to update our **pyreact.py** module to include the necessary React methods. So lets add `React.createContext()` and `React.useContext()` to that file:

React to Python

Listing 21-2 File: *pyreact.py*

```python
# Load React and ReactDOM JavaScript libraries into local namespace
React = require('react')
ReactDOM = require('react-dom')

# Map React javaScript objects to Python identifiers
createElement = React.createElement
useState = React.useState
useEffect = React.useEffect
createContext = React.createContext
useContext = React.useContext


def render(root_component, props, container):
    def main():
        ReactDOM.render(
            React.createElement(root_component, props),
            document.getElementById(container)
        )

    document.addEventListener('DOMContentLoaded', main)


# JavaScript function mappings
alert = window.alert


def setTitle(title):
    document.title = title
```

Now that we have those React methods available to us, let's take the example we just did and use a React context to store the `testVal` value instead of passing it down as props all the way through the component tree:

Listing 21-3 File: *app.py*

```python
from pyreact import render, useState, createElement as el
from pyreact import useContext, createContext
from pymui import Box, TextField

Ctx = createContext()
```

Chapter 21 - React Context Hook | 169

```python
def ROTextField(props):
    new_props = {'fullWidth': True,
                 'variant': 'outlined',
                 'InputLabelProps': {'shrink': True},
                 'InputProps': {'margin': 'dense'},
                 'margin': 'dense',
                 'disabled': True
                 }

    new_props.update(props)
    return el(TextField, new_props)

def Component2(props):
    return el(Box, None,
              el(ROTextField, {'label': 'Row 2', 'value': 'Row Two'}),
              el(Component3, None)
              )

def Component3(props):
    return el(Box, None,
              el(ROTextField, {'label': 'Row 3', 'value': 'Row Three'}),
              el(Component4, None)
              )

def Component4(props):
    return el(Box, None,
              el(ROTextField, {'label': 'Row 4', 'value': 'Row Four'}),
              el(Component5, None)
              )

def Component5(props):
    ctx = useContext(Ctx)
    testVal = ctx['testVal']
    return el(Box, None,
              el(ROTextField, {'label': 'Copy From Row 1',
                               'value': testVal}
                 ),
              )

def App():
    testVal, setTestVal = useState("")

    def handleChange(event):
        target = event['target']
        setTestVal(target['value'])
```

```
    return el(Ctx.Provider, {'value': {'testVal': testVal, 'otherVal': 42}},
              el(Box, {'key': 'App', 'style': {'width': '200px'}},
                  el(TextField, {'label': 'Row 1',
                                 'value': testVal,
                                 'onChange': handleChange}
                  ),
                  el(Component2, None)
              )
          )

render(App, None, 'root')
```

You'll notice that we no longer pass any props down our component tree, yet the component at the bottom of the tree still has access to the data it needs.

The first thing we needed to do here was to create a React context variable. This gives us a reference to a specific context and provides the actual functionality. This variable can be created in the same file we use it in, or we can create it in another module and just import it into the module where it is used. In this case, we only have one module:

```
Ctx = createContext()
```

The next step is to "inject" the context into the component tree by using the `Provider` method of the React context object, and provide any value that we want to use further down the tree as a prop. This can be a single value, or you can use a dictionary to pass multiple values as we did here:

```
el(Ctx.Provider, {'value': {'testVal': testVal, 'otherVal': 42}}
```

Finally, to get to the context values where we need to use them, we access the context with the `React.useContext()` hook method:

```
ctx = useContext(Ctx)
```

Then we can access any values in the context dictionary just like we do for props:

```
testVal = ctx['testVal']
```

And be aware that just like props, context variables are also immutable.

21.3 Summary

Now we have three ways to store and move data around our application: *State*, *Props*, and *Context*. Generally speaking, that is also the order in which they are used. While it may be tempting to use context instead of props for all of your components, it's really better to use props for the same reason global variables are bad in general. Context variables should be reserved for either truly global information like a *username* that might need to be accessed from multiple components, or in a case where the component nesting is deep and you don't want to have to pass the data down through each level when the intermediate components don't utilize that data.

Chapter Review:

1. Update source file (Nested Components):
   app.py

2. Build the application for development with:
   ```
   npm run dev
   ```

3. Open the application:
   http://localhost:8080

4. Update source files (Context Variables):
   app.py
   pyreact.py

References:

- Chapter code
  https://github.com/rtp-book/code/tree/main/ch21

Chapter 22 – Transcrypt Miscellany

Since the focus of Transcrypt is on applications that run in web browsers and not desktop applications, it is intended to be used more with JavaScript libraries rather than Python libraries. As such, it does not have a full set of standard Python modules available to it. However, in addition to supporting most of Python's built-ins, there are also a few standard Python modules that have been added to the Transcrypt distribution that can be imported into your python module.

22.1 Standard Library

This list is bound to grow over time as the Transcrypt project matures, but for now, we only have these modules from the standard library available to us:

- math
- cmath
- time (does not have sleep function for web browser use)
- datetime
- itertools
- logging
- warnings
- random (partially)
- re (partially)
- turtle

In addition to the above, there is also a separate project called Numscrypt under development that is porting the Python numpy library as well.

Python `dataclasses` is one language construct that works really well with React for storing component state. Though while being syntactically supported, as of this writing, none of the methods like `replace()` or `asdict()` for `dataclasses` have been implemented in Transcrypt yet. So if you want to use them, you will have to provide that additional functionality yourself for now.

22.2 Built-in Functions

Despite the limitations of not having full Python standard library functionality, you will find that most of the other Python-related language constructs have been implemented. Working with standard Python objects like lists, dictionaries, strings, and more will feel just like Python should. There are only a few Python built-ins that have yet to be implemented, namely exec and eval, which are likely not needed in a web browser environment anyway. Then there are a few others like bin, oct, and hex for converting numbers, but those can easily be replaced with the toString(radix) method in JavaScript:

```
bin_val = int(val).toString(2)
oct_val = int(val).toString(8)
hex_val = int(val).toString(16)
```

In general, Transcrypt does not support third-party Python libraries, and as we've seen, only a few of the standard library modules. That said, if a third party library is pure Python (no dependencies on C libraries) and conforms to the general limitations of Transcrypt, you should be able to transpile it to JavaScript and use it. However, note that the Transcrypt limitations would apply to the full dependency tree of that library in order for it to work.

Since Python was never designed to run in a web browser environment, some coding techniques may feel a bit foreign. And when mimicking JavaScript code examples, you may have to take a step back and rewrite some of that example code in a more Pythonic way so that you don't fall into the trap of just writing JavaScript code with a Python syntax. Though in the end, with the methodology we are using here, you should be able to write your front-end web applications without having to think about JavaScript very much at all.

22.3 Keyword Args

By default, unpacking keyword arguments with **kwargs in a function does not work out of the box in Transcrypt. This is because it would lead to bloated code when it gets transpiled to JavaScript. Fortunately, Transcrypt provides us with a compiler directive that will selectively enable that feature for just when it is needed. Here is a simple example:

```
# __pragma__('kwargs')

def test_function(**kwargs):
    for key, val in kwargs.items():
        print(key, ":", val)

# __pragma__('nokwargs')
```

So you basically just have to wrap your function that uses **kwargs in the __pragma__ compiler directives to turn it on, then turn it off again. Transcrypt will then handle making sure that the function is transpiled into JavaScript with that capability enabled.

If you do try and use **kwargs without the __pragma__ compiler directives, you might see an error similar to this in the web browser console at runtime:

```
ReferenceError: kwargs is not defined
```

So if you do get that error, check to make sure that you let Transcrypt know about the use of the kwargs language construct.

Speaking of the __pragma__ compiler directive, you can see in this example that we actually put it behind a Python comment. Transcrypt will still process it the way we expect, but putting it in a comment form has the added advantage that the Python linter doesn't complain about an unknown function called __pragma__(). Transcrypt also supports a single-line version of its compiler directives in some cases, which you can get more information on in the Transcrypt documentation.

22.4 Immutability

We talked about immutability several times so far, and how to work with React in that regard. Whenever changes to state happen, React needs to know about it so it can appropriately re-render components. To prevent developers from bypassing the mechanisms React uses to detect these changes in state that are made through an update function, it makes variables, specifically props and context variables, immutable so that they can't be updated via a direct assignment of value.

In order to make changes to an immutable variable, we must make a copy of it and then make changes to the copy. There are several ways to accomplish this in Python, one of which we have already used in our composition component examples:

```python
def StyledTextField(props):
    new_props = {'type': 'text',
                 'fullWidth': True,
                 'variant': 'outlined'}

    new_props.update(props)
    return el(TextField, new_props)
```

Here, we are creating a new Python dictionary, then adding the prop values in the immutable JavaScript object into it. If we tried doing it the other way around by first converting the JavaScript object to a Python dictionary and then tried to add in the new values, we would get an error at runtime similar to this:

```
Uncaught TypeError: Cannot define property __class__, object is not extensible
```

Which essentially means we tried to modify an immutable object.

Another way to accomplish the task of updating an immutable object is to use a deepcopy() function to create a completely unrelated clone of the object. While this feature exists in Python with the copy.deepcopy() function, the Python copy module has yet to be made available to Transcrypt, and will currently generate an error during build time if you try to use it.

But since Transcrypt is intended to be used with JavaScript libraries, if we look, we'll find that indeed there is a JavaScript deepcopy library that exists for exactly the purpose we intend to use it for. You can install it with:

```
$ npm install deepcopy
```

Then add it to the **jsutils.py** module with:

```python
deepcopy = require('deepcopy')
```

Now we can use it in a Python module. Taking the example we just looked at, we can do this:

```
from jsutils import deepcopy

def StyledTextField(props):
    props_copy = dict(deepcopy(props))
    new_props = {'type': 'text',
                 'fullWidth': True,
                 'variant': 'outlined'}

    props_copy.update(new_props)
    return el(TextField, props_copy)
```

Even though both of these methods of making a mutable copy of an immutable JavaScript object accomplish the same thing, depending on what you need to update in the immutable props object, one will likely be easier than the other to implement. The order you do the update in will also determine whether the new props override the old ones or the other way around. And if you have another dictionary inside of the props dictionary, like the `style` property for example, you will have to add extra code to explicitly merge those values in a way that achieves the desired outcome, instead of having one completely override the other.

On a related note, when a dictionary-like object is returned from a JavaScript function, it is just a plain key/value store and must be explicitly converted to a Python dictionary if you want to use the methods or properties of one. This is most easily achieved by using the Python `dict()` function to turn the generic JavaScript object that has no methods into a valid Python dictionary, as we did above.

22.5 Truthiness

As we brought up in an earlier chapter, there is a difference in truthiness between Python and JavaScript when it comes to empty lists, dictionaries, and sets. For example, in Python an empty list evaluates to False, whereas in JavaScript it evaluates to True. If you use the condition of a list being empty in an expression to determine program flow, you may not get the result you intended. As previously mentioned, the most straightforward and recommended way to deal with this difference in truthiness is to check if your list or dictionary has a length of zero. For example, the expression len([]) > 0 will always evaluate to False in both Python and JavaScript. The second way is to use a Transcrypt compiler directive that tells the transpiler to explicitly use Python-based truthiness:

```
__pragma__ ('tconv')
my_list = []
if not my_list:
    print("Empty List")
__pragma__ ('notconv')
```

Using the tconv compiler directive will cause an empty list, empty dictionary, or empty set, to evaluate as False when it is transpiled. The downside to this is that it adds additional code cruft and can actually slow down the execution of your code. Unless you need your Python code to behave the same way in CPython as it does when transpiled to JavaScript, it's best just to avoid the ambiguity altogether and explicitly check the length of a list rather than rely on its truthiness value implicitly.

22.6 Types

While we don't get into using Python type hints in this book, it should be pointed out that Transcrypt does support type annotations, and can even run static type validation at compile time by using the --dstat command line option:

```
transcrypt --nomin --map --dstat my_annotated_app
```

22.7 Summary

One of the core premises of Transcrypt is that it acts as a bridge between your Python code and the myriad of JavaScript libraries that are available for web application development. At the same time, it facilitates letting you code in Python as much as possible, and when it makes more sense to do so. While it is certainly already useful, Transcrypt is still in an early development stage and doesn't have full implementation of all Python standard libraries yet. It is best to keep checking the Transcrypt GitHub repository and project documentation for any updates to standard library support.

References:

- Chapter code
  https://github.com/rtp-book/code/tree/main/ch22

- Numscrypt Project
  http://www.transcrypt.org/numscrypt/numscrypt.html
- Python Dataclasses
  https://docs.python.org/3/library/dataclasses.html
- Transcrypt Compiler Directives
  https://www.transcrypt.org/docs/html/special_facilities.html#the-pragma-mechanism
- Transcrypt GitHub Repository
  https://github.com/QQuick/Transcrypt
- Transcrypt Python Language Support
  https://www.transcrypt.org/docs/html/supported_constructs.html

Chapter 23 – Application Versioning

When you are working on an application, it's always good to know if you have deployed the version you think it is. While code repositories like GitHub are great for versioning in general, that versioning doesn't always carry through to the deployment of the application. What we'll present here is one way to tackle that issue.

23.1 NPM Version

As it turns out, the Node Package Manager that we are already using has a built-in feature to version your application. If you look at the **package.json** file, you'll see a value that holds a *semver* formatted version number:

```
"version": "1.0.0"
```

The three numbers in the semantic versioning string represent the Major, Minor, and Patch version. Conveniently, npm has version commands that will increment each of these:

```
npm version patch
npm version minor
npm version major
```

When you run one of these commands, it will update the appropriate part of the semver version value in the **package.json** file. If you update the minor version it will set the patch version to 0. So version 1.0.3 becomes 1.1.0. Likewise, if you update the major version, the minor and patch versions will both get set to 0.

In addition to updating the version in **package.json**, if npm finds a **.git** folder, it will also integrate with git and automatically commit and tag the version update when you run the command. However, it does have a prerequisite that the git working directory needs to be clean. If it isn't clean, the npm version command will fail.

One extra point to make is that due to a bug (or quirky feature?), if your project's root folder is at a lower level than where the root folder for your git repository is (as might be the case if you have multiple projects in one git repository), you will need to add an *empty* **.git** folder to your project folder for the git integration to work properly with the `npm version` command.

So if, for example, you have a full-stack application in one git repository with separate client and server projects in it, your folder structure might look like this:

```
full_stack_app/
├── .git/   <--(actual git repo)
├── client/
│   ├── .git/   <--(empty folder)
│   ├── node_modules/
│   └── src/
└── server/
    └── src/
```

23.2 Application Version

To easily get the current **package.json** version into your application, we can add another script to **package.json** to write the version to a Python file. With that, we can directly import the semver version number into our application. Let's add the version script entry in the script section of **package.json**:

```
"start": "NODE_ENV=development parcel --log-level 4 index.html --out-dir
    dist/dev",
"build": "NODE_ENV=production parcel --log-level 4 build index.html
    --no-source-maps --out-dir dist/prod",
"dev": "node dev-server.js",
"version": "echo \"version = '$npm_package_version'\" > ./version.py;git add
    ./version.py",
```

Now when you run one of the `npm version` commands, it will also run this script and create a **version.py** module that contains the version number. This script will also automatically include the updated **version.py** file with the git version commit. The generated Python file only has one global variable in it:

```
version = '1.0.1'
```

Now from any other Python module, you can import the current version as needed:

```
from version import version
```

If, for example, you have an "About" view component for your application, you can display this version number on it to verify the version that is actually deployed, and be able to match it up to a tag in the git repository.

Note that because this script is using git, you must have git installed and configured, or you will get errors when running it. If you are *not* using git, then you can remove the last command from the script:

```
"version": "echo \"version = '$npm_package_version'\" > ./version.py",
```

This will still update the **package.json** file and create or update the **version.py** file when you run it.

23.3 Summary

Using the approach presented in this chapter, with the `version` command of npm, you can automatically tie a tagged `git` version, the **package.json** version, and your application version together.

Chapter Review:

1. Update the build scripts in **package.json**:

    ```
    "version": "echo \"version = '$npm_package_version'\" > ./version.py;git
    ↪   add ./version.py",
    ```

3. Update the application version with one of these:
   npm version patch
   npm version minor
   npm version major

References:

- Chapter code
  https://github.com/rtp-book/code/tree/main/ch23
- npm Version Documentation
  https://docs.npmjs.com/cli/v6/commands/npm-version

Chapter 24 – Google Analytics

It is fundamentally important to understand how your application gets utilized by users. One of the most popular tools for doing this is Google Analytics. While it is geared primarily towards marketing, we can still use it to gather information about which parts of our application are being utilized the most, and to keep a watch for performance issues. The Google Analytics application itself can be an overwhelming tool to use, so we won't go too deep into that aspect of it. But we *will* show you how to get analytic information from your application into Google Analytics.

24.1 ReactGA

Unsurprisingly, there is an existing react-ga JavaScript library that specifically works within the React framework that we can utilize to collect usage data from our application. Like most other JavaScript libraries, we can use npm to install it:

```
$ npm install react-ga
```

To use Google Analytics, you will need to have an account with Google. The good news is that any Gmail account will do. What we will need is a Google Analytics ID or GAID that will identify what account the analytic data we send from your application will be associated with. To get that, while logged into your Google account, go to:

> https://analytics.google.com

At the *Welcome* screen, click the "*Set up for free*" button that should take you to the analytics *Account setup* screen. Give the account a name and click *Next*. Under *Property setup* (property is equivalent to a project) specify a name for the application. Click the *Show advanced options* link and turn on the *Create a Universal Analytics property*. Fill in the Website URL as 127.0.0.1 and select the *Create a Universal Analytics property only* option. Click *Next*, then in the *Business information* section, you can fill in the business demographic information as you wish. Click the *Create* button, then read and accept the terms in the pop-up window. You may get another pop-up screen that asks about email preferences. If so, change those settings as desired and close the pop-up.

React to Python

At this point, what we are looking for is the *Tracking ID* that has been assigned. This should be an ID that starts with "UA-" (for Universal Analytics). Note that a GA4 Measurement ID will not work for our purposes. We will eventually need to add this Google Analytics ID to our application, so make a note of it.

Getting back to our code, we will need to add the `react-ga` library to our **pyreact.py** module:

Listing 24-1 File: *pyreact.py*

```
# Load React and ReactDOM JavaScript libraries into local namespace
React = require('react')
ReactDOM = require('react-dom')
ReactGA = require('react-ga')

# Map React javaScript objects to Python identifiers
createElement = React.createElement
useState = React.useState
useEffect = React.useEffect
createContext = React.createContext
useContext = React.useContext


def render(root_component, props, container):
    def main():
        ReactDOM.render(
            React.createElement(root_component, props),
            document.getElementById(container)
        )

    document.addEventListener('DOMContentLoaded', main)


# JavaScript function mappings
alert = window.alert


def setTitle(title):
    document.title = title
```

The only line we had to add to **pyreact.py** was to import ReactGA:

Chapter 24 - Google Analytics   185

React to Python

```
ReactGA = require('react-ga')
```

Now we're ready to add analytics to our previous asynchronous request example:

Listing 24-2 File: *app.py*

```python
from pyreact import render, useState, useEffect, createElement as el
from pyreact import ReactGA
from pymui import Box, TextField
from jsutils import fetch

GAID = 'UA-100000000-1'   # Substitute your own GA Tracking ID here
ReactGA.initialize(GAID, {'titleCase': False, 'debug': False,
                          'gaOptions': {'siteSpeedSampleRate': 100}}
                  )

...

    def getUser():
        def _getUser(data):
            user_info = data if data else {}
            if len(user_info) > 0:
                setFirstName(user_info['FirstName'])
                setLastName(user_info['LastName'])
                setUsername(user_info['Username'])
            else:
                setFirstName("")
                setLastName("")
                setUsername("")

        if len(userID) > 0:
            ReactGA.event({'category': 'User',
                           'action': 'Select',
                           'label': userID}
                         )
            fetch(f"/api/user/{userID}", _getUser)

    def getUsers():
        def _getUsers(data):
            user_list = data if data else []
            user_list.sort(key=lambda user: user[1])
            ReactGA.event({'category': 'App',
                           'action': 'Load',
                           'label': 'Users',
                           'nonInteraction': True}
```

Part II - Building Blocks

```
                )
        setUsers(user_list)
        setUserID("")

    fetch("/api/users", _getUsers)

    useEffect(getUser, [userID])
    useEffect(getUsers, [])

...

render(App, None, 'root')
```

ReactGA makes collecting data for Google Analytics pretty easy. The first step is to initialize ReactGA:

```
ReactGA.initialize(GAID, {'titleCase': False, 'debug': False,
                          'gaOptions': {'siteSpeedSampleRate': 100}}
                  )
```

The GAID is the Tracking ID we grabbed from the Google Analytics screen when we set up the account. Then we set a few options like `titlecase`, which by setting it to `False` means it won't automatically change the character case on the strings we send to Google Analytics like it does by default. And then there's `debug`, which will output analytic information directly to the web browser console window when set to `True`. The last option we provide `gaOptions`, is a dictionary with more detailed settings. The one we provide `siteSpeedSampleRate`, has to do with timing and making sure we capture all speed measurements, like the one we'll do next.

Once you build and run this (and don't forget to start the Flask back-end REST server), and then select a few different names from the list, they should start showing up in the Google Analytics dashboard. If you go back to your analytics account dashboard, and on the left side go to *Reports -> Realtime -> Events* you should start to see events from your application showing up. You may need to change from *Active Users* to *Events* for the Viewing option just above the list of events.

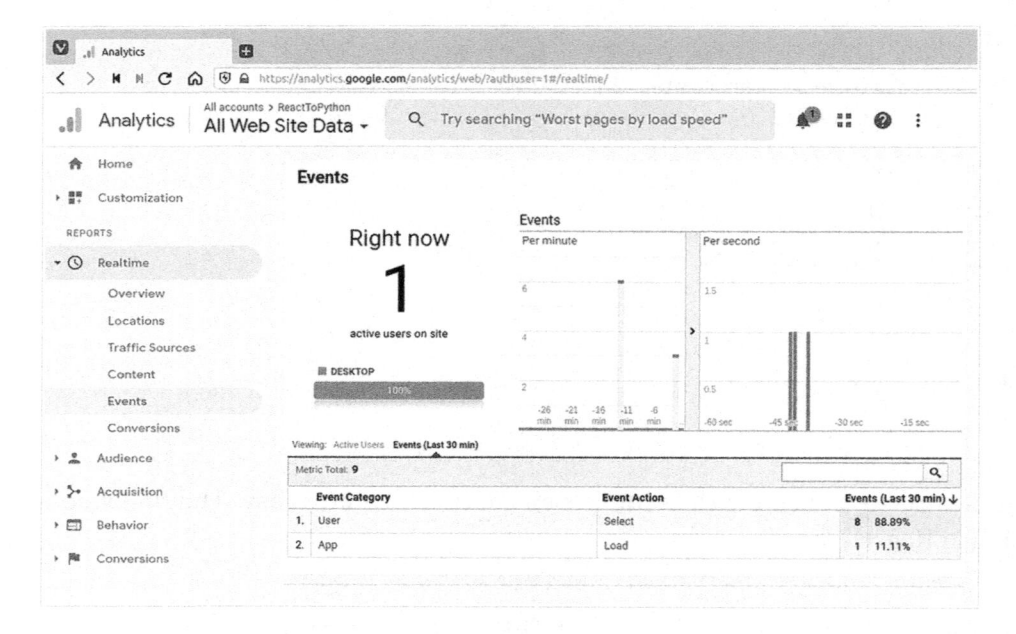

To see more data than just the last 30 minutes, you can also go to *Reports -> Behavior -> Events -> Overview* to see historical data as well. The date range for that view can be changed in the upper right corner.

If you look at the *Network* tab of the web browser developer console, every time you select a new user, along with the HTTP request to the Flask web server, you should also see a beacon request being sent to Google Analytics.

The calls to the `ReactGA.event()` method is what sends those beacon requests to Google Analytics:

```
ReactGA.event({'category':  'User',
               'action':    'Select',
               'label':     userID}
             )
```

In addition to sending analytics for user events like clicks, with ReactGA you can also specifically track pageviews by URL, modalview where the URL doesn't change, exceptions, and timing. We'll cover all of these in the last section of the book, but we can also try capturing timing events right now.

24.2 Request Timing

One of the big performance metrics that you might want to capture is how long it takes to retrieve data from your back-end REST server. We can do that pretty easily with ReactGA by adding a timing event to our Python `fetch()` function.

Listing 24-3 File: *jsutils.py*

```
import time
from pyreact import ReactGA


console = window.console

deepcopy = require('deepcopy')

polyfill = require("@babel/polyfill")  # required by async/await

async def fetch(url, callback):
    t_start = time.time()
    try:
        response = await window.fetch(url)
        if response.status != 200:
            console.error('Fetch error - Status Code: ' + response.status)
        else:
            data = await response.json()
            t_elapsed = time.time() - t_start
            ReactGA.timing({'category': 'API',
                            'variable': 'fetch',
                            'value': int(t_elapsed * 1000),
                            'label': url}
                          )
            callback(data)
    except object as e:
        console.error(e)
```

Whenever a fetch request is made, using the `time` module, we first save the starting time as `t_start` before the call to the back-end server. Then when we have the requested data in hand, based on the start time and current time, we calculate the elapsed time as `t_elapsed`.

Once we have our timing data, we make a call to `ReactGA.timing()` to send it off to Google Analytics along with the actual URL that was requested by our application. After generating some data in the application, you can see the timing results on the Google Analytics dashboard under *Reports -> Behavior -> Site Speed -> User Timings*. And again, you can set the date range to explore in the upper right corner of the dashboard.

If you've generated some data, you should see the *API* category that we specified in our code. Clicking on *API* and drilling down, you will then see the variable *fetch* that we specified. Then clicking on *fetch* and drilling down some more, you will finally see the actual URLs and the corresponding average timing in seconds for each one.

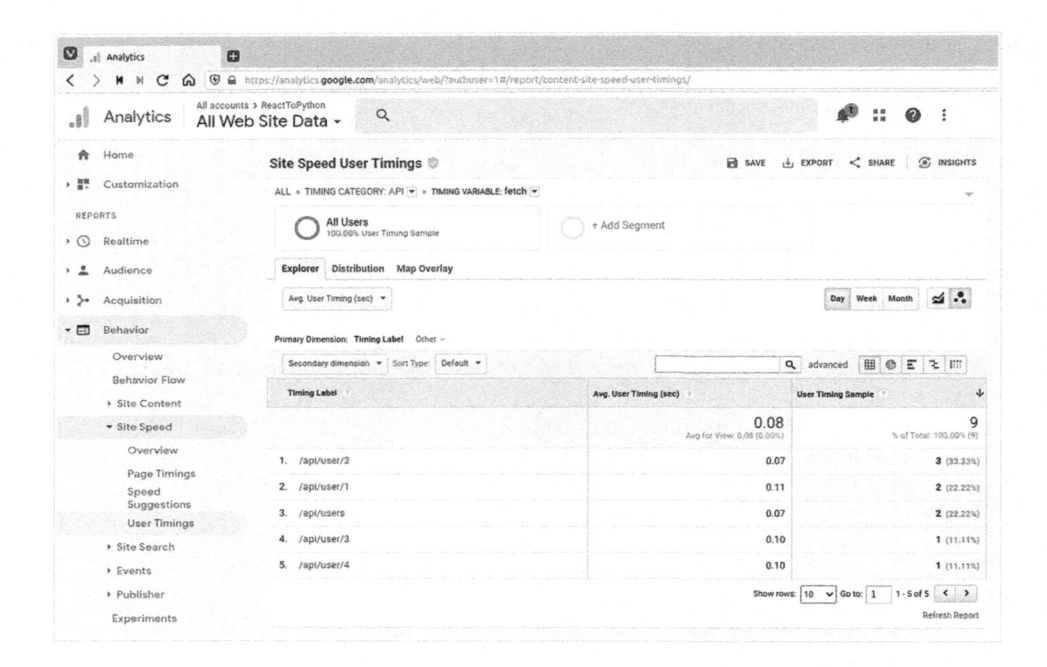

24.3 Summary

Getting usage data from your application can help you better understand how it is being utilized and potentially identify performance bottlenecks. The ReactGA JavaScript library makes collecting analytics from your application very easy. You can pretty much insert a call to ReactGA at any point in your application to capture as much analytical usage and timing data as you like.

Chapter Review:

1. Install ReactGA package:
   `npm install react-ga`

2. Update source files (GA Event):
   pyreact.py
   app.py

3. Build the application for development with:
   `npm run dev`

4. Open the application:
   http://localhost:8080

5. Update source files (GA Timing):
   jsutils.py

References:

- Chapter code
  https://github.com/rtp-book/code/tree/main/ch24

- Google Analytics
  https://analytics.google.com

- ReactGA JavaScript Library
  https://www.npmjs.com/package/react-ga

Chapter 25 – Developer Tools

There are a few developer tools that I've found to come in handy when developing React applications with Python.

25.1 Bundle Visualizer

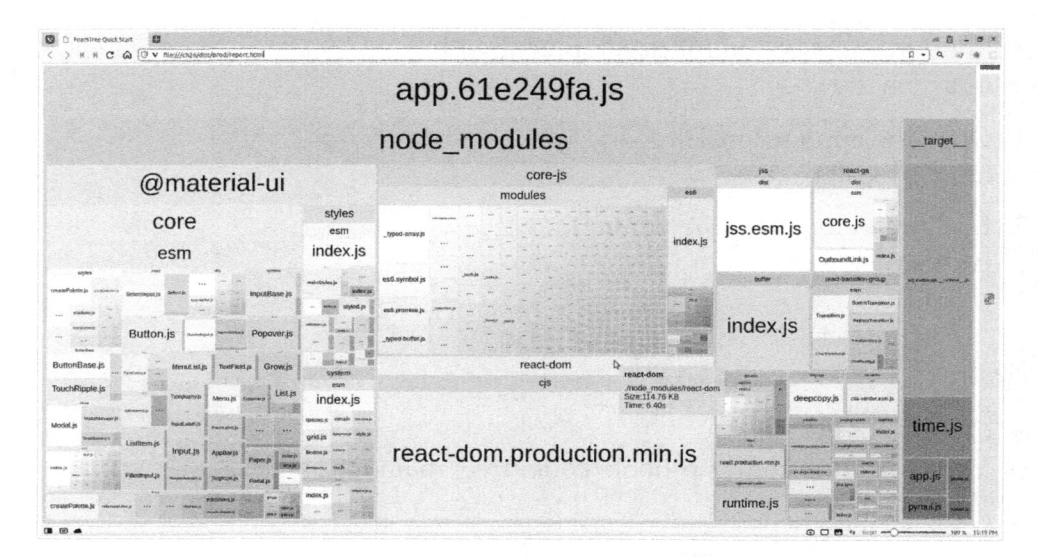

The first developer tool we'll look at is the `parcel-plugin-bundle-visualiser` that lets you see how the generated JavaScript bundle that Parcel produces utilizes space, organized by JavaScript library. This is a build-time tool that generates a report based on the production build of your application.

The first step is to install the JavaScript library using `npm`:

(venv) $ `npm install parcel-plugin-bundle-visualiser --save-dev`

Then, just run the production build script for your application with:

(venv) $ `npm run build`

As long as `NODE_ENV=production` is set in the build script, the visualizer will generate a brilliantly self-contained HTML report in your project folder in:

./dist/prod/report.html

If you open up this HTML file, the report will show you the relative size of each JavaScript module included in the production bundle, as well as give you more detailed information about each one when you hover your mouse over it. The report is fully pannable by clicking and dragging, and is zoomable with the mouse wheel to drill down to some of the smaller libraries.

You can use this report to optimize the production build of your application by looking for large libraries that you are not actually using. You might also find data or image files that could benefit from compression to further reduce the size of your application download to the web browser. Or you can use the report to see what the download burden is of a specific library that you might not really need.

If you run it on our last example application, you'll see that your transpiled Python code is a very small part of the bundle and that the vast majority is taken up by Material-UI and the React library, as well as all of their dependencies. This is the reason that we import individual components from Material-UI and not the entire library, which would bloat the JavaScript bundle even more with unused components. That said, you might see components that you didn't explicitly import yourself. In that case, they may be dependencies of other components that you *did* import.

You might also notice that the Transcrypt JavaScript runtime library is only about 35KB, and doesn't add too much to the size of the deployment relative to some of the other JavaScript dependencies. So in terms of deployment size, using Python and Transcrypt to develop your applications doesn't have a significant disadvantage compared to applications that were developed directly in JavaScript.

25.2 React Chrome Extension

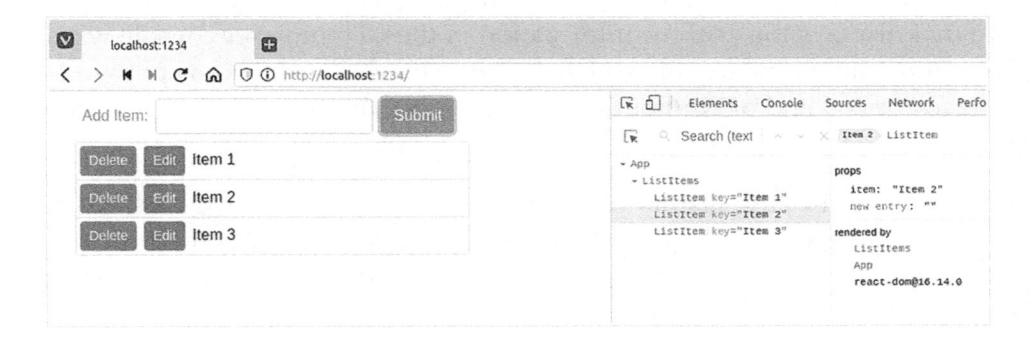

React Developer Tools is a web browser extension for Chrome available in the Chrome Web Store, that helps you to visualize your component tree, and to see, add, and modify component props in real-time right in the web browser.

It also has a profiler you can use to see how often a particular component gets re-rendered and how long each render takes. If your application seems sluggish for certain interactions, you can use this tool to help identify where in your component tree the delay is coming from. Having this information will help you pinpoint what part of your application needs to be optimized for performance.

25.3 GA Debug Chrome Extension

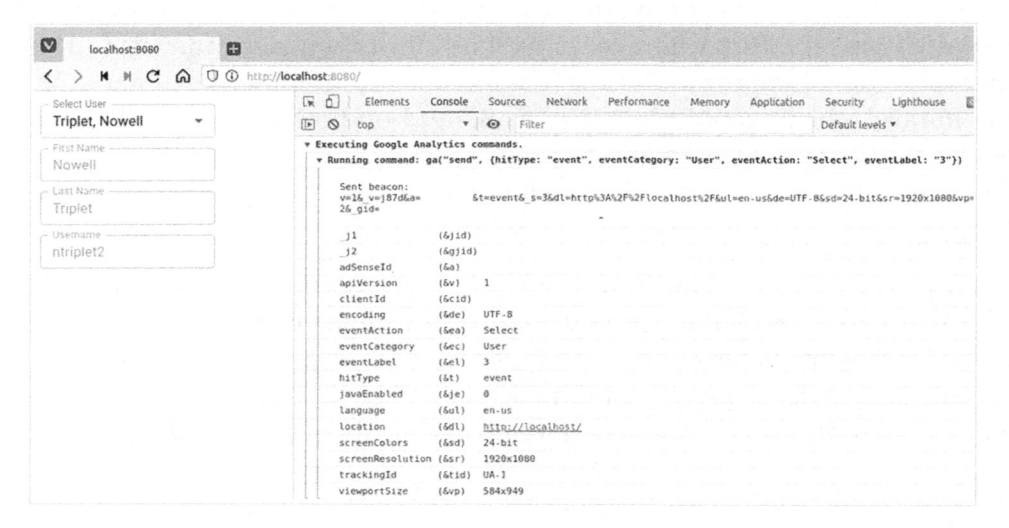

If you use Google Analytics, they have made a Google Analytics Debugger you can get in the Chrome Web Store, which lets you turn on the Google Analytics debug feature that displays the analytic information in the web browser console window. The nice thing about having the web browser extension installed, is that you can turn the feature on and off without having to modify the Google Analytics settings in your code.

If you are not seeing the results you are expecting from your application in the Google Analytics dashboard, you can use the Google Analytics Debugger extension to make sure that your application is actually sending the analytics data that you think it is.

25.4 Debug CSS Chrome Extension

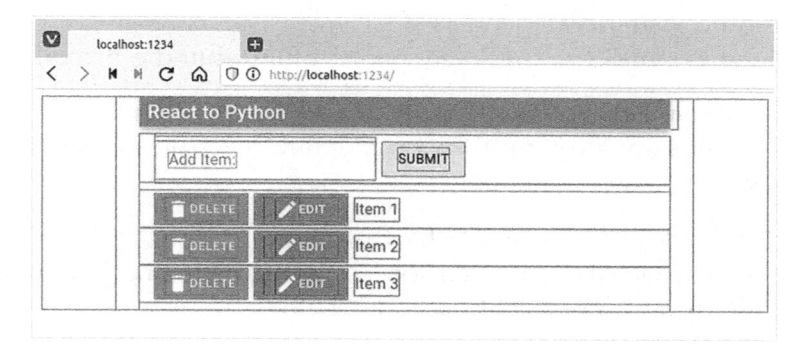

The last developer tool we'll mention here is one that can significantly help you with CSS layout issues. The Debug CSS chrome extension, also available from the Chrome Web Store, when activated, will outline every displayed HTML element in the web browser. This lets you visually see how your margins, padding, and width settings are affecting your layout.

Holding the *Ctrl* or *Command* key while hovering over an element will also display basic information about that element.

25.5 Summary

There are many useful developer tools available to help optimize your application. These were just a few that you might find useful for just about every Python React application you develop.

Chapter Review:

1. Install Parcel Bundle Visualizer package:
   npm install parcel-plugin-bundle-visualiser --save-dev

2. Build the application for production with:
   npm run build

3. Open the generated HTML file in:
   ./dist/prod/report.html

References:

- Parcel Bundle Visualizer
  https://www.npmjs.com/package/parcel-plugin-bundle-visualiser

- React Chrome Extension
  https://chrome.google.com/webstore/detail/react-developer-tools/fmkadmapgofadopljbjfkapdkoienihi

- Google Analytics Debug Chrome Extension
  https://chrome.google.com/webstore/detail/google-analytics-debugger/jnkmfdileelhofjcijamephohjechhna

- Debug CSS Chrome Extension
  https://chrome.google.com/webstore/detail/debug-css/igiofjnckcagmjgdoaakafngegecjnkj

Chapter 26 – Section Summary

While the examples we used in this section were very basic, the concepts they demonstrate can be used as building blocks to construct much more complex applications. In review, we covered the following concepts:

- *Working with text input, rendering lists, and using HTML forms*
- *Using React, JSX, and converting JavaScript code*
- *CSS and Material-UI styling options*
- *Working with back-end web services and using asynchronous communication*
- *Developer insights including details of using Transcrypt, analytics, and versioning*

In the next section, we will leverage what we have learned in this one to build a functional multi-featured application from the ground up, that demonstrates how all of these individual building blocks can be put together and utilized in a cohesive way.

– Part III –

Putting it all Together

To give further context to the concepts previously presented in the book and to provide a few more tips and tricks when using Python to create React web applications, this section will build a sample web application from the ground up. The intent here is to show you what the process of building a React web application with Python looks like, step-by-step.

While this section is quite code-heavy, it reflects the requirements of a typical data-centric CRUD (Create, Read, Update, Delete) type of application, and demonstrates how to accomplish the common programming tasks required of such.

Chapter 27 – Project Outline

The premise of the project we will be building up in this section is a personal library management system that stores a catalog of books.

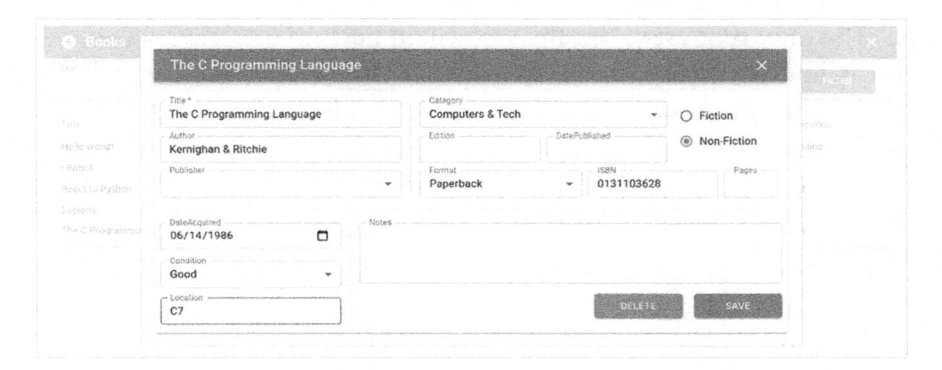

The single-page application will consist of several editing and viewing screens, and allow for user session management. For the back-end service, we will use an SQLite database that will be accessed via a Flask based REST service.

We will be utilizing just about everything we've already learned so far in this book. In addition to diving a bit further into React and Material-UI, we will also introduce a few other JavaScript libraries that will help you create feature-rich applications.

Being that we have already covered a lot of what we'll be using in this project, we won't be going into too many details about what has already been touched on in earlier chapters. But I do encourage you to read through every code example as we build up this project and make sure you understand how it all fits together. Once you grasp how each piece works, you can start modifying it to suit your own needs.

While building a project like this inevitably includes quite a bit of refactoring of code in order to stay organized as the application grows, we will try and minimize that as much as possible to avoid confusion. Each chapter will end with a functioning application, with all the features we added up to that point.

27.1 Application Structure

Applications like the one we are building here are an ideal candidate to structure as a single-page application or SPA. What this means is that instead of using server-rendered web pages that use server-side templating for views, we send the entire application with all the views in it to the web client all at once - as a single "page". Any changes in views or required rendering is then handled client-side. The only requests from the web client back to the server once the initial application is loaded is just for data, typically received in the form of JSON or XML. So while the initial application load may be a bit slower than server-rendered pages, subsequent re-renderings are very fast since there is no round-trip to the server and back for UI information. This architecture also allows for excellent web browser caching optimizations as well.

We will be building several views for our application, including:

- Landing Page
- Login Modal Form
- About Modal View
- Book View / Edit
- Book Search / List
- Lookup Table View / Edit

We will be incorporating a number of ancillary features like snackbar notifications, modal forms, filtered lists, menus, session management, page routing, and more.

This application will rely on a RESTful back-end server that we will implement using Flask. While we won't spend a lot of time on the implementation details of the Flask application, we will need to incorporate a few specific features to properly support our front-end application. For the back-end database, we will be using SQLite, which is part of the Python standard library.

We will also spend some time digging further into features of the Material-UI library to show you some more ways to add functionality to your React applications.

27.2 Folder Structure

Before starting the project, let's discuss the overall project folder structure. This is a topic that tends to not have a definitive best practice and is highly up to personal preference. But for the purposes of this book, we'll use this general folder structure:

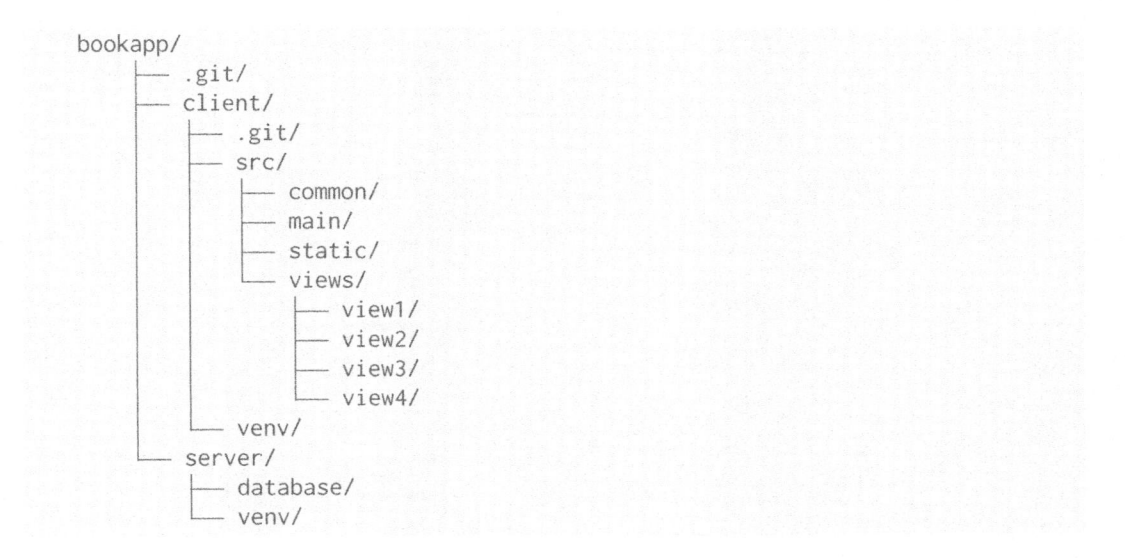

```
bookapp/
    ├── .git/
    ├── client/
    │      ├── .git/
    │      ├── src/
    │      │    ├── common/
    │      │    ├── main/
    │      │    ├── static/
    │      │    └── views/
    │      │           ├── view1/
    │      │           ├── view2/
    │      │           ├── view3/
    │      │           └── view4/
    │      └── venv/
    └── server/
           ├── database/
           └── venv/
```

In the main **bookapp/** project folder, we actually have two separate application folders: **server/**, where we will have our back-end Flask application, and **client/**, which is where our Python React application will reside. Each of these will be considered the root folder for each of their respective applications. I also prefer to keep separate Python virtual environments for each of the two applications. While this might complicate the setup a little bit, it serves to maintain a separation of concerns between the two applications and allows them to run independently of one another. That said, we will use just one git repository for the entire project, located at the root of the project under **bookapp/**. As mentioned in the earlier chapter on versioning, we will also have any empty **.git/** folder in the **client/** folder to facilitate the proper functioning of the `npm version` command that we will use for our client application.

The **src/common/** folder will hold shared application modules like `pyreact` and `jsutils` that have functions used throughout the application. These mostly contain the code for loading JavaScript modules, and have the Python-to-JavaScript function mapping. The **src/main/** folder has components that are global to the application like the `Login` and `About` forms, as well as the Material-UI theme and application data. The **src/static/** folder has resources like image files that get embedded into the application. Lastly, the **src/view/** folder has subfolders related to individual views within the application, each representing a specific view or page and containing the necessary components to render each view.

Chapter 28 – Environment Setup

We'll start this project with a clean slate and walk through each step to set up the development environment. It is assumed you already have Python 3.6 or 3.7, and the Node.js server that is needed for npm, still installed from earlier in the book since those should have been installed at the system level.

The environment setup described here is from the perspective of issuing commands from a terminal window. If you are using an IDE, you can adjust the instructions as necessary to work within the parameters of the one you use.

This chapter is essentially a compact version of the entire first section of the book. So if there are parts that aren't clear, you can review the appropriate earlier chapter.

28.1 Initial Setup

Based on the folder structure we saw earlier, start by creating the main **bookapp/** project folder. Then after making this folder current, initialize a git repository from a command prompt with:

```
$ git init
```

To make sure we don't commit any generated files to the repository, create a git ignore file in the **bookapp/** folder:

Listing 28-1 File: *.gitignore*

```
.idea/

*.pyc
*.bak
*.log

database/
venv/
__target__/
dist/
.cache/
node_modules/
__pycache__/
```

I prefer to not commit my IDE settings to the project's git repository, so I added the PyCharm **.idea/** folder to the **.gitignore** file. Likewise, I keep the Python virtual environments out of the code repository as well. If the virtual environment needs to be recreated, a **requirements.txt** file can be used to automatically install any needed Python library dependencies. This is also a similar case with the JavaScript libraries, so we ignore anything in the **node_modules/** folder. Installing the JavaScript libraries from scratch can be done with npm and the **package.json** file. We also don't want to commit the database either, so we add that folder to the ignore list.

Next, go ahead and create the two application folders: **server/** and **client/**. Then after making the **bookapp/server/** folder the current folder, set up the virtual environment for the back-end server using Python 3.6 or higher. Remember that you may need to use python3 or python3.7 (or py -3.7 on windows) instead of just python depending on what version(s) of Python you have installed:

```
$ python -m venv venv
```

Then activate the virtual environment using the appropriate command for your operating system:

For Windows:
```
C:\> venv\Scripts\activate
```

For Mac or Linux
```
$ source venv/bin/activate
```

And since we know we are going to be using Flask, let's go ahead and install that now, as well as the Flask-Login plug-in:

```
(venv) $ pip install Flask
(venv) $ pip install Flask-Login
```

And then exit the virtual environment:

```
(venv) $ deactivate
```

Now change the working folder to **bookapp/client/** and repeat the above steps using:

```
C:\> python -m venv venv
C:\> venv\Scripts\activate
```

or

```
$ python -m venv venv
$ source venv/bin/activate
```

Then for the web application, we know we are going to be using Transcrypt, so install that into the virtual environment:

```
(venv) $ pip install transcrypt
```

We then want to create the **src/** source code folder for **bookapp/client/**. And finally, to allow npm `version` to work properly with our folder structure, add an empty **.git/** folder to **bookapp/client/**.

At this point, the project folder structure should now look like this:

```
bookapp/
    ├── .git/
    ├── client/
    │   ├── .git/
    │   ├── src/
    │   └── venv/
    └── server/
        └── venv/
```

That takes care of the Python side of things, next we'll take care of the JavaScript side.

28.2 Parcel Setup

With the assumption that you already have Node.js installed from earlier in the book, we can install some of the JavaScript libraries that we know we're going to need. While in the **bookapp/client/** folder, we first need to initialize npm:

```
$ npm init
```

This will ask you a series of questions, mostly related to general information about the project. Just using the defaults is OK, but feel free to update the information.

Next, we can install the JavaScript libraries we'll use as part of our development toolchain:

```
$ npm install parcel-bundler parcel-plugin-transcrypt --save-dev
$ npm install parcel-plugin-bundle-visualiser --save-dev
$ npm install express http-proxy-middleware --save-dev
```

Before we can use the Transcrypt plug-in, we need to manually update one of the plug-in's JavaScript files as a workaround for a Parcel version incompatibility. The file that needs to be updated is:

./node_modules/parcel-plugin-transcrypt/asset.js

In that file, change line 2 that loads the Parcel Logger module from this:
```
const logger = require('parcel-bundler/src/Logger');
```
to this:
```
const logger = require('@parcel/logger/src/Logger');
```

Once this modification is made, the Transcrypt plug-in for Parcel should be working.

NOTE FOR WINDOWS USERS:

For those of you using Windows, there are two more changes that need to be made to the **asset.js** file for it to work in Windows environments.

Change line 14 that defines the Transcrypt command to simply use `python` instead of `python3`, changing it from this:

```
"command": "python3 -m transcrypt",
```

to this:

```
"command": "python -m transcrypt",
```

Then on line 143, make an inline modification to the file path for Windows environments using the `replace()` method, changing this line:

```
this.content = `export * from "${this.importPath}";`;
```

to this:

```
this.content = `export * from "${this.importPath.replace(/\\/g, '/')}";`;
```

Part III - Putting it all Together

Now we'll install some of the JavaScript libraries that we know we'll be using in the application itself:

```
$ npm install react@16 react-dom@16 react-ga
$ npm install @material-ui/core @material-ui/icons
$ npm install @babel/polyfill deepcopy
```

We've already used all of these JavaScript libraries in the previous section of the book, and later on we'll be adding a few more as we need them.

Next, we need to add our build scripts. We can add these scripts to the existing *scripts* section (once again, mind where the commas go):

```
"start": "NODE_ENV=development parcel --log-level 4 src/index.html
   --no-cache --out-dir dist/dev",
"build": "NODE_ENV=production parcel --log-level 4 build src/index.html
   --no-source-maps --out-dir dist/prod --no-hmr --public-url ./",
"dev": "node dev-server.js",
"version": "echo \"version = '$npm_package_version'\" > ./src/version.py;git
   add ./src/version.py",
```

These four scripts cover the development and production builds, running the development proxy server, and handling our git integrated version updates.

28.3 Application Entry Point

We will need an **index.html** file to act as the application entry point that we will be hooking into with React. We can pretty much use one just like we were using in the last section of the book, so add this to the **bookapp/client/src/** folder:

Listing 28-2 File: *index.html*

```html
<!DOCTYPE html>
<html lang="en">
  <head>
    <meta charset="utf-8"/>
    <meta name="viewport"
          content="minimum-scale=1, initial-scale=1, width=device-width"
    />
    <link rel="shortcut icon"
          href="./static/favicon.ico"
    />
```

```
    <link rel="stylesheet"
        href="https://fonts.googleapis.com/css?
family=Roboto:300,400,500,700&display=swap"
    />
    <link rel="stylesheet"
        href="https://fonts.googleapis.com/icon?family=Material+Icons"
    />
    <title id="title">Python React App</title>
  </head>
  <body>
    <noscript>You need to enable JavaScript to run this app.</noscript>
    <div id="root">Loading...</div>
    <script src="app.py"></script>
  </body>
</html>
```

We added just a few extras in this version of **index.html** over what we had earlier in the book. Namely, a `meta` tag for configuring the display area for different devices, a link for a custom **favicon.ico** file, and a few defaults like `title` and a temporary message that is displayed while your React application is loading the component tree. This temporary "*Loading...*" message in the innerHTML part of the *root* `div`, will get replaced with the HTML elements generated by React once it finishes loading components.

While Transcrypt can recognize and parse direct calls to JavaScript functions in our Python code without requiring us to define them, Python linters, like what you might find in most IDEs, aren't so accommodating and will generate warnings about unknown identifiers. To get around this, we can define some stub classes and functions so that the Python linter will be happy, but then use a Transcrypt compiler directive to tell Transcrypt to ignore those stubs during the compilation process.

Since these JavaScript stub identifiers are only used by the modules in the **src/common/** folder, it makes sense to define these stubs right in the **__init__.py** file that we use to identify the **src/common/** folder as a Python package. So after creating the folder **common/** in the **src/** folder, add this file to it:

Listing 28-3 File: *__init__.py*

```
# __pragma__ ('skip')

"""
```

These JavaScript builtin function and object stubs are just to
quiet the Python linter and are ignored by transcrypt as long
as they are imported inside of pragma skip/noskip lines.
"""

```
def require(lib):
    return lib

def __new__(obj):
    return obj

class JSON:
    stringify = None

class document:
    title = None
    getElementById = None
    addEventListener = None

class window:
    class console:
        log = None
        error = None
        warn = None

    alert = None
    confirm = None
    fetch = None
    history = None
    location = None
    addEventListener = None
    dispatchEvent = None
    PopStateEvent = None
    URLSearchParams = None
    encodeURIComponent = None

# __pragma__ ('noskip')
```

This stubs out all of the built-in JavaScript functions that we will be calling from other modules in the **src/common/** folder. They don't have to actually do anything, which is why they are all set equal to None, but are just used to fill in Python namespace gaps. We then use the skip/noskip Transcrypt compiler directives at the beginning and end of the module to ignore this block of code at compile time.

React to Python

Next, let's create our **pyreact.py** module that has all of our React specific JavaScript-to-Python mappings in it. We will put modules like this in the **src/common/** folder:

Listing 28-4 File: *pyreact.py*

```python
# __pragma__ ('skip')
from common import require, document
# __pragma__ ('noskip')


# Load React and ReactDOM JavaScript libraries into local namespace
React = require('react')
ReactDOM = require('react-dom')
ReactGA = require('react-ga')

# Map React javaScript objects to Python identifiers
createElement = React.createElement
useState = React.useState
useEffect = React.useEffect
createContext = React.createContext
useContext = React.useContext

Fragment = React.Fragment


def render(root_component, props, container):
    def main():
        ReactDOM.render(
            React.createElement(root_component, props),
            document.getElementById(container)
        )

    document.addEventListener('DOMContentLoaded', main)
```

This is pretty much just like we had before, with a few additions. First, we added the `React.Fragment` component that allows us to return multiple elements from a component instead of just one, without adding unnecessary extra nodes to the DOM. Then, we also added an import for a few Python stubs at the top to quiet the Python linter about the JavaScript functions we are calling here. Since we put the skip/noskip compiler directives in, Transcrypt will ignore these imports when it does its transpiling.

While we are in the common folder, let's also add our **jsutils.py** module that maps miscellaneous JavaScript utilities in there as well:

Listing 28-5 File: *jsutils.py*

```
# __pragma__ ('skip')
from common import require, document, window
# __pragma__ ('noskip')

console = window.console
alert = window.alert
confirm = window.confirm

deepcopy = require('deepcopy')

def setTitle(title):
    document.title = title
```

In our **index.html** file, we have the page using a custom favicon so we'll need something for it to use. As a placeholder for now, we can use the Python icon and download it into the **src/static/** folder using the wget command (or you can download it manually if you prefer). This will also create the **src/static/** folder for us:

```
$ wget -P ./src/static/ https://www.python.org/static/favicon.ico
```

Lastly, we just need a basic React application to start from to test our setup. We'll use a slightly modified version of our first React application, just with updates to the import paths. So add this **app.py** file to the **bookapp/client/src/** folder:

Listing 28-6 File: *app.py*

```
from common.pyreact import useState, render, createElement as el
from common.jsutils import alert

def App():
    phrase, setPhrase = useState("")

    def handleSubmit():
        alert(f"Test phrase is : {phrase}")
        setPhrase("")

    def handleChange(event):
        target = event['target']
        setPhrase(target['value'])
```

React to Python

```
    return el('div', None,
            el('label', {'htmlFor': 'testPhrase'}, "Test Phrase: "),
            el('input', {'id': 'testPhrase',
                         'onChange': handleChange,
                         'value': phrase
                        }
              ),
            el('button', {'onClick': handleSubmit}, "Submit"),
           )

render(App, None, 'root')
```

You can see that since we have the **__init__.py** file in our **src/common/** folder, it treats it as a Python package, and we can refer to the modules in that folder with dot notation when we import them.

Our project folder structure now looks like this with **client/** as the current application root, along with the files we created:

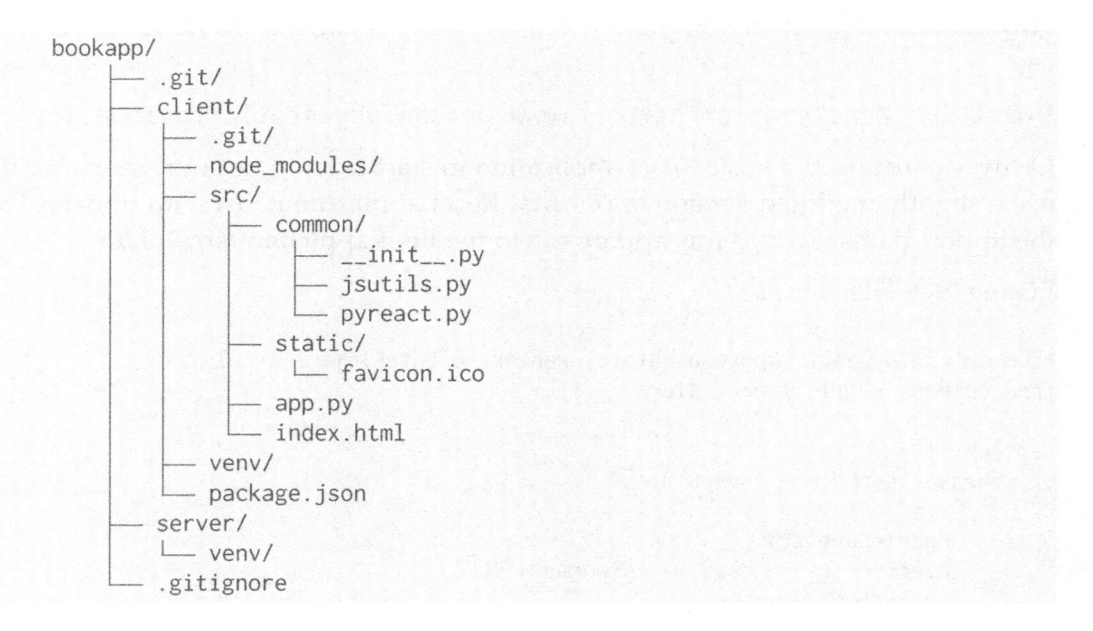

```
bookapp/
    ├── .git/
    ├── client/
    │   ├── .git/
    │   ├── node_modules/
    │   ├── src/
    │   │   ├── common/
    │   │   │   ├── __init__.py
    │   │   │   ├── jsutils.py
    │   │   │   └── pyreact.py
    │   │   ├── static/
    │   │   │   └── favicon.ico
    │   │   ├── app.py
    │   │   └── index.html
    │   ├── venv/
    │   └── package.json
    ├── server/
    │   └── venv/
    └── .gitignore
```

If everything looks good, go ahead and run:

(venv) $ `npm start`

212 | Part III - Putting it all Together

which will build the application, and start up the Parcel development web server. When it finishes, you should be able to open it in a web browser with:

http://localhost:1234/

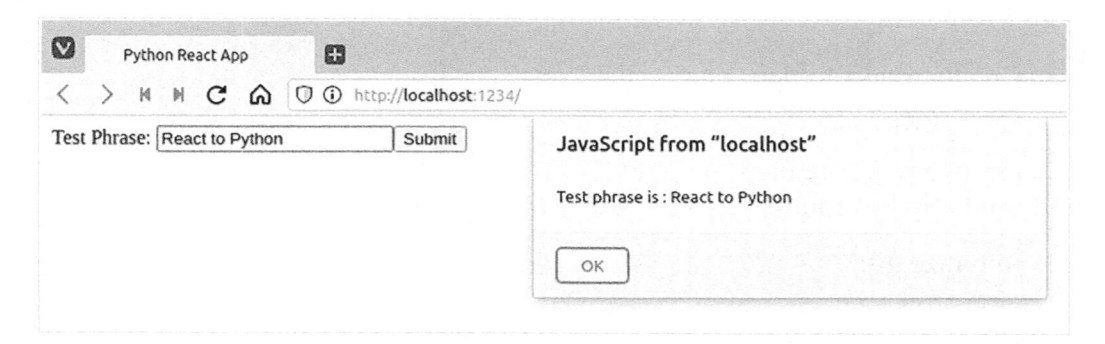

If it doesn't load, here are a few things to check:

- Check the code for syntax errors.
- Check the Parcel/Transcrypt build log for errors.
- Check the web browser developer console for errors.
- See if all of the files are loading successfully in the network tab of the web browser console.
- Check to make sure that npm is working with npm -v to show the version.
- To start with a clean build slate, try deleting the **.cache/**, **dist/**, and **src/__target__/** folders and rebuild the application.

Once the application loads successfully, we are ready to move forward and start building the application. But before that, if you haven't already done so, now would be a good time to add the **package.json** file and the files in the **./src/** folder (without the **__target__/** folder) to git and commit the files to the local repository.

One last note for this chapter, I generally keep the Parcel development web server (or later, the proxy web server) running while I'm developing. It will automatically detect changes to the entry point file (in our case **app.py**) and reload the application in the web browser for you. For me, this speeds up the development loop quite a bit, even if I have to manually touch the **app.py** file (usually by just putting a space on an empty line) to trigger the application rebuild process by Parcel. It may seem a little kludgy (and it is), but it is easier than manually stopping and restarting each time. The other benefit is that doing a full stop and restart rebuilds the entire application, but the automatic rebuild is incremental and only rebuilds what has actually changed, so it is *much* faster.

Chapter Review:

1. Create project folder:
   bookapp/

2. Create git ignore file:
   bookapp/.gitignore

3. Initialize git:
   `git init`

4. Create application folders:
   bookapp/client/
   bookapp/server/

5. Create a Python virtual environment in **bookapp/server/**:
   `python -m venv venv`

6. Activate the virtual environment:
   `venv\Scripts\activate` (Windows)
   `source venv/bin/activate` (Mac/Linux)

7. Install Flask:
   `pip install Flask`
   `pip install Flask-Login`

8. Deactivate the virtual environment:
   `deactivate`

9. Create a Python virtual environment in **bookapp/client/**:
   `python -m venv venv`

10. Activate the virtual environment:
    `venv\Scripts\activate` (Windows)
    `source venv/bin/activate` (Mac/Linux)

11. Install Transcrypt:
    `pip install transcrypt`

12. Create client folders:
    client/src/
    client/.git/

13. Initialize npm:
    ```
    npm init
    ```

14. Install development JavaScript libraries:
    ```
    npm install parcel-bundler parcel-plugin-transcrypt --save-dev
    npm install parcel-plugin-bundle-visualiser --save-dev
    npm install express http-proxy-middleware --save-dev
    ```

15. Fix the logger library location in the Transcrypt plug-in file:
    ./node_modules/parcel-plugin-transcrypt/asset.js
    ```
    const logger = require('@parcel/logger/src/Logger');
    ```

16. Install application JavaScript libraries:
    ```
    npm install react@16 react-dom@16 react-ga
    npm install @material-ui/core @material-ui/icons
    npm install @babel/polyfill deepcopy
    ```

17. Add build scripts to **package.json**:
    ```
    "start": "NODE_ENV=development parcel --log-level 4 src/index.html
      ↪ --no-cache --out-dir dist/dev",
    "build": "NODE_ENV=production parcel --log-level 4 build src/index.html
      ↪ --no-source-maps --out-dir dist/prod --no-hmr --public-url ./",
    "dev": "node dev-server.js",
    "version": "echo \"version = '$npm_package_version'\" > ./src/version.py;git
      ↪ add ./src/version.py",
    ```

18. Create source file:
    client/src/index.html

19. Create common folder:
    client/src/common/

20. Create source files:
    client/src/common/__init__.py
    client/src/common/pyreact.py
    client/src/common/jsutils.py

21. Create static folder:
    client/src/static/

22. Add **favicon.ico** image file to **client/src/static/**:
    https://www.python.org/static/favicon.ico

23. Create source file:
    client/src/app.py

24. Build the application for development with:
    `npm start`

25. Open the application:
    http://localhost:1234

References:

- Chapter code
  https://github.com/rtp-book/project/tree/step01

Chapter 29 – Landing Page

The first part of building our application will be focused on several generic framework features like handling user logins, session management, theming, and a landing page that can be used as a launching point for any web application.

Our landing page will be pretty sparse to start out with since we don't have any views for it to link to, but we can put some placeholders on it for now to give us a platform to build from.

29.1 Material-UI Theme

Since we are going to be using Material-UI as our styling framework, let's go ahead and set up a basic theme for our application. If you recall, we had previously set up a **pymui.py** module that had our JavaScript-to-Python mappings in it for the Material-UI library. So let's start by adding that to the **src/common/** folder:

Listing 29-1 File: *pymui.py*

```
# __pragma__ ('skip')
from common import require
# __pragma__ ('noskip')


# Icons
MenuIcon  = require('@material-ui/icons/Menu')['default']
CloseIcon = require('@material-ui/icons/Close')['default']
AddIcon   = require('@material-ui/icons/AddCircle')['default']

# Basic components
Button        = require('@material-ui/core/Button')['default']
ButtonGroup   = require('@material-ui/core/ButtonGroup')['default']
IconButton    = require('@material-ui/core/IconButton')['default']
InputLabel    = require('@material-ui/core/InputLabel')['default']
OutlinedInput = require('@material-ui/core/OutlinedInput')['default']
TextField     = require('@material-ui/core/TextField')['default']
Select        = require('@material-ui/core/Select')['default']
Box           = require('@material-ui/core/Box')['default']
Toolbar       = require('@material-ui/core/Toolbar')['default']
AppBar        = require('@material-ui/core/AppBar')['default']
Typography    = require('@material-ui/core/Typography')['default']
```

```
Divider = require('@material-ui/core/Divider')['default']
Container = require('@material-ui/core/Container')['default']
Input = require('@material-ui/core/Input')['default']
Tooltip = require('@material-ui/core/Tooltip')['default']
Menu = require('@material-ui/core/Menu')['default']
MenuItem = require('@material-ui/core/MenuItem')['default']
Paper = require('@material-ui/core/Paper')['default']
CircularProgress = require('@material-ui/core/CircularProgress')['default']
Link = require('@material-ui/core/Link')['default']
Radio = require('@material-ui/core/Radio')['default']
RadioGroup = require('@material-ui/core/RadioGroup')['default']
FormControl = require('@material-ui/core/FormControl')['default']
FormLabel = require('@material-ui/core/FormLabel')['default']
FormControlLabel = require('@material-ui/core/FormControlLabel')['default']

# Tables
TableContainer = require('@material-ui/core/TableContainer')['default']
Table = require('@material-ui/core/Table')['default']
TableHead = require('@material-ui/core/TableHead')['default']
TableBody = require('@material-ui/core/TableBody')['default']
TableFooter = require('@material-ui/core/TableFooter')['default']
TableRow = require('@material-ui/core/TableRow')['default']
TableCell = require('@material-ui/core/TableCell')['default']

# Theming
ThemeProvider = require('@material-ui/styles/ThemeProvider')['default']
createMuiTheme = require('@material-ui/core/styles/createMuiTheme')['default']
useTheme = require('@material-ui/styles/useTheme')['default']
styled = require('@material-ui/styles/styled')['default']
makeStyles = require('@material-ui/styles/makeStyles')['default']
colors = require('@material-ui/core/colors')
```

This module has all of the Material-UI components we had used previously, plus a few more that we will also be employing later on. That said, it would be a good idea to eventually comment out the libraries that are not actually used by your application to ensure that they don't get added to the JavaScript bundle unnecessarily during the production build process. Doing so will help keep the size of the deployed JavaScript bundle as small as possible.

Next, we can create a Python module for our theme, which will be based on the same theme that we experimented with earlier in the book. Since we'll eventually want to access this from multiple points in our application, create a folder called **main/** under **client/src/**, and in that new folder, add an empty **__init__.py** file to identify the folder as a Python package. This will later allow us to import from modules that are in that folder.

Once that folder structure is set up, add this file to the **client/src/main/** folder:

Listing 29-2 File: *appTheme.py*

```python
from common.pyreact import createElement
from common.pymui import createMuiTheme, colors
from common.pymui import Box, styled, TextField

theme = createMuiTheme({
    'overrides': {
        'MuiDivider': {
            'root': {
                'margin': '0.8rem',
            }
        },
        'MuiTextField': {
            'root': {
                'marginRight': '0.5rem',
            }
        },
    },
    'palette': {
        'primary': colors['teal'],
        'secondary': colors['pink'],
        'altPrimary': {
            'main': colors['cyan'][700],
            'contrastText': colors['common']['white'],
        },
        'altSecondary': {
            'main': colors['cyan'][400],
            'contrastText': colors['common']['white'],
        },
        'warning': colors['yellow'],
        'error': colors['red'],
    },
    'props': {
        'MuiButton': {
            'variant': 'contained',
            'color': 'primary',
            'style': {'minWidth': '6rem', 'margin': '0.3rem'},
        },
        'MuiTextField': {
            'variant': 'outlined',
```

```python
                'type': 'text',
                'fullWidth': True,
                'InputLabelProps': {'shrink': True},
                'InputProps': {'margin': 'dense'},
                'margin': 'dense',
            },
            'MuiPaper': {
                'elevation': 2
            },
            'MuiTable': {
                'stickyHeader': True,
                'size': 'small'
            },
            'MuiTableCell': {
                'size': 'small'
            },
        },
    },
})


def ROTextField(props):
    new_props = {'type': 'text', 'fullWidth': True, 'disabled': True}
    new_props.update(props)
    return createElement(TextField, new_props)


Flexbox = styled(Box)({
    'display': 'flex',
})
FlexboxCenter = styled(Box)({
    'display': 'flex',
    'alignItems': 'center',
    'justifyContent': 'center'
})
```

Here, we have created a Material-UI theme just as we did before using the `createMuiTheme()` function of Material-UI. The theme itself is broken up into three sections: `overrides` for setting default styles, `palette` for defining the color scheme, and `props` that set default component properties for Material-UI components.

We also added the composition component `ROTextField` for a read-only text box, and two styled `Box` components that have the CSS display property already set to display: flex. The Flexbox styled component is meant for general use, and the FlexboxCenter component is intended for centered content. All three of these custom components can be used throughout our application.

29.2 Starting Point

Now, we'll put together a basic landing page for our application that will incorporate the Material-UI theming we just created that we can use as a starting point. Since **app.py** will be the main entry point for our application, it should remain in the **src/** folder, so we are just updating the one that is already there:

Listing 29-3 File: *app.py*

```python
from common.pyreact import render, createElement as el
from common.pymui import ThemeProvider, Paper, Typography, Container, Link
from common.jsutils import setTitle
from main.appTheme import theme, Flexbox, FlexboxCenter

APP_NAME = "Library Management System"

def App(props):
    setTitle(props['title'])

    return el(ThemeProvider, {'theme': theme},
            el(Container, {'maxWidth': 'md'},
                el(Paper, {'style': {'padding': '1rem'}},
                    el(Flexbox, {'alignItems': 'center'},
                        el(Typography, {'variant': 'h5'}, APP_NAME)
                    )
                ),
                el(Paper, {'style': {'padding': '0.5rem',
                                     'marginTop': '1rem'}
                          },
                    el(FlexboxCenter, None,
                        el(Link, {'href': '#', 'variant': 'h5'}, "Books")
                    ),
                    el(FlexboxCenter, None,
                        el(Link, {'href': '#', 'variant': 'h5'}, "About")
                    ),
                    el(FlexboxCenter, None,
                        el(Link, {'href': '#', 'variant': 'h5'}, "Login")
                    )
                )
```

```
            )
        )
render(App, {'title': "Books"}, 'root')
```

Right now, this doesn't actually do much, but you can start to see how the use of theming and styled-components helps keep down some of the CSS noise in the return statement that defines our element tree.

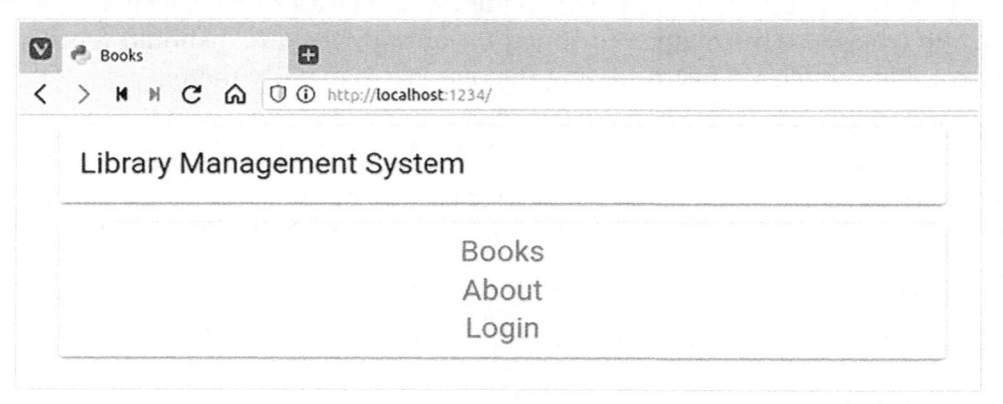

In addition to using our `Flexbox` and `FlexboxCenter` styled-components, we also introduced the Material-UI `Link` component. This is a wrapper around the standard HTML anchor tag that also incorporates a `Typography` component for text styling purposes. The `variant` prop of the Link component gets passed through to its underlying `Typography` component, and the `href` prop ends up getting passed to the HTML anchor tag. In this case, we don't have any other content to link to yet, so we just used # as a placeholder on the `href` props.

It is common to use some minor inline CSS styling for padding and margins on components. Ideally, if a component is going to be using the same styling most of the time, you should create a styled component to reuse instead and not repeat the same inline styling over and over for a given component. But for one-off component usage, inline styling is generally fine.

29.3 Versioning

Before we get too much further, let's start versioning our application using the method we presented earlier in the book. We already put the `npm version` script in place in the **package.json** file, so once the git working directory is clean, run the npm command:

$ npm version patch

This will update the version in **package.json**, create a **version.py** file in the **client/src/** folder, and perform a git commit tagged with the new version number.

As a point of reference, our **client/** application folders should now look like this:

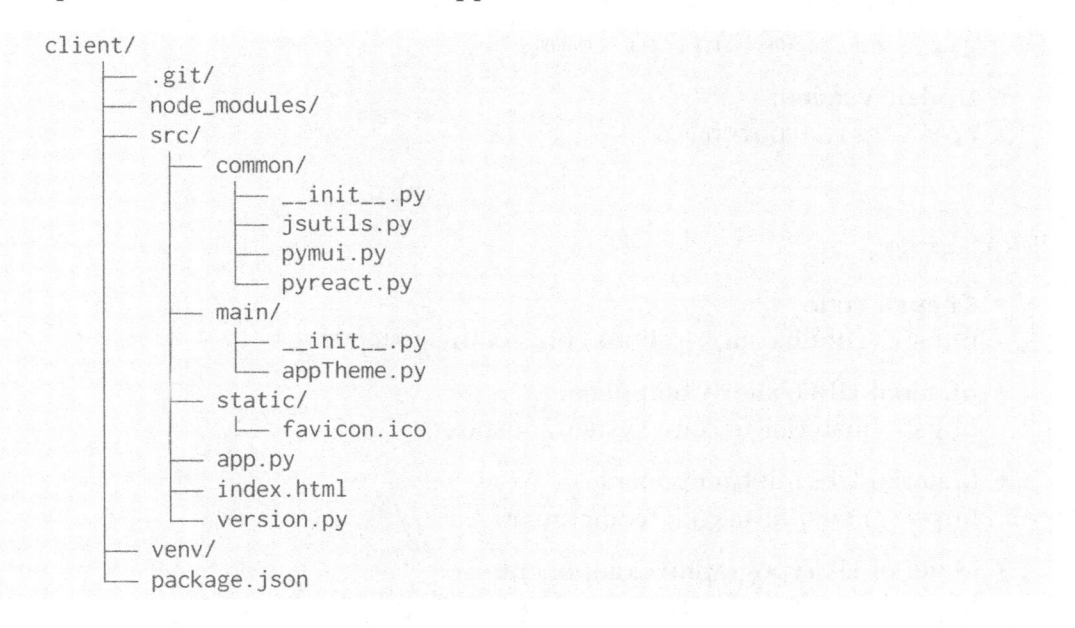

```
client/
    ├── .git/
    ├── node_modules/
    ├── src/
    │       ├── common/
    │       │       ├── __init__.py
    │       │       ├── jsutils.py
    │       │       ├── pymui.py
    │       │       └── pyreact.py
    │       ├── main/
    │       │       ├── __init__.py
    │       │       └── appTheme.py
    │       ├── static/
    │       │       └── favicon.ico
    │       ├── app.py
    │       ├── index.html
    │       └── version.py
    ├── venv/
    └── package.json
```

Chapter Review:

1. Add source file:
   client/src/common/pymui.py

2. Create main folder:
   client/src/main/

3. Add source files:
   client/src/main/__init__.py
   client/src/main/appTheme.py

4. Update source file:
   client/src/app.py

5. Build the application for development with:
   `npm start`

6. Open the application:
   http://localhost:1234

7. Add and commit files to git (from **src/client/** folder):
   ```
   git add ../.gitignore
   git add .
   git commit -m "initial commit"
   ```

8. Update version:
   `npm version patch`

References:

- Chapter code
  https://github.com/rtp-book/project/tree/step02

- Material-UI Flexbox Component
  https://material-ui.com/system/flexbox/

- Material-UI Link Component
  https://material-ui.com/components/links/

- Material-UI Typography Component
  https://material-ui.com/components/typography/

- Anchor Element
  https://html.spec.whatwg.org/multipage/interactive-elements.html#using-the-a-element-to-define-a-command

Chapter 30 – Modal View

In this chapter, we will add a modal *About* view to our application. It will be a small window showing basic application information that is conditionally displayed.

30.1 Application Data

To make our *About* view look fancy, and perhaps more importantly, show you how to easily incorporate images into your application, we need an image file. Here's one you can download right to the **src/static/** folder either manually or with wget, saving it as **app_logo.jpg**:

```
wget -O ./src/static/app_logo.jpg
    https://free-images.com/sm/40ec/book_read_old_literature.jpg
```

Then to help keep things organized, let's make a Python module in **src/main/** for storing general application information that we'll eventually display in our *About* view:

Listing 30-1 File: *appData.py*

```
# __pragma__ ('skip')
from common import require
# __pragma__ ('noskip')


applogo = require("../static/app_logo.jpg")
appname = "Library Management System"

gaid = 'UA-100000000-1'
```

We moved the name of our application from our main Python module to here, and we also load the image file in the **src/static/** folder that we just downloaded, into a Python variable. By using the require() function in this way with the image file, we can just refer to it by its variable name when used, and import it just like any other Python object.

We also added the Google Analytics ID that we will be using later on to this module (don't forget to substitute your own tracking ID).

30.2 Modality

In web applications, it is frequently desirable to pop-up a window over the active application to display some information. In doing so, the main application underneath gets grayed out and disabled until the pop-up window is closed. Doing this manually can take a lot of effort. So to make things easy on ourselves in making a modal view, we can take advantage of another JavaScript library called react-modal that has a modal component for React. This lets us easily display a modal window on top of our main application whenever we need to. First, we install it using npm:

```
$ npm install react-modal
```

Then we add the JavaScript-to-Python mapping in our **pyreact.py** module to give us access to it from our Python modules:

Listing 30-2 File: *pyreact.py*

```
# __pragma__ ('skip')
from common import require, document
# __pragma__ ('noskip')


# Load React and ReactDOM JavaScript libraries into local namespace
React = require('react')
ReactDOM = require('react-dom')
ReactGA = require('react-ga')

Modal = require('react-modal')

# Map React javaScript objects to Python identifiers
createElement = React.createElement
useState = React.useState
useEffect = React.useEffect
createContext = React.createContext
useContext = React.useContext

Fragment = React.Fragment


def render(root_component, props, container):
    def main():
        ReactDOM.render(
            React.createElement(root_component, props),
```

```
        document.getElementById(container)
    )

document.addEventListener('DOMContentLoaded', main)
```

Because this JavaScript library has a default export for the Modal object, we didn't need to do anything special with the require() function to bring it into the Python namespace.

Since we will be reusing the modal component in a few places, we'll put the basic style information for the Modal component in our **appTheme.py** module. We don't have to do anything special with this. It's just a normal Python dictionary that we assign to a variable that we can import into other modules later on. Add the modalStyles dictionary statement to the end of the **appTheme.py** module:

Listing 30-3 File: *appTheme.py*

```
from common.pyreact import createElement
from common.pymui import createMuiTheme, colors
from common.pymui import Box, styled, TextField

theme = createMuiTheme({

...

FlexboxCenter = styled(Box)({
    'display': 'flex',
    'alignItems': 'center',
    'justifyContent': 'center'
})

modalStyles = {
    'overlay': {'zIndex': 1000},
    'content': {
        'top': '35%',
        'left': '50%',
        'right': 'auto',
        'bottom': 'auto',
        'marginRight': '-50%',
        'transform': 'translate(-50%, -50%)'
    }
}
```

The content style attribute of the Modal component mostly has to do with the positioning of the modal window when it opens. The `overlay` attribute is there to ensure that the modal window always opens on top of any other content.

30.3 About Component

Now we can actually build the *About* modal component, which will consist of the following when it opens:

- Window title
- Close button
- Image
- Application name
- Application version

Since we may eventually want to access this from multiple points in our application, we will add the About component module to the **client/src/main/** folder:

Listing 30-4 File: *aboutModal.py*

```
from common.pyreact import createElement as el, Modal
from common.pymui import Paper, Typography, IconButton, CloseIcon, Divider
from main.appData import applogo, appname
from main.appTheme import Flexbox, FlexboxCenter, modalStyles
from version import version


def About(props):
    modalState = props['modalState']
    onClose = props['onClose']

    return el(Modal, {'isOpen': modalState,
                      'onRequestClose': onClose,
                      'style': modalStyles,
                      'ariaHideApp': False,
                     },
              el(Flexbox, {'justifyContent': 'space-between',
                           'alignItems': 'center'
                          },
                 el(Typography, {'variant': 'h6', 'color': 'primary'}, "About"),
                 el(IconButton, {'edge': 'end',
                                 'color': 'primary',
                                 'onClick': onClose
                                }, el(CloseIcon, None)
```

228 | Part III - Putting it all Together

```
            ),
          ),
        el(Paper, {'style': {'padding': '1rem'}},
          el(FlexboxCenter, {'maxWidth': '400px'},
            el('img', {'src': applogo, 'width': '80%'})
          ),
        ),
        el(Paper, {'style': {'padding': '0.5rem', 'marginTop': '1rem'}},
          el(FlexboxCenter, None,
            el(Typography, {'variant': 'h5'}, appname)
          ),
          el(Divider, {'style': {'marginTop': '0.5rem',
                                 'marginBottom': '0.5rem'}
                      }
          ),
          el(FlexboxCenter, None,
            el(Typography, {'variant': 'h5'}, f"Version: {version}")
          ),
        )
    )
)
```

The most important property of the Model component is the isOpen prop. This determines whether the Modal component is rendered based on if it is set to True or False. The onRequestClose prop determines what happens when the modal is closed, which happens if you click away from it, for example. The ariaHideApp prop needs to be set as a workaround to avoid a console warning. It has to do with an ARIA (Accessible Rich Internet Applications) web accessibility setting.

The IconButton component is just a Button component that uses a Material-UI icon for its UI representation. Here we use the Material-UI CloseIcon, which is just a graphical "X" that we put in the upper right-hand corner of the modal window. The onClick event calls an onClose() function that needs to be passed into the About component that will set the isOpen prop of the Modal component to False, which hides it. That value is passed in as the modalState prop that the Modal component uses to determine whether or not it should render itself.

We should mention here that it is a good practice to destructure the props that are passed into a component at the beginning of the component code and create local variables. In addition to some possible performance gains by doing so, it also helps to make your Python code a little cleaner when you use the prop values. But even more useful, is that it identifies what props the component is expecting to have passed into it. If you follow this practice, when you go to use one of your own components, you won't have to search the code of the entire component just to figure out what you need to pass into it. By doing this, all the necessary props that need to be passed in will be right near the top of the component function definition.

As mentioned earlier, we were able to just import the **app_logo.jpg** image like any other data, and apply it right to the src attribute of the standard HTML img tag element. Additionally, we also introduced the Divider component here, which is a stylized wrapper around the standard HTML hr (horizontal rule) tag.

30.4 About Link

Now that we have a modal *About* view component, we need a way to open and close it. As mentioned above, we need to pass two things into the aboutModal component: a modalState prop and an onClose() function. We add both of those items, as well as an onClick handler function for the *About* link on the landing page in the **app.py** module:

Listing 30-5 File: *app.py*

```
from common.pyreact import render, useState, createElement as el
from common.pymui import ThemeProvider, Paper, Typography, Container, Link
from common.jsutils import setTitle
from main.appTheme import theme, Flexbox, FlexboxCenter
from main.aboutModal import About
from main.appData import appname

def App(props):
    setTitle(props['title'])

    aboutShow, setAboutShow = useState(False)

    def handleClickAbout(event):
        event.preventDefault()
        setAboutShow(True)

    return el(ThemeProvider, {'theme': theme},
            el(Container, None,
                el(Paper, {'style': {'padding': '1rem'}},
                    el(Flexbox, {'alignItems': 'center'},
                        el(Typography, {'variant': 'h5'}, appname)
                    )
```

```
                ),
                el(Paper, {'style': {'padding': '0.5rem',
                                     'marginTop': '1rem'}
                          },
                    el(FlexboxCenter, None,
                        el(Link, {'href': '#', 'variant': 'h5'}, "Books")
                    ),
                    el(FlexboxCenter, None,
                        el(Link, {'href': '#', 'variant': 'h5',
                                  'onClick': handleClickAbout
                                 }, "About")
                    ),
                    el(FlexboxCenter, None,
                        el(Link, {'href': '#', 'variant': 'h5'}, "Login")
                    )
                ),
                el(About, {'onClose': lambda: setAboutShow(False),
                           'modalState': aboutShow}
                ),
            )
        )

render(App, {'title': "Books"}, 'root')
```

To handle the state of the About component, we create a state variable like we've done several times before:

```
aboutShow, setAboutShow = useState(False)
```

Then, we have a function that takes care of the onClick event of the *About* link on the landing page:

```
def handleClickAbout(event):
    event.preventDefault()
    setAboutShow(True)
```

The event.preventDefault() function call is there to stop the web browser URL from changing because of the href attribute of the Link component. This is important, because a change in the URL can actually cause the entire application to reload, causing our application to lose track of its current state.

When we call setAboutShow() to change the value of the aboutShow state variable to True, it causes the App component to re-render, sending the new value of aboutShow to the About component, which in turn causes that component to re-render and make itself visible.

For the Modal component to be shown, we need to add it to the component tree. Here, we just tacked it on to the end of everything else inside the Container component. Because of the way it renders in the DOM, it doesn't matter too much where it is in the component tree, it just has to be there.

As we mentioned earlier, the About component expects two props to be passed in. And as you can see here, we pass in the value of the aboutShow state variable as modalState. And then, for the onClose function prop, we actually send the setAboutShow() function with the parameter to close the modal view already filled in. We used a Python lambda to wrap the function, in this case, to prevent it from getting called right away since we have the parenthesis after the function name. By doing it this way, the About component doesn't need to know about any of the implementation details. It just calls a function that doesn't take any parameters.

After a rebuild of the application, the *About* link on the landing page should be working, and clicking it should open the About modal view. Clicking the "X" icon in the upper right corner of the modal window should close it, as should just clicking anywhere that is off the modal view itself (which triggers the onRequestClose event).

At the end of this chapter, our **client/** folders and files looks like this:

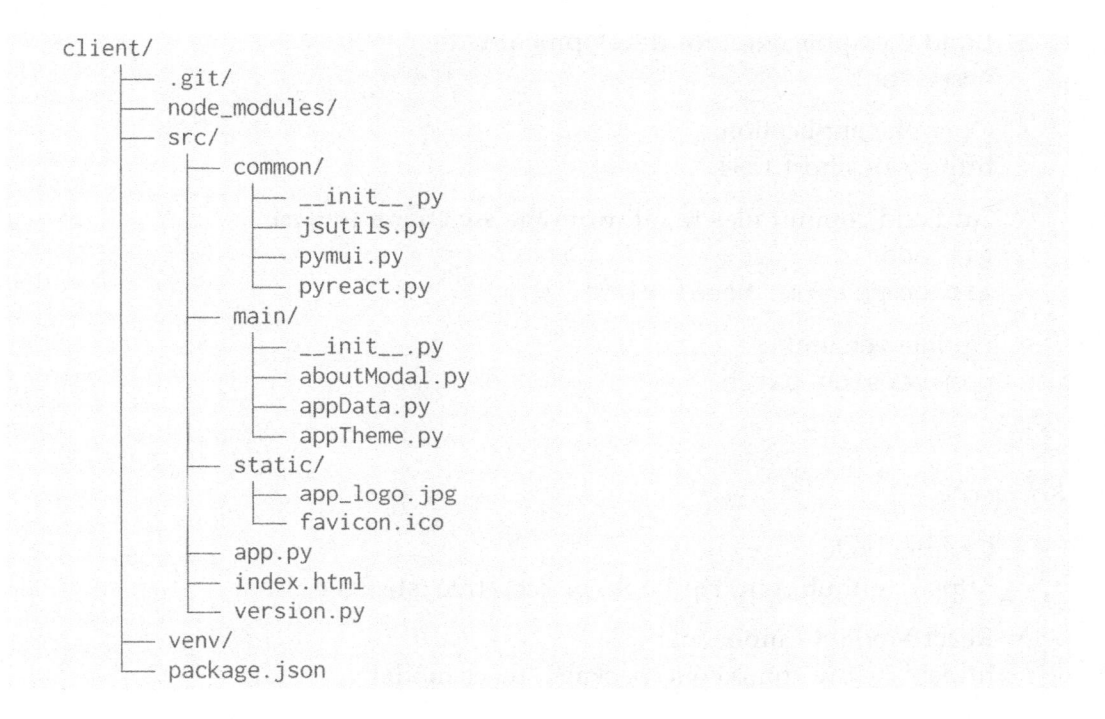

```
client/
├── .git/
├── node_modules/
├── src/
│   ├── common/
│   │   ├── __init__.py
│   │   ├── jsutils.py
│   │   ├── pymui.py
│   │   └── pyreact.py
│   ├── main/
│   │   ├── __init__.py
│   │   ├── aboutModal.py
│   │   ├── appData.py
│   │   └── appTheme.py
│   ├── static/
│   │   ├── app_logo.jpg
│   │   └── favicon.ico
│   ├── app.py
│   ├── index.html
│   └── version.py
├── venv/
└── package.json
```

Before getting into the next chapter, commit any new or updated files to the git repository, and then run `npm version patch` after the git working directory is clean to update the application version again.

Chapter Review:

1. Add **app_logo.jpg** image file to **client/src/static/**:
   https://free-images.com/sm/40ec/book_read_old_literature.jpg

2. Install React Modal package:
   `npm install react-modal`

3. Add source files:
   client/src/main/appData.py
   client/src/main/aboutModal.py

4. Update source files:
   client/src/common/pyreact.py
   client/src/main/appTheme.py
   client/src/app.py

5. Build the application for development with:
   `npm start`

6. Open the application:
   http://localhost:1234

7. Add and commit files to git (from the **src/client/** folder):
   `git add .`
   `git commit -m "Modal View"`

8. Update version:
   `npm version patch`

References:

- Chapter code
  https://github.com/rtp-book/project/tree/step03

- React Modal Component
  https://www.npmjs.com/package/react-modal

- Material-UI Button Component
  https://material-ui.com/components/buttons/

- Material-UI Icons
  https://material-ui.com/components/material-icons/

- Material-UI Divider Component
  https://material-ui.com/components/dividers/

Chapter 31 – REST Service

Since we can't do too much more with our client web application until we have some data to work with, let's switch gears and move over to the server application and get a basic Flask REST service up and running. As mentioned before, the back-end server isn't the focus of this book so we won't go into too many details about it, but we'll try and point out some of the interesting code bits in this chapter anyway.

The first step is to `deactivate` the `client` virtual environment if it is active, change to the **bookapp/server/** folder, then `activate` the `server` virtual environment. You will know you forgot to switch over later if you get an error message when you try and run the Flask application saying:

`ModuleNotFoundError: No module named 'flask'`.

That indicates that the virtual environment that we installed Flask into earlier, is not active.

31.1 The Database

For us to serve up data from a REST service, it has to come from somewhere. For this application, we will be using an SQLite database. SQLite is a serverless file-based database. It is quick to set up and is included in the Python standard library, so we don't need to install any extra libraries to use it.

We are not going to do anything too fancy with database access. We will open up a new connection anytime we need to do database reads or writes, and we won't worry about maintaining a database connection pool. While this is certainly not considered best practices for a production server, for our simple demo application, it will do. On the initial connection, if the database doesn't exist, it will be created and optionally populated with some test data.

Be warned that there is a lot of SQL code in this chapter, but nothing too fancy. Here is the first module that we'll use for creating and accessing the database. It should go into the **server/** folder:

Listing 31-1 File: *dbutils.py*

```python
import sqlite3
import os
import logging


DB_LOC = './database'
DB_NAME = 'books.db'
DB_FILE = os.path.join(DB_LOC, DB_NAME)

if __name__ == "__main__":
    fmt = "[%(asctime)s]|%(levelname)s|[%(module)s]:%(funcName)s()|%(message)s"
    logging.basicConfig(format=fmt, level=logging.DEBUG)
log = logging.getLogger(__name__)


def create_db(autopopulate):
    if not os.path.exists(DB_LOC):
        os.mkdir(DB_LOC)

    with sqlite3.connect(DB_FILE) as conn:
        cur = conn.cursor()

        # sqlite foreign key support is off by default
        cur.execute("PRAGMA foreign_keys = ON")
        conn.commit()

        # Create tables
        cur.execute("CREATE TABLE Categories ("
                    "ID INTEGER PRIMARY KEY NOT NULL, "
                    "Category TEXT UNIQUE)")
        cur.execute("CREATE TABLE Publishers ("
                    "ID INTEGER PRIMARY KEY NOT NULL, "
                    "Publisher TEXT UNIQUE)")
        cur.execute("CREATE TABLE Conditions ("
                    "ID INTEGER PRIMARY KEY NOT NULL, "
                    "Code TEXT UNIQUE, "
                    "Condition TEXT)")
        cur.execute("CREATE TABLE Formats ("
                    "ID INTEGER PRIMARY KEY NOT NULL, "
                    "Format TEXT UNIQUE)")
        cur.execute("CREATE TABLE Users ("
                    "ID INTEGER PRIMARY KEY NOT NULL, "
                    "Username TEXT UNIQUE, "
                    "Password TEXT)")
```

```python
            conn.commit()

            cur.execute("CREATE TABLE Books ("
                "ID INTEGER PRIMARY KEY NOT NULL,"
                "Title TEXT NOT NULL,"
                "Author TEXT,"
                "Publisher TEXT "
                  "REFERENCES Publishers(Publisher) "
                  "ON UPDATE CASCADE ON DELETE RESTRICT,"
                "IsFiction BOOLEAN DEFAULT 0,"
                "Category TEXT "
                  "REFERENCES Categories(Category) "
                  "ON UPDATE CASCADE ON DELETE RESTRICT,"
                "Edition TEXT,"
                "DatePublished TEXT,"
                "ISBN TEXT,"
                "Pages INTEGER,"
                "DateAcquired DATE,"
                "Condition TEXT "
                  "REFERENCES Conditions(Code) "
                  "ON UPDATE CASCADE ON DELETE RESTRICT,"
                "Format TEXT "
                  "REFERENCES Formats(Format) "
                  "ON UPDATE CASCADE ON DELETE RESTRICT,"
                "Location TEXT,"
                "Notes TEXT"
                ")"
            )
            conn.commit()
            cur.close()

            if autopopulate:
                from testdata import populate_db
                populate_db(conn)


def connect(autopopulate=False):
    if not os.path.exists(DB_FILE):
        log.warning("Creating new DB")
        create_db(autopopulate)


def execute(stmt, params=()):
    try:
        with sqlite3.connect(DB_FILE) as conn:
```

```python
            conn.execute("PRAGMA foreign_keys = ON")
            curs = conn.cursor()
            curs.execute(stmt, params)
            rowcount = curs.rowcount
            curs.close()
            conn.commit()
        return 'success', rowcount
    except Exception as e:
        log.error(e)
        return 'error', str(e)


def select(stmt, params=()):
    try:
        with sqlite3.connect(DB_FILE) as conn:
            curs = conn.cursor()
            curs.execute(stmt, params)
            desc = curs.description
            cols = [fld[0] for fld in desc]
            rowset = curs.fetchall()
            rows = [dict(zip(cols, row)) for row in rowset]
            curs.close()
        return 'success', rows
    except Exception as e:
        log.error(e)
        return 'error', str(e)


def _main():
    with sqlite3.connect(DB_FILE) as conn:
        cur = conn.cursor()
        sql = "SELECT name FROM sqlite_master WHERE type = ?"
        cur.execute(sql, ('table',))
        data = cur.fetchall()
        print('Tables:', [tbl[0] for tbl in data])


if __name__ == '__main__':
    connect(True)
    _main()
```

The first part of the module deals with creating the database tables and establishing the relationships between them. We use a `connect()` function to ensure that the database exists before trying to use it. If the `autopopulate` variable is True, then it will put some test data into the tables as well. It is only necessary to call this function once. Since we are going to reconnect for every database call, it is not actually needed for anything else. But we can use it to make sure our REST server has a database to connect to when it starts up.

If you run this module (after creating the **testdata.py** module), it will create the database and fill it with the test data. The _main() function will then print out the list of tables in the database as a confirmation of success.

```
(venv) $ python -m dbutils

[2020-11-12 14:28:53,872]|WARNING|[dbutils]:connect()|Creating new DB
Tables: ['Categories', 'Publishers', 'Conditions', 'Formats', 'Users', 'Books']
(venv) $
```

The other two functions, execute() and select(), are what we will use from the Flask server to run queries against the database. The execute() function is for queries that do not return data but affect rows, specifically for inserts, updates, and deletes. And the select() function is used for queries that return rows from the database. Both functions take an SQL statement and an optional tuple of SQL parameter values as arguments. The return value from both of these functions is a tuple that indicates whether it was successful or not, and then the result of the database operation.

To use the autopopulate option and add some test data to the database, you'll need to create the **testdata.py** module and put it into the **server/** folder:

Listing 31-2 File: *testdata.py*

```python
def populate_db(conn):
    cur = conn.cursor()

    # Populate lookup tables
    conditions = {'F': 'Fine/Like New',
                  'NF': 'Near Fine',
                  'VG': 'Very Good',
                  'G': 'Good',
                  'FR': 'Fair',
                  'P': 'Poor'}
    for code, cond in conditions.items():
        cur.execute(f"INSERT INTO Conditions(Code, Condition) "
                    f"values('{code}', '{cond}')")
```

```python
formats = ['Hardcover', 'Paperback', 'Oversized', 'Pamphlet', 'E-book']
for item in formats:
    cur.execute(f"INSERT INTO Formats(Format) values('{item}')")

categories = ['Computers & Tech',
              'Biographies',
              'Sci-Fi & Fantasy',
              'Arts & Music',
              'History']
for item in categories:
    cur.execute(f"INSERT INTO Categories(Category) values('{item}')")

cur.execute(f"INSERT INTO Publishers(Publisher) values('No Starch Press')")
cur.execute(f"INSERT INTO Publishers(Publisher) values('Del Rey Books')")
conn.commit()

# Populate main table
cur.execute("INSERT INTO Books(Title, Author, IsFiction, "
            "Category, DateAcquired, Condition, Location) "
            "values('React to Python', 'Sheehan', 0, "
            "'Computers & Tech', '2020-12-01', 'F', 'A3')")
cur.execute("INSERT INTO Books(Title, Author, Publisher, "
            "ISBN, IsFiction, Category, Format) "
            "values('I Robot', 'Isaac Asimov', 'Del Rey Books', "
            "'055338256X', 1, 'Sci-Fi & Fantasy', 'Paperback')")
cur.execute("INSERT INTO Books(Title, Author, ISBN, IsFiction, Category) "
            "values('The C Programming Language', 'Kernighan & Ritchie', "
            "'0131103628', 0, 'Computers & Tech')")
conn.commit()

cur.execute(f"INSERT INTO Users(Username, Password) values('admin', '')")
conn.commit()
```

This function executes a number of SQL INSERT statements, putting sample data records into each of the tables. Since we don't have a UI to actually create records with yet, this will give us a few records right off the bat to help design our client application UI with.

31.2 The REST Server

Now that we have the database in place, let's work on the back-end Flask server that will access it. Like the others, this module needs to go into the server folder:

Listing 31-3 File: *appserver.py*

```python
from flask import Flask, jsonify, request, Response, session
import flask_login
import logging
import os
from datetime import timedelta

import dbutils as db
from admin_routes import admin_api, User
from db_routes import import db_api


fmt = "[%(asctime)s]|%(levelname)s|[%(module)s]:%(funcName)s()|%(message)s"
logging.basicConfig(format=fmt)
log = logging.getLogger()
log.setLevel(logging.INFO)

SESSION_TIMEOUT = 60

app = Flask(__name__)
app.register_blueprint(admin_api)
app.register_blueprint(db_api)

login_manager = flask_login.LoginManager()
login_manager.init_app(app)

app.config.update(
    SECRET_KEY=os.urandom(16),
    SESSION_COOKIE_HTTPONLY=True,
    SESSION_COOKIE_SAMESITE='Lax',
)

app.permanent_session_lifetime = timedelta(minutes=SESSION_TIMEOUT)

# Create the database if it doesn't exist
db.connect()


@login_manager.user_loader
def load_user(user_id):
    return User(user_id)


@login_manager.unauthorized_handler
def unauthorized_callback():
```

```
        log.warning(f"UNAUTHORIZED [{request.method}] {request.full_path}")
        return Response("UNAUTHORIZED", 401)


@app.errorhandler(404)
def request_not_found(err):
    return jsonify({'error': str(err)})


@app.before_request
def request_log():
    log.info(f"[{request.method}] {request.full_path}")


@app.before_request
def refresh_session():
    session.modified = True


@app.after_request
def apply_headers(response):
    response.headers['Access-Control-Allow-Origin'] = '*'
    if request.blueprint == 'db_api':
        response.headers['Cache-Control'] = 'no-store'
    return response


@app.route('/', methods=['GET'])
def index():
    return Response("OK", 200)


if __name__ == "__main__":
    app.run(debug=True, port=8000)
```

We first set up some logging and set a few constants, then call the connect() function in the **database.py** module to make sure the database exists before we try to use it. The actual routes for our REST API are in separate modules that we set up as Flask blueprints: one for general admin use and one for database access.

In this module, we also set up user session management using Flask-Login, the response headers, and default handlers for unauthorized and unknown requests. The only actual route we have set up here is just the / default route, which returns an OK response to show that the Flask server is alive.

React to Python

For the administrative routes like those for login, logout, and to refresh the session, we have this Flask blueprint module that needs to go into the **server/** folder:

Listing 31-4 File: *admin_routes.py*

```python
from flask import jsonify, request, Response, session, Blueprint
from werkzeug.security import check_password_hash, generate_password_hash
import flask_login
import logging

log = logging.getLogger(__name__)

admin_api = Blueprint('admin_api', __name__, url_prefix='/api')


class User(flask_login.UserMixin):
    def __init__(self, userid):
        self.id = userid


@admin_api.route('/login', methods=['POST'])
def login():
    record = request.get_json()
    pwd = record.pop('password', "")
    username = record.pop('username', "")
    username = username.lower()

    if validateLogin(username, pwd):
        flask_login.login_user(User(username))
        session.permanent = True
        return jsonify({"OK": 200})
    else:
        log.warning(f"Failed login attempt for user '{username}'")
        flask_login.logout_user()
        return Response("UNAUTHORIZED", 401)


def validateLogin(user, pwd):
    # TODO: Use db.Users table for user validation
    SECRET_PASSWORD = generate_password_hash('123')
    return user == 'admin' and check_password_hash(SECRET_PASSWORD, pwd)


@admin_api.route('/logout', methods=['GET'])
@flask_login.login_required
def logout():
```

```
    flask_login.logout_user()
    return jsonify({"OK": 200})


@admin_api.route('/whoami', methods=['GET'])
@flask_login.login_required
def getUser():
    user = ''
    if flask_login.current_user.is_authenticated:
        user = flask_login.current_user.get_id()
    return jsonify({'success': {'user': user}})


@admin_api.route('/ping', methods=['GET'])
@flask_login.login_required
def keepAlive():
    return jsonify({"OK": 200})
```

The /api/login route uses a function validateLogin() to validate the user/password combination. Right now, it just has a placeholder that is hard-coded to *admin/123*. At some point, you would instead want it to check the Users table in the database to compare the calculated hash of the given password with the hash that would be stored in the database for each user. We will leave that as an exercise for another time however. Note that the /api/login route does require a POST request.

Since you can only manually test GET requests from a web browser, I would recommend using the Postman application if you need to test other REST requests like POST and DELETE.

The /api/logout route invalidates the current session, and the /api/ping route resets the timeout clock on the current session. The /api/whoami route is used when the application gets reloaded in the web browser. If there is an active valid session, the application can retrieve the name of the user that is currently still logged in.

The last module needed for our REST API is the Flask blueprint that handles routes that interact with the SQLite database. This module goes in the **server/** folder as well:

Listing 31-5 File: *db_routes.py*

```python
from flask import jsonify, request, Blueprint
import flask_login
import logging

import dbutils as db

log = logging.getLogger(__name__)

db_api = Blueprint('db_api', __name__, url_prefix='/api')


LOOKUPS = ['Categories', 'Publishers', 'Conditions', 'Formats']


@db_api.route('/lookup/<string:name>', methods=['GET'])
def get_lookup(name):

    if name in LOOKUPS:
        result, data = db.select(f"SELECT * FROM {name}")
        return jsonify({result: data})

    return jsonify(None)


@db_api.route('/lookup/<string:name>', methods=['POST'])
@flask_login.login_required
def update_lookup(name):
    if name in LOOKUPS:
        record = request.get_json()
        record_id = record.pop('ID', None)
        fields = record.keys()
        values = tuple([record[field] for field in fields])

        if record_id:
            fields = ','.join([f"{field}=?" for field in fields])
            sql = f"UPDATE {name} SET {fields} WHERE ID=?"
            values = values + (record_id,)
        else:
            fields = ','.join(record.keys())
            params = ','.join(['?']*len(record.keys()))
            sql = f"INSERT INTO {name} ({fields}) VALUES ({params})"
```

Chapter 31 - REST Service   245

```python
        result, data = db.execute(sql, values)

        return jsonify({result: data})

    return jsonify(None)


@db_api.route('/lookup/<string:name>', methods=['DELETE'])
@flask_login.login_required
def delete_lookup(name):
    if name in LOOKUPS:
        record = request.get_json()
        record_id = record.pop('ID', None)

        if record_id:
            sql = f"DELETE FROM {name} WHERE ID=?"
            values = (record_id,)
            result, data = db.execute(sql, values)
            return jsonify({result: data})

    return jsonify(None)


@db_api.route('/book', methods=['GET'])
def get_book():
    book_id = request.args.get('id', "")
    if len(book_id) > 0:
        result, data = db.select(f"SELECT * FROM Books WHERE ID=?", (book_id,))
        return jsonify({result: data[0]} if len(data) > 0 else None)

    return jsonify(None)


@db_api.route('/book', methods=['POST'])
@flask_login.login_required
def update_book():
    record = request.get_json()
    if record:
        record_id = record.pop('ID', None)
        fields = record.keys()
        values = tuple([record[field] if len(f"{record[field]}") > 0 else None
                        for field in fields]
                      )

        if record_id:
```

```python
            fields = ','.join([f"{field}=?" for field in fields])
            sql = f"UPDATE Books SET {fields} WHERE ID=?"
            values = values + (record_id,)
        else:
            fields = ','.join(record.keys())
            params = ','.join(['?']*len(record.keys()))
            sql = f"INSERT INTO Books ({fields}) VALUES ({params})"

        result, data = db.execute(sql, values)
        return jsonify({result: data})

    return jsonify(None)


@db_api.route('/book', methods=['DELETE'])
@flask_login.login_required
def delete_book():
    record = request.get_json()
    if record:
        record_id = record.pop('ID', None)

        if record_id:
            sql = f"DELETE FROM Books WHERE ID=?"
            values = (record_id,)
            result, data = db.execute(sql, values)
            return jsonify({result: data})

    return jsonify(None)


@db_api.route('/books', methods=['GET'])
def get_books():
    params = dict(request.args)
    fields = params.keys()

    if 'IsFiction' in fields:
        params['IsFiction'] = int(params['IsFiction'])
    if 'Title' in fields:
        params['Title'] = f"%{params['Title']}%"
    if 'Author' in fields:
        params['Author'] = f"%{params['Author']}%"

    values = tuple([params[field] if len(f"{params[field]}") > 0 else None
                    for field in fields]
                   )
```

```python
    def get_operator(field):
        return ' LIKE ' if field in ['Title', 'Author'] else '='

    wc = ' AND '.join([f"{field}{get_operator(field)}?" for field in fields])
    if len(wc) > 0:
        wc = f" WHERE {wc}"
    result, data = db.select(f"SELECT * FROM Books{wc}", values)
    return jsonify({result: data} if len(data) > 0 else None)
```

If you now run the **appserver.py** module, Flask will start up in debug mode on port 8000 and allow you to access the REST API.

(venv) $ python -m appserver

Routes in this module for working with the lookup tables in the database start with /api/lookup/ followed by the name of the lookup table. Read requests use GET, inserts and updates use a POST request, and deletions use a DELETE request.

For example, if you want to get the values in the *Categories* table, you can use this:

http://localhost:8000/api/lookup/Categories

Which returns a JSON response:

```
{"success":[
 {"Category": "Computers & Tech", "ID": 1},
 {"Category": "Biographies", "ID": 2},
 {"Category": "Sci-Fi & Fantasy", "ID": 3},
 {"Category": "Arts & Music", "ID": 4},
 {"Category": "History", "ID": 5}
]}
```

Since we are injecting the passed in table name directly into our SQL statement instead of using an SQL parameter, the routes do a sanity check to make sure that the requested table name is valid before running the query.

For POST and DELETE requests, the lookup table record to be inserted, updated, or deleted is provided in the body of the POST or DELETE request. If a POST is used and there is no ID field present, the REST API will do a database INSERT, otherwise it will do an UPDATE.

React to Python

To retrieve a single book record from the Books table, the request uses /api/book, where the ID of the book record is provided as a URL query parameter. For example:

http://localhost:8000/api/book?id=3

Returns a JSON response:

```
{"success": {
"Author": "Kernighan & Ritchie",
"Category": "Computers & Tech",
"Condition": null,
"DateAcquired": null,
"DatePublished": null,
"Edition": null,
"Format": null,
"ID": 2,
"ISBN": "0131103628",
"IsFiction": 0,
"Location": null,
"Notes": null,
"Pages": null,
"Publisher": null,
"Title": "The C Programming Language"
}}
```

As it is for the lookup tables, inserting, updating, and deleting book records in the Books table uses POST and DELETE requests with the information about the record provided in the body of the request.

The last route implemented to get all the books is simply:

http://localhost:8000/api/books

Query parameters can be provided in the URL of the /api/books request to filter the data that is returned in the response. For example, to only return books that have a category of *Computers & Tech*, you could use this (note the URL encoding):

http://localhost:8000/api/books?Category=Computers%20%26%20Tech

That is the extent of the REST API that we will be needing for our demo application. Note that this REST implementation is not necessarily robust, secure, or scalable, and is only provided as a rudimentary platform to build our example application off of.

React to Python

As a check, this is what the **server/** folders and files should look like now:

```
server/
    ├── database/
    │   └── books.db
    ├── venv/
    ├── admin_routes.py
    ├── appserver.py
    ├── db_routes.py
    ├── dbutils.py
    └── testdata.py
```

Chapter Review:

1. Deactivate the **bookapp/client/** virtual environment:
   `deactivate`

2. Switch to the **bookapp/server/** folder and activate the virtual environment:
   `venv\Scripts\activate` (Windows)
   `source venv/bin/activate` (Mac/Linux)

3. Add source files:
   server/dbutils.py
   server/testdata.py

4. Create the database:
   `python -m dbutils`

5. Add source files:
   server/appserver.py
   server/admin_routes.py
   server/db_routes.py

6. Start the web server:
   `python -m appserver`

7. Test the web service:
   http://localhost:8000/api/lookup/Categories
   http://localhost:8000/api/book?id=3
   http://localhost:8000/api/books
   http://localhost:8000/api/books?Category=Computers%20%26%20Tech

8. Add and commit files to git (from the **src/server/** folder):
   git add .
   git commit -m "REST Service"

References:

- Chapter code
  https://github.com/rtp-book/project/tree/step04
- SQLite Database
  https://www.sqlite.org/index.html
- Flask
  https://flask.palletsprojects.com/en/1.1.x/
- Flask-Login
  https://flask-login.readthedocs.io/en/latest/
- Postman REST Client
  https://www.postman.com/downloads/

Chapter 32 – Books

Now that we have our REST service in place, let's switch back over to our client application and try getting some data from it.

The first step once again, is to deactivate the server virtual environment if it is active, switch back to the **bookapp/client/** folder, then activate the client virtual environment.

32.1 Proxy Server

With the back-end server now running, the next step will be to start using the development proxy server to serve up content for both the Flask server and the Parcel server. Earlier, we added a script to **package.json** to run it, and we already installed the necessary JavaScript libraries via npm. Now we just need the actual proxy server script, which we add to the client application client/ root folder:

Listing 32-1 File: *dev-server.js*

```javascript
const Bundler = require('parcel-bundler');
const express = require('express');
const { createProxyMiddleware } = require('http-proxy-middleware');

const app = express();

const apiProxy = createProxyMiddleware('/api', {
  target: 'http://localhost:8000'
});
app.use(apiProxy);

// parcel options
const options = {minify:false, cache: false, outDir: 'dist/dev', logLevel: 4};

const bundler = new Bundler('src/index.html', options);
app.use(bundler.middleware());

bundler.on('buildEnd', () => {
  console.log('Parcel proxy server has started at: http://localhost:8080');
});

app.listen(8080);
```

You can look at the Parcel Web Proxy chapter if you want to review the details of how this works. The only changes we made from the previous version, is that the directory for the application entry point file is now **src/** instead of just the current directory, and we are going to leave the /api prefix in place on the URL for calls to the REST service.

We start the development proxy server with:

(venv) $ npm run dev

Then, you can test the proxy to the back-end server with:

http://localhost:8080/api/books

Note the change in port number from 8000 for the Flask server to 8080 for the proxy server.

32.2 Updated Fetch

In the **jsutils.py** module we previously created for this project, we left out the fetch() function that we used earlier in the book. Since we will ultimately be creating several other URL related functions, let's put our fetch() function into a new module called **urlutils.py**, which we can add to the **client/src/common/** folder:

Listing 32-2 File: *urlutils.py*

```
import time
from common.pyreact import ReactGA
from common.jsutils import console

# __pragma__ ('skip')
from common import require, window, JSON
# __pragma__ ('noskip')

polyfill = require("@babel/polyfill")  # required by async/await

# __pragma__ ('kwargs')
async def fetch(url, callback=None, **kwargs):
    ReactGA.event({'category': 'api', 'action': 'request', 'label': url})
    t_start = time.time()
```

```
        on_error = kwargs.pop('onError', None)
        method = kwargs.pop('method', 'GET')
        try:
            if method == 'POST' or method == 'DELETE':
                data = kwargs.pop('data', None)
                headers = {'Content-Type': 'application/json;'}  # __:jsiter
                response = await window.fetch(url, {'method': method,
                                                   'headers': headers,
                                                   'body': JSON.stringify(data)
                                                  }
                                             )
            else:
                kw_params = kwargs.pop('params', {})
                params = buildParams(kw_params)
                response = await window.fetch(f"{url}{params}")

            if response.status != 200:
                console.error('Fetch error - Status Code: ' + response.status)
                if on_error:
                    on_error()
            else:
                json_data = await response.json()
                t_elapsed = time.time() - t_start
                ReactGA.timing({'category': 'API',
                                'variable': 'fetch',
                                'value': int(t_elapsed * 1000),
                                'label': url}
                              )

                error = dict(json_data).get('error', None)
                if error:
                    raise Exception(error)
                else:
                    result = dict(json_data).get('success', None)
                    if callback:
                        callback(result)
        except object as e:
            console.error(str(e))
            if on_error:
                on_error()

# __pragma__ ('nokwargs')

def buildParams(param_dict: dict):
    param_list = [f"&{key}={window.encodeURIComponent(val)}"
```

```
                for key, val in param_dict.items() if val]
    params = ''.join(param_list)
    return f"?{params[1:]}" if len(params) > 0 else ''
```

In this version of our `fetch()` function, we added a few more capabilities. One is that it now looks for a `method` keyword passed into it that determines the type of HTTP request that should be made. It still defaults to a GET request if not provided though. The other new feature is that it also looks for an `onError` keyword where you can specify a function that will be called if there is an error that occurs during the `fetch()` call. By default, it will always print an error message to the web browser console if something goes wrong. But if provided, the `onError` callback function allows you to do any extra cleanup that might be required if an error does occur during the fetch process.

Lastly, in addition to the call to Google Analytics that we already had in place to record the timing of the HTTP request, we also added another call to Google Analytics that will record every URL that is requested by the client application.

At the end of the file, we also added the `buildParams()` convenience method that turns a regular Python dictionary into a URL query string that is properly encoded and delineated. This allows us to easily add query parameters to a request URL if needed.

32.3 Book List

Now that we have a way to call our REST API, let's create a view component that will display all of the books in our database as a formatted list. Doing that will require several aspects:

```
Container component
    ├── Title bar
    │     ├── Title
    │     └── Close button
    ├── Table component
    │     ├── Column headings
    │     └── Rows of book records
    ├── Function to get data on load
    ├── Function to sort data
    └── Wait icon to display while getting data
```

In creating the individual components that make up this view, you have the option of creating them as separate files, or combining them all into one file. In this case, we will use two files: one for the main view, and a second one just for the list itself. To organize the views we will be building, create a folder **views/** under **client/src/**. Then add an empty **__init__.py** file in that folder so that Python recognizes it as a package. For our first view, under **client/src/views/**, create a folder called **bookList/**, and in that, add an **__init__.py** file there as well. Finally, put this Python module that represents the entire view into the **client/src/views/bookList/** folder:

Listing 32-3 File: *bookListView.py*

```
from common.pyreact import useState, useEffect, createElement as el
from common.pymui import Typography, AppBar, Toolbar, IconButton, CloseIcon
from common.pymui import Container, Box, Paper, CircularProgress
from common.urlutils import fetch
from views.bookList.bookListTable import BooksTable


def BookList(props):
    setBooksShow = props['setBooksShow']

    books, setBooks = useState([])
    sortKey, setSortKey = useState('Title')
    showProgress, setShowProgress = useState(False)

    def sortBooks():
        book_list = [dict(tmp_book) for tmp_book in books]
        if len(book_list) > 0:
            setBooks(sorted(book_list, key=lambda k: k[sortKey] or ""))

    def on_fetch_error():
        setShowProgress(False)

    def getBooks():
        isPending = True

        def _getBooks(data):
            book_list = data if data else []
            if isPending:
                if len(book_list) > 0:
                    setBooks(sorted(book_list, key=lambda k: k[sortKey]))
                else:
                    setBooks([])
```

```python
            setShowProgress(False)

    def abort():
        nonlocal isPending
        isPending = False

    setShowProgress(True)
    fetch("/api/books", _getBooks, onError=on_fetch_error)
    return abort

useEffect(getBooks, [])
useEffect(sortBooks, [sortKey])

return el(Container, None,
        el(AppBar, {'position': 'static',
                    'style': {'marginBottom': '0.5rem'}
                    },
            el(Toolbar, {'variant': 'dense'},
                el(Box, {'width': '100%'},
                    el(Typography, {'variant': 'h6'}, "Books")
                ),
                el(IconButton, {'edge': 'end',
                                'color': 'inherit',
                                'onClick': lambda: setBooksShow(False)
                                }, el(CloseIcon, None)
                ),
            ),
        ),
        el(Paper, {'style': {'padding': '0.5rem', 'marginTop': '0.8rem'}},
            el(BooksTable, {'books': books, 'setSortKey': setSortKey})
        ),
        el(CircularProgress,
            {'style': {'position': 'absolute',
                        'top': '30%',
                        'left': '50%',
                        'marginLeft': -12}
        }) if showProgress else None
)
```

This component needs one prop `onClose` passed into it, which is a function that is called when the close button is clicked. We will use this for the `onClick` event of the `IconButton` in the `AppBar`. This is similar to what we did for the `About` modal component.

It also uses three state variables:

- books - a list that stores the book records
- sortKey - a string that holds the column name to sort on
- showProgress - a boolean value that indicates if the wait icon should be shown or not

To get the list of books from the REST service, we used the same approach that we did in the previous chapter on Asynchronous Requests. Utilizing a React.useEffect() hook function with an empty list, the getBooks() function will be called when the BookList component completes loading. That in turn calls our fetch() function, which then calls the internal _getBooks() function as a callback to update the component state.

Normally, once the fetch is complete, it deactivates the waiting icon by setting the showProgress state to False. But if something goes wrong with the call to fetch(), we still want the wait icon to go away. This is where the onError keyword for our updated fetch() function comes into play. By passing setShowProgress(False) as a value for onError to the fetch() function, it will be called if an error occurs that would otherwise end up bypassing our normal call to turn off the wait icon.

If there are a lot of books in our database, it could take a second or so to retrieve the data. To let the user know our application is in a waiting state, we use the CircularProgress component, and display it for the duration of the call to fetch(). To make that work, we add the CircularProgress component to the element tree code, and use a state variable to decide if it should be shown or not. In this case, we used an inline ternary statement to provide that logic. If we don't need to show it, the ternary statement returns a value of None, which is a valid return value from a React component to indicate it should not be added as a node in the DOM.

Note that because we only have a few books in our database for testing, it might not be enough time for the progress indicator to even show. If you want to test it, you can try adding a 5-second delay using a call to time.sleep() in the /api/books route on the Flask server.

One nuanced detail of the getBooks() function is the addition of a flag variable:

```
isPending = True
```

This is used to flag whether or not the HTTP request is still valid and that the component hasn't been closed before the response from the server has been received. If React tries to update a state variable after the component has been removed from the DOM, you will see an error message similar to this:

```
Warning: Can't perform a React state update on an unmounted component. This is
a no-op, but it indicates a memory leak in your application. To fix, cancel all
subscriptions and asynchronous tasks in a useEffect cleanup function.
    in BookList (created by App)
```

By passing the `abort()` function back to `useEffect()` when the HTTP request is made, it will be called when React is removing the component from the DOM and give us a chance to set `isPending` to `False`. This prevents the `books` state variable from being updated after it no longer exists, which would otherwise cause it to generate the above error.

We also created a function that is used to sort the list of books. And thanks to the call to `useEffect`, it will be called whenever the `sortKey` variable is updated:

```
useEffect(sortBooks, [sortKey])
```

The other parts of the `BookList` component include an `AppBar` component that displays a title and has an `IconButton` component for closing the view. And finally, it has a `BooksTable` component that builds the element tree for the list of books.

This leads us to the second module that we need to implement. The view module above references a `BooksTable` component that we still need to define. So in the **client/src/views/bookList/** folder, create this module:

Listing 32-4 File: *bookListTable.py*

```
from common.pyreact import createElement as el
from common.pymui import Box, Link, Tooltip
from common.pymui import TableContainer, Table
from common.pymui import TableHead, TableBody, TableRow, TableCell
```

```python
def BookRowVu(props):
    book = props['book']

    title = book['Title']
    author = book['Author']
    book_type = "Fiction" if book['IsFiction'] else "Non-Fiction"
    category = book['Category']
    book_fmt = book['Format']
    location = book['Location']

    return el(TableRow, None,
            el(TableCell, None,
                el(Tooltip, {'title': title if title else ''},
                    el(Box, {'width': '10rem',
                            'textOverflow': 'ellipsis',
                            'overflow': 'hidden',
                            'whiteSpace': 'nowrap'}, title),
                )
            ),
            el(TableCell, None,
                el(Box, {'width': '6rem', 'whiteSpace': 'nowrap'}, author)),
            el(TableCell, None,
                el(Box, {'width': '5rem'}, book_type)),
            el(TableCell, None,
                el(Box, {'width': '8rem'}, category)),
            el(TableCell, None,
                el(Box, {'width': '6rem'}, book_fmt)),
            el(TableCell, None,
                el(Box, {'width': '5rem'}, location)),
            )


def BooksTable(props):
    books = props['books']
    setSortKey = props['setSortKey']

    def bookToRow(book):
        return el(BookRowVu, {'key': book['ID'], 'book': book})

    def BookRows():
        if len(books) > 0:
            return [bookToRow(book) for book in books if book]
        else:
            return el(TableRow, {'key': '0'})
```

```
    def HeaderSort(props_):
        field = props_['field']

        def handleSort(event):
            event.preventDefault()
            setSortKey(field)

        return el(TableCell, None,
                el(Link, {'href': '#', 'onClick': handleSort}, field)
                )

    return el(TableContainer, {'style': {'maxHeight': '30rem'}},
            el(Table, None,
                el(TableHead, None,
                    el(TableRow, None,
                        el(HeaderSort, {'field': 'Title'}),
                        el(HeaderSort, {'field': 'Author'}),
                        el(HeaderSort, {'field': 'Genre'}),
                        el(HeaderSort, {'field': 'Category'}),
                        el(HeaderSort, {'field': 'Format'}),
                        el(HeaderSort, {'field': 'Location'}),
                        ),
                    ),
                el(TableBody, None,
                    el(BookRows, None)
                    )
                )
            )
```

This module contains two components: the main BooksTable component that includes the table header, and a second BookRowVu component representing the view for one row in the table.

The BooksTable component expects two props to be passed in: the list of books to display, and a function for setting the sortKey state variable in the main view component. This component uses the Material-UI Table component, starting with the static TableHeader section, and then dynamically adds Rows to the TableBody. It has an inner function component BookRows, that will either iterate through the list of book records generating a BookRowVu for each book in the list, or if the list is empty, will return a placeholder Row to maintain the structure of the UI if there are no records to display.

Since we want the header column to be clickable to sort the table, we create an inner

HeaderSort component that incorporates the function that updates the sortKey state variable using the function that was passed in as a prop. Each header is contained in a TableCell component. This component uses closure to include a function that has the sort value embedded in the function itself that is unique for each column header.

That leads us to the second component in the module, the BookRowVu component. When the BooksTable component iterates through the list of books via BookRows, it adds a new BookRowVu component for every book record, passing in a single book record as a prop. The BookRowVu component assembles a list of TableCells based on the fields in a single book record, and returns a single TableRow.

In the setup for this component, we turn the book's IsFiction boolean value into a corresponding string by using a Python ternary statement so that we actually display a word instead of just the stored numeric representation of the value.

For demonstration purposes, in the code for the *title* TableCell, we changed the attributes of the Box component so that it will cut off any excess text of a long string and show an ellipsis at the end if it does get cut off. This behavior is achieved using a combination of the standard CSS attributes textOverflow, overflow, and whiteSpace. Then, to be able to see the full text string, we wrapped the Box component in a Tooltip component that will display the full string when the mouse hovers over it.

32.4 View Control

Adding another view requires us to think about how we switch between views. In this case, we only have the landing page and the new book list that we are creating. Thinking about this in a simplistic way, we generally want to show the landing page unless the book list view is being shown. This is essentially the same behavior our modal view used in the last chapter with the isOpen prop of the Modal component.

So let's mimic that behavior by adding a booksShow prop to the landing page in **app.py**:

Listing 32-5 File: *app.py*

```python
from common.pyreact import render, useState, createElement as el, ReactGA
from common.pymui import ThemeProvider, Paper, Typography, Container, Link
from common.jsutils import setTitle
from main.appTheme import theme, Flexbox, FlexboxCenter
from main.aboutModal import About
from main.appData import appname, gaid
from views.bookList.bookListView import BookList

ReactGA.initialize(gaid, {'titleCase': False, 'debug': False,
                    'gaOptions': {'siteSpeedSampleRate': 100}}
                )


def App(props):
    setTitle(props['title'])

    aboutShow, setAboutShow = useState(False)
    booksShow, setBooksShow = useState(False)

    def handleClickAbout(event):
        event.preventDefault()
        setAboutShow(True)

    return el(ThemeProvider, {'theme': theme},
            el(Container, None,
                el(Paper, {'style': {'padding': '1rem'}},
                    el(Flexbox, {'alignItems': 'center'},
                        el(Typography, {'variant': 'h5'}, appname)
                    )
                ),
                el(Paper, {'style': {'padding': '0.5rem',
                                    'marginTop': '1rem'}
                            },
                    el(FlexboxCenter, None,
                        el(Link, {'href': '#',
                                    'variant': 'h5',
                                    'onClick': lambda: setBooksShow(True)
                                }, "Books")
                    ),
                    el(FlexboxCenter, None,
                        el(Link, {'href': '#', 'variant': 'h5',
                                    'onClick': handleClickAbout
                                }, "About")
                    ),
```

```
                el(FlexboxCenter, None,
                    el(Link, {'href': '#', 'variant': 'h5'}, "Login")
                )
            ),
            el(About, {'onClose': lambda: setAboutShow(False),
                       'modalState': aboutShow}
            ),
        ) if not booksShow else None,
        el(BookList, {'setBooksShow': setBooksShow}
        ) if booksShow else None,
    )

render(App, {'title': "Books"}, 'root')
```

This is the same landing page we previously built up in the main App component. The main difference is that we added another state variable booksShow to keep track of if the BookList component should be shown or not. We then use the booksShow state variable in ternary statements at the end of the element tree code to determine if the landing page element tree should be used, or if we should show the BookList component instead.

At the top of the module, we import the BookList component itself, and also initialize the Google Analytics feature since we are using that whenever we make a call to the back-end REST API now. The account ID for Google Analytics is imported from the **appData.py** module where we had previously added it.

To test what we did in this chapter, if it is not already running, we again start the development proxy server with:

(venv) $ `npm run dev`

Then, as long as the Flask application is already running on port 8000, we can test our client application with:

http://localhost:8080

Title	Author	Genre	Category	Format	Location
I Robot	Isaac Asimov	Fiction	Sci-Fi & Fantasy	Paperback	
React to Python	Sheehan	Non-Fiction	Computers & Tech		A3
The C Programming La...	Kernighan & Ritchie	Non-Fiction	Computers & Tech		

By using the proxy server to serve up our application, we are able to both open the front-end client, and also allow the application to fetch any needed data from the back-end Flask server.

With the new bookList view added, our **client/** folders and files now look like this:

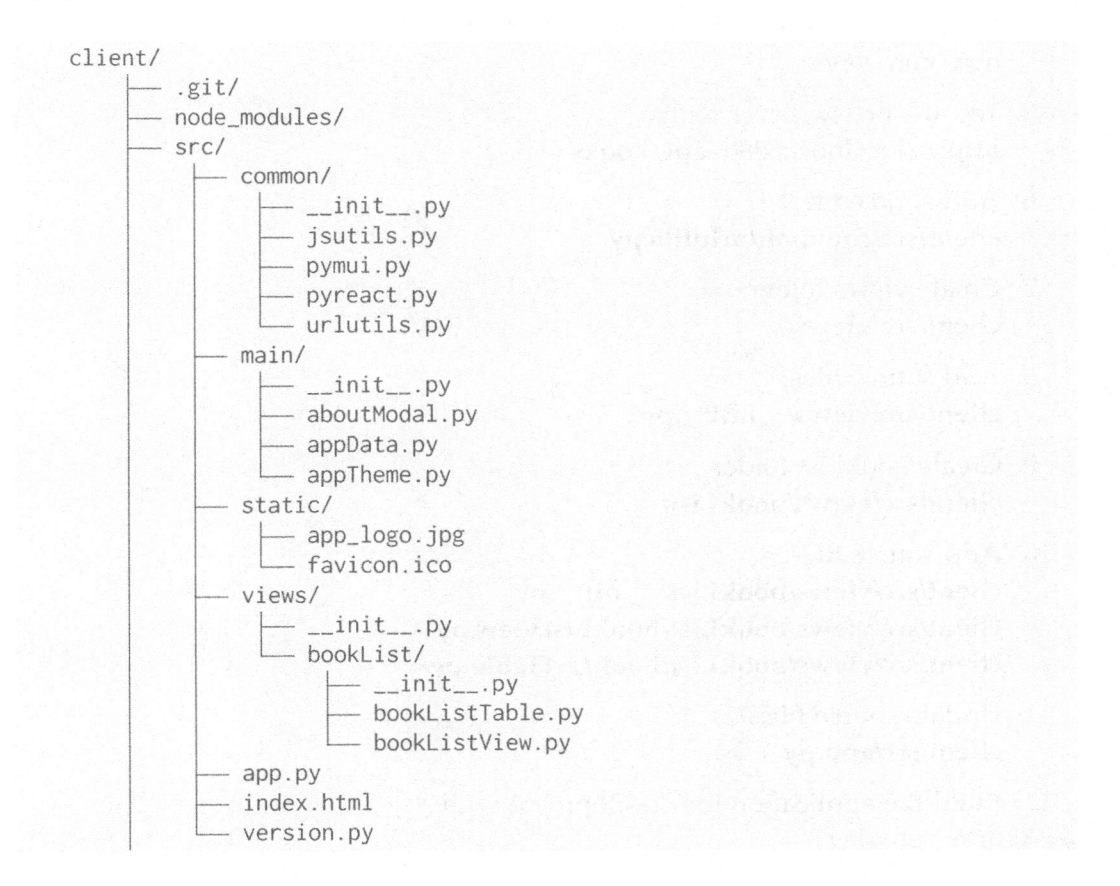

```
client/
    ├── .git/
    ├── node_modules/
    ├── src/
        ├── common/
            ├── __init__.py
            ├── jsutils.py
            ├── pymui.py
            ├── pyreact.py
            └── urlutils.py
        ├── main/
            ├── __init__.py
            ├── aboutModal.py
            ├── appData.py
            └── appTheme.py
        ├── static/
            ├── app_logo.jpg
            └── favicon.ico
        ├── views/
            ├── __init__.py
            └── bookList/
                ├── __init__.py
                ├── bookListTable.py
                └── bookListView.py
        ├── app.py
        ├── index.html
        └── version.py
```

```
├── venv/
└── package.json
```

Chapter Review:

1. Deactivate the **bookapp/server/** virtual environment:
   `deactivate`

2. Switch to the **bookapp/client/** folder and activate the virtual environment:
   `venv\Scripts\activate` (Windows)
   `source venv/bin/activate` (Mac/Linux)

3. Add proxy server source file:
   client/dev-server.js

4. Build the application for development with:
   `npm run dev`

5. Test the proxy server with:
   http://localhost:8080/api/books

6. Add source file:
   client/src/common/urlutils.py

7. Create views folder:
   client/src/views/

8. Add source files:
   client/src/views/__init__.py

9. Create bookList folder:
   client/src/views/bookList/

10. Add source files:
    client/src/views/bookList/__init__.py
    client/src/views/bookList/bookListView.py
    client/src/views/bookList/bookListTable.py

11. Update source file:
    client/src/app.py

12. Build the application for development with:
    `npm run dev`

13. Open the application:
    http://localhost:8080

14. Add and commit files to git (from the **src/client/** folder):
    ```
    git add .
    git commit -m "Books"
    ```

15. Update version:
    ```
    npm version patch
    ```

References:

- Chapter code
  https://github.com/rtp-book/project/tree/step05

- Material-UI CircularProgress Component
  https://material-ui.com/components/progress/

- Material-UI Table Component
  https://material-ui.com/components/tables/

Chapter 33 – Menus

Menus are a clean way of giving the user several navigation options in an application without cluttering up the user interface too much. As you might expect, Material-UI has us covered in that department.

Looking at the structure of our application, we currently have two main views: the landing page, and the book list. Since we only need to show one of these at a time, and they are independent of one another, we should separate them out further and not have them stuck in the same element tree as we have now in our current **app.py** module.

33.1 Landing Page Revisited

The BookList component that shows us all of the books in the database is already self-contained, but let's do the same for the landing page and make that self-contained as well, separating it from the **app.py** application entrance point. This will allow us to load either the book list or the landing page independent of one another.

Start by making another folder under **src/views/** called **landingPage/**, then add an empty **__init__.py** file to indicate to Python that this is a package. The first step is to move the landing page elements that we currently have in the **app.py** module into its own module, which we will create in the **src/views/landingPage/** folder:

Listing 33-1 File: *landingPageView.py*

```
from common.pyreact import useState, createElement as el
from common.pymui import Container, Paper, Typography
from common.pymui import IconButton, MenuIcon, Link
from main.appTheme import Flexbox, FlexboxCenter
from main.aboutModal import About
from main.appData import appname
from views.landingPage.landingPageMenu import LandingPageMenu


def LandingPage(props):
    setBooksShow = props['setBooksShow']

    mainMenu, setMainMenu = useState(None)
```

```python
    aboutShow, setAboutShow = useState(False)

    def mainMenuOpen(event):
        setMainMenu(event['currentTarget'])

    def mainMenuClose():
        setMainMenu(None)

    def aboutModalOpen():
        setAboutShow(True)

    return el(Container, {'maxWidth': 'md'},
            el(Paper, {'style': {'padding': '1rem'}},
                el(Flexbox, {'alignItems': 'center'},
                    el(IconButton, {'edge': 'start',
                                    'color': 'inherit',
                                    'onClick': mainMenuOpen
                                }, el(MenuIcon, None)
                    ),
                    el(Typography, {'variant': 'h5'}, appname)
                )
            ),
            el(LandingPageMenu, {'mainMenu': mainMenu,
                                'mainMenuClose': mainMenuClose,
                                'aboutModalOpen': aboutModalOpen}
            ),
            el(Paper, {'style': {'padding': '0.5rem',
                                'marginTop': '1rem'}
                    },
                el(FlexboxCenter, None,
                    el(Typography, {'variant': 'h5'},
                        el(Link, {'href': '#',
                                'variant': 'h5',
                                'onClick': lambda: setBooksShow(True)
                            }, "Books")
                    ),
                ),
                el(FlexboxCenter, None,
                    el(Typography, {'variant': 'h5'},
                        el(Link, {'href': '#'}, "Login")
                    )
                ),
            ),
            el(About, {'onClose': lambda: setAboutShow(False),
                    'modalState': aboutShow}
```

```
        )
    )
```

We will leave the logic for deciding which view to show in the **app.py** module, but we need to be able to control it from the landing page. To accomplish this, we still maintain the state that determines which view to show in the main App component, and pass in the function `setBooksShow` as a prop to the `LandingPage` component that we can use to set it.

The significant new feature we added here is the "hamburger" menu (called that because it looks sort of like the layers of a hamburger) that we added to the left side of our landing page title bar. Because there is a lot of functionality tied into the menu as a whole, we decomposed that part into a separate `LandingPageMenu` component, which we put into another Python module located in the **src/views/landingPage/** folder:

Listing 33-2 File: *landingPageMenu.py*

```
from common.pyreact import useState, createElement as el, Fragment
from common.pymui import Menu, MenuItem

lookup_tables = ['Categories', 'Publishers', 'Conditions', 'Formats']


def LandingPageMenu(props):
    mainMenu = props['mainMenu']
    mainMenuClose = props['mainMenuClose']
    aboutModalOpen = props['aboutModalOpen']

    lookupMenu, setLookupMenu = useState(None)

    def lookupMenuOpen(event):
        setLookupMenu(event['currentTarget'])

    def lookupMenuClose():
        setLookupMenu(None)
        mainMenuClose()

    def handleLookup(event):
        value = event['currentTarget']['textContent']
        lookupMenuClose()
        print("Lookup Table:", value)
```

```python
    def handleAbout():
        mainMenuClose()
        aboutModalOpen()

    def handleLogout():
        mainMenuClose()
        print("Logout")

    return el(Fragment, None,
            el(Menu, {'id': 'main-menu',
                      'anchorEl': mainMenu,
                      'keepMounted': True,
                      'open': bool(mainMenu),
                      'onClose': mainMenuClose,
                     },
                el(MenuItem, {'onClick': lookupMenuOpen}, "Lookup Tables"),
                el(MenuItem, {'onClick': handleAbout}, "About"),
                el(MenuItem, {'onClick': handleLogout,
                              'disabled': True}, "Logout"),
            ),
            el(Menu, {'id': 'lookup-menu',
                      'anchorEl': lookupMenu,
                      'keepMounted': True,
                      'open': bool(lookupMenu),
                      'onClose': lookupMenuClose,
                      'transformOrigin': {'vertical': 'top',
                                          'horizontal': 'center'},
                     },
                [el(MenuItem, {'key': table,
                               'onClick': handleLookup
                              }, table) for table in lookup_tables
                ],
            )
        )
```

The LandingPageMenu component expects three props to be passed into it: the anchor point for the main menu, a function to close the main menu, and a function to open the About modal view. As with most of these types of functions, all they need to do is set the value of a state variable, and React handles the re-rendering of the user interface for you.

Since the sub-menu that handles showing the lookup tables is contained within this component, we created a new state variable lookupMenu that determines where and if that menu should be shown. If we set it to a DOM element to be used as an anchor point, the lookup menu will be visible. And if we set it to None, it will be hidden.

Every menu item has an onClick event handler assigned to it that determines what action to take when it is selected. Generally speaking, when a menu item is clicked, whether it is on the main menu or a sub-menu, in addition to performing whatever action is required by it, we also then close any open menus afterward. So if a menu item on the lookup menu is clicked, the event handler for the item will perform the specified action, and then also set both the lookupMenu state variable and the mainMenu state variable to None. This causes both the main menu and lookup menu to close when we set the value of the open property of the menus. Since anything not None will evaluate to True, and None evaluates to False, we indirectly control the visibility of the menus using the element anchor point value instead of creating an additional state variable just to indicate visibility.

This Material-UI Menu component uses MenuItem components as child elements to form the items in each menu. One of the key properties of the Menu component is anchorEl that identifies the anchor element in the DOM tree to attach the menu to. Any positional properties that are set, like transformOrigin that we use on the nested lookup menu, are relative to this anchor point.

For the lookup menu, we provide a list of table names that we iterate through to produce a new MenuItem component for each table in the list. For now, we are just printing the table name in the console as a placeholder for the menu action, but we will come back to this later on once we have an actual lookup table view that we can show.

For the *Logout* MenuItem component, we are using the disabled property to make it unselectable in the main menu. Later on, we will use the login state to determine whether this menu item should be enabled or not (since you can't log out if you're not logged in).

The logic for the About modal view stays the same as what we had before, but instead of using a Link component to show it, we have moved it to our menu instead.

You'll notice that because our LandingPageMenu component returns several top-level elements instead of just one, we wrapped them in a React Fragment component to return a single mount point for the element tree being returned without having to add any additional element nesting (by wrapping them in an HTML div for example).

33.2 View Routing

Now that we have both the landing page and book list as independent components, we still have to determine which one to show at any given time. We will continue to do that in the **app.py** module:

Listing 33-3 File: *app.py*

```
from common.pyreact import render, useState, createElement as el, ReactGA
from common.pymui import ThemeProvider
from common.jsutils import setTitle
from main.appTheme import theme
from main.appData import gaid
from views.bookList.bookListView import BookList
from views.landingPage.landingPageView import LandingPage


ReactGA.initialize(gaid, {'titleCase': False, 'debug': False,
                    'gaOptions': {'siteSpeedSampleRate': 100}}
                   )

def App(props):
    setTitle(props['title'])

    booksShow, setBooksShow = useState(False)

    pathname = '/books' if booksShow else '/'

    router = {
        '/': LandingPage,
        '/books': BookList,
    }

    return el(ThemeProvider, {'theme': theme},
              el(router[pathname], {'setBooksShow': setBooksShow})
              )


render(App, {'title': "Books"}, 'root')
```

Since the value of the booksShow state variable determines whether we show the LandingPage component or the BookList component, we can use that to assign a pseudo URL path that can be used for view routing that gives us a bit of context to a given route. With that, we can route as we do in Flask based on the URL.

If we then create a Python dictionary that uses these routes as keys, and the React component that we want to show as the value, we in effect create a kind of switch statement view routing mechanism that is extensible, allowing us to add additional view component options later on. So to show the desired view, we use the pseudo URL path as a key to look up the appropriate view component in the router dictionary.

Since the App component is effectively the entry point and container of our entire client application, we keep the outer theme-component in place regardless of which view is being shown since that is utilized application-wide. With all that refactoring, we now have a UI with a menu navigation option and componentized views:

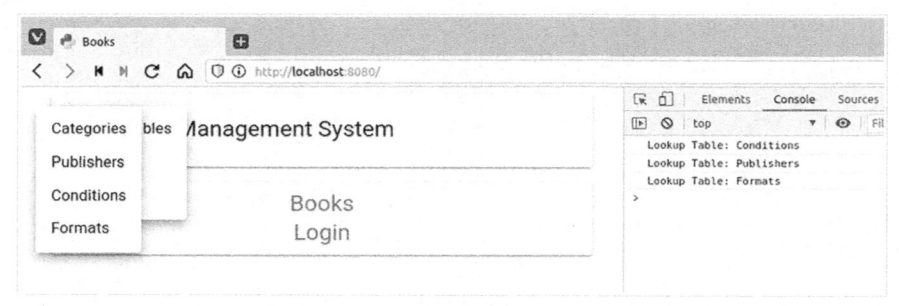

After adding the landingPage view, our **client/** folder structure should now look like this:

```
client/
    ├── .git/
    ├── node_modules/
    ├── src/
            ├── common/
                    ├── __init__.py
                    ├── jsutils.py
                    ├── pymui.py
                    ├── pyreact.py
                    └── urlutils.py
            ├── main/
                    ├── __init__.py
                    ├── aboutModal.py
                    ├── appData.py
                    └── appTheme.py
```

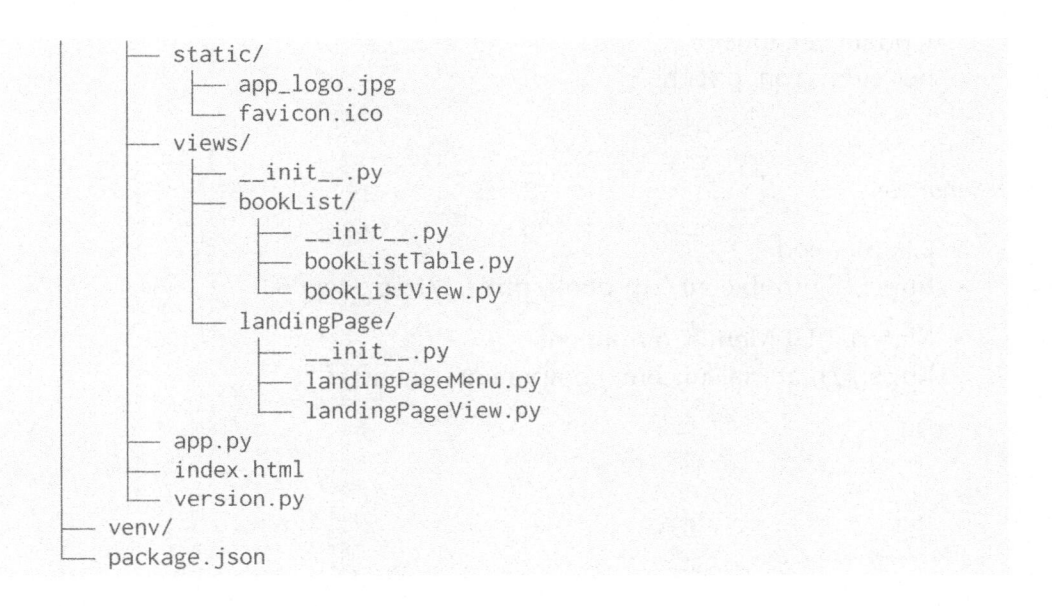

```
        ├── static/
        │   ├── app_logo.jpg
        │   └── favicon.ico
        ├── views/
        │   ├── __init__.py
        │   ├── bookList/
        │   │   ├── __init__.py
        │   │   ├── bookListTable.py
        │   │   └── bookListView.py
        │   └── landingPage/
        │       ├── __init__.py
        │       ├── landingPageMenu.py
        │       └── landingPageView.py
        ├── app.py
        ├── index.html
        └── version.py
    ├── venv/
    └── package.json
```

Chapter Review:

1. Create landingPage folder:
   client/src/views/landingPage/

2. Add source files:
   client/src/views/landingPage/__init__.py
   client/src/views/landingPage/landingPageView.py
   client/src/views/landingPage/landingPageMenu.py

3. Update source file:
   client/src/app.py

4. Build the application for development with:
   npm run dev

5. Open the application:
   http://localhost:8080

6. Add and commit files to git (from the **src/client/** folder):
   git add .
   git commit -m "Menus"

7. Update version:
   `npm version patch`

References:

- Chapter code
  https://github.com/rtp-book/project/tree/step06
- Material-UI Menu Component
  https://material-ui.com/components/menus/

Chapter 34 – User Login

Before we get too much further into our application, let's create a modal view we can use as a login form. Our REST API already supports managing user sessions using the following routes:

- /api/login [POST]
- /api/logout [GET] (login required)
- /api/ping [GET] (login required)
- /api/whoami [GET] (login required)

Once we can establish a user session, we will use that on the client-side to determine whether the user will be allowed to edit data or not, and we will update the user interface accordingly.

Just a warning that this is one of the more involved chapters of the book because of how many places the session management touches. Fortunately, most of it is boilerplate code that, once you have it working, can be reused on other projects.

34.1 Snackbar

One feature we can add to give the user better feedback, is a small tab that pops up briefly to provide the user with information about what your application is doing. This UI treatment is called a snackbar (or sometimes called a toast), and we can use a pre-built component that performs this task. We will use it in this chapter to indicate whether or not the login was successful.

To use the snackbar feature, we will need to add a JavaScript library that implements it. To do that, from the terminal window run this npm command:

```
(venv) $ npm install notistack
```

This will download the notistack library to the **node_modules/** folder and save the requirement to the **package.json** file.

Since it is a UI feature, we can add the mapping for the notistack library to the end of the existing **pymui.py** module in the **src/common/** folder:

Listing 34-1 File: *pymui.py*

```python
# __pragma__ ('skip')
from common import require
# __pragma__ ('noskip')


# Icons
MenuIcon  = require('@material-ui/icons/Menu')['default']
CloseIcon = require('@material-ui/icons/Close')['default']
AddIcon   = require('@material-ui/icons/AddCircle')['default']

...

# Theming
ThemeProvider  = require('@material-ui/styles/ThemeProvider')['default']
createMuiTheme = require('@material-ui/core/styles/createMuiTheme')['default']
useTheme       = require('@material-ui/styles/useTheme')['default']
styled         = require('@material-ui/styles/styled')['default']
makeStyles     = require('@material-ui/styles/makeStyles')['default']
colors         = require('@material-ui/core/colors')


# notistack
notistack = require('notistack')

SnackbarProvider = notistack.SnackbarProvider
useSnackbar      = notistack.useSnackbar
```

Here we add the notistack `require` statement to import the library into the namespace, and then add two Python-to-JavaScript mappings that we will use later in our Python modules. This component works in a way similar to a React context variable in that the `SnackbarProvider` component is added to the component tree near the top, and then the `useSnackbar()` function is used to obtain a reference to it where it is needed. We'll see this in action in just a bit.

34.2 Session User

The actual calls to the REST API that facilitate logging in are handled in the App component. We can modify that existing module like this:

React to Python

Listing 34-2 File: *app.py*

```python
from common.pyreact import render, createElement as el, ReactGA
from common.pyreact import useState, useEffect
from common.pymui import ThemeProvider, SnackbarProvider
from common.jsutils import setTitle, console
from common.urlutils import fetch
from main.appTheme import theme
from main.appData import gaid
from views.bookList.bookListView import BookList
from views.landingPage.landingPageView import LandingPage


ReactGA.initialize(gaid, {'titleCase': False, 'debug': False,
                         'gaOptions': {'siteSpeedSampleRate': 100}}
                  )


def App(props):
    user, setUser = useState("")

    setTitle(props['title'])

    booksShow, setBooksShow = useState(False)

    pathname = '/books' if booksShow else '/'

    router = {
        '/': LandingPage,
        '/books': BookList,
    }

    isLoggedIn = len(user) > 0

    def login(username):
        setUser(username)

    def logout():
        setUser("")
        fetch('/api/logout')

    def validateSession():
        def validated():
            def _setuser(data):
                login(data['user'])
```

```python
            if not isLoggedIn:
                fetch('/api/whoami', _setuser,
                    onError=console.error,
                    redirect=False
                )

        def notValidated(error):
            if len(user) > 0:
                setUser("")

        fetch('/api/ping', validated, onError=notValidated, redirect=False)

    useEffect(validateSession, [])

    return el(ThemeProvider, {'theme': theme},
            el(SnackbarProvider, {'maxSnack': 3},
                el(router[pathname], {'setBooksShow': setBooksShow,
                                    'login': login,
                                    'logout': logout,
                                    'isLoggedIn': isLoggedIn
                                    }
                )
            )
        )

render(App, {'title': "Books"}, 'root')
```

We start by adding a state variable called user to store the name of the user that is logged in. If there is no current login session, then the user state variable is set to an empty string.

After that, we have three simple helper functions. The isLoggedIn() function is just a boolean indicating if there is a stored user name. The login() function is really just an alias for the setUser() state function. And lastly, the logout() function resets the user state variable back to an empty string and makes a call to the back-end server to invalidate the session.

When the application loads for the first time or is reloaded by the user, we don't want to have the user need to re-login if they already have a valid session established with the back-end server. So one of the first things we do when the application loads, is to call our validateSession() function via a React useEffect() hook function. Since we are passing it an empty watch list, it will be called just once, right after the App component is loaded.

What the `validateSession()` function will do, is send a small request to the back-end server. If the response is an HTTP 401 *Unauthorized* code, then we know there is no currently established session because of the way the Flask `/api/ping` route is set up in our REST server. On the other hand, if the response is an HTTP 200 *OK* code, then we do have a valid session. In that case, we send another request using the `/api/whoami` route to obtain the username that is tied to the current session. Once we receive that back, we take that information and set the `user` state variable in the App component.

Finally, we get to the return value of the App component. In addition to passing the `isLoggedIn()`, `login()`, and `logout()` functions as props down the component tree, we also inject the functionality of the snackbar feature into the component tree by nesting the `SnackbarProvider` component. This works in the same way our `ThemeProvider` does, in that it will allow us to access the functionality in any component further down the tree. The `maxSnack` property we pass into the `SnackbarProvider` component indicates the maximum number of stacked snackbars to show at any time, which in this case is three.

34.3 Login Modal

In order to log in, we will need a place to enter the username and password. For that, we'll create a simple modal view that has two text boxes and a submit button. You can put this module in the **src/main/** folder:

Listing 34-3 File: *loginModal.py*

```python
from common.pyreact import createElement as el, Modal
from common.pymui import Box, Paper, TextField, Button, Typography
from common.pymui import IconButton, CloseIcon
from main.appData import appname
from main.appTheme import Flexbox, FlexboxCenter, modalStyles


def Login(props):
    onClose = props['onClose']
    onLogin = props['onLogin']
    username = props['username']
    password = props['password']
    setUsername = props['setUsername']
```

```python
    setPassword = props['setPassword']
    modalState = props['modalState']

    def login(event):
        event.preventDefault()
        onLogin()

    def handleUsernameChange(event):
        target = event['target']
        setUsername(target['value'])

    def handlePasswordChange(event):
        target = event['target']
        setPassword(target['value'])

    return el(Modal, {'isOpen': modalState,
                      'onRequestClose': onClose,
                      'style': modalStyles,
                      'ariaHideApp': False,
                     },
            el(FlexboxCenter, {'maxWidth': '300px'},
              el(Box, None,
                el(Flexbox, {'justifyContent': 'space-between',
                             'alignItems': 'center'},
                  el(Typography, {'variant': 'h6',
                                  'width': '40%',
                                  'color': 'primary'}, appname),
                  el(IconButton, {'edge': 'end',
                                  'color': 'primary',
                                  'onClick': onClose}, el(CloseIcon, None))
                ),
                el(Paper, {'elevation': 2, 'style': {'padding': '1rem'}},
                  el('form', {'onSubmit': login},
                    el(TextField, {'label': 'Login Name',
                                   'variant': 'outlined',
                                   'fullWidth': True,
                                   'value': username,
                                   'onChange': handleUsernameChange,
                                   'autoFocus': True
                                  }
                    ),
                    el(TextField, {'label': 'Password',
                                   'variant': 'outlined',
                                   'fullWidth': True,
                                   'type': 'password',
```

```
                            'value': password,
                            'onChange': handlePasswordChange
                        }
                ),
                el(Button, {'type': 'submit',
                            'fullWidth': True,
                            'style': {'minWidth': '10rem',
                                      'marginRight': '1rem',
                                      'marginTop': '1rem'},
                        }, "Login"
                ),
            )
        )
    )
)
```

This view is set up as an HTML form with two input boxes and a submit button. Any state that it requires is passed in as props from its parent component, which in this case will be the LandingPage component. It does not maintain any state of its own.

That said, it does take several props, starting with an onClose function to hide the modal view, and a doLogin function for processing the values that were entered. The username and password props and their corresponding update functions work in conjunction with the two TextField components. Then lastly, there is the modalState prop that the Modal component uses to show or hide the modal Login view.

Other than a few functions for handling the state update of the username and password text boxes, most of the heavy lifting for handling the login will be dealt with by the onLogin() function that is passed in as a prop.

34.4 Login Functionality

Next up, we need to refactor the existing LandingPage component in **src/views/landingPage/** to add the state variables required by the Login component, provide a DOM attachment point for the Login component, and define the required login functionality:

Listing 34-4 File: *landingPageView.py*

```python
from common.pyreact import useState, createElement as el, useEffect
from common.pymui import Container, Paper, Typography, useSnackbar
from common.pymui import IconButton, MenuIcon, Link
from common.urlutils import fetch
from main.appTheme import Flexbox, FlexboxCenter
from main.aboutModal import About
from main.appData import appname
from main.loginModal import Login
from views.landingPage.landingPageMenu import LandingPageMenu


def LandingPage(props):
    setBooksShow = props['setBooksShow']
    login = props['login']
    logout = props['logout']
    isLoggedIn = props['isLoggedIn']

    mainMenu, setMainMenu = useState(None)
    aboutShow, setAboutShow = useState(False)
    loginModal, setLoginModal = useState(False)
    username, setUsername = useState("")
    password, setPassword = useState("")

    snack = useSnackbar()

    def doLogin():
        def _login():
            login(username)
            snack.enqueueSnackbar("Login succeeded!", {'variant': 'success'})

        def _loginFailed():
            setLoginModal(True)
            snack.enqueueSnackbar("Login failed, please try again",
                        {'variant': 'error'}
            )

        fetch("/api/login", _login,
            data={'username': username, 'password': password},
            method='POST',
            onError=_loginFailed
            )
```

```python
        setLoginModal(False)

    def clearUser():
        if loginModal:
            setUsername("")
            setPassword("")

    def mainMenuOpen(event):
        setMainMenu(event['currentTarget'])

    def mainMenuClose():
        setMainMenu(None)

    def aboutModalOpen():
        setAboutShow(True)

    useEffect(clearUser, [loginModal])

    return el(Container, {'maxWidth': 'md'},
            el(Paper, {'style': {'padding': '1rem'}},
                el(Flexbox, {'alignItems': 'center'},
                    el(IconButton, {'edge': 'start',
                                    'color': 'inherit',
                                    'onClick': mainMenuOpen
                                   }, el(MenuIcon, None)
                    ),
                    el(Typography, {'variant': 'h5'}, appname)
                  )
            ),
            el(LandingPageMenu, {'mainMenu': mainMenu,
                                 'mainMenuClose': mainMenuClose,
                                 'aboutModalOpen': aboutModalOpen,
                                 'logout': logout,
                                 'isLoggedIn': isLoggedIn}
            ),
            el(Paper, {'style': {'padding': '0.5rem',
                                 'marginTop': '1rem'}
                      },
                el(FlexboxCenter, None,
                    el(Typography, {'variant': 'h5'},
                        el(Link, {'href': '#',
                                  'variant': 'h5',
                                  'onClick': lambda: setBooksShow(True)
                                 }, "Books")
                    ),
```

```
            ),
        el(FlexboxCenter, None,
            el(Typography, {'variant': 'h5'},
                el(Link, {'href': '#',
                          'onClick': lambda: setLoginModal(True)
                         }, "Login")
               ) if not isLoggedIn else None
            ),
        ),
        el(Login, {'onClose': lambda: setLoginModal(False),
                   'onLogin': doLogin,
                   'password': password,
                   'username': username,
                   'setUsername': lambda usr: setUsername(usr),
                   'setPassword': lambda pwd: setPassword(pwd),
                   'modalState': loginModal,
                  }
          ),
        el(About, {'onClose': lambda: setAboutShow(False),
                   'modalState': aboutShow}
          )
    )
```

We start by destructuring the three additional props related to logging in that we passed in from the main App component, storing them in local variables. Then we add three state variables: `loginModal` to keep track of whether the login form should be shown or not, and `username` and `password` to hold the values that are entered into the login form.

To utilize the snackbar feature that we added earlier, we get a reference to it with this line:

```
snack = useSnackbar()
```

This is a hook function that pulls a reference from the `SnackbarProvider` we injected into the component tree in the App component.

The `doLogin()` function is the cornerstone of this section and is what actually performs the login process. It first makes a call to the `/api/login` route of the rest API, passing it the `username` and `password` collected from the login form in the body of an HTTP POST request. It then immediately sets the modal state of the Login component to `False` so that it is no longer shown.

If the response from the REST server is successful, it calls the `login()` function that was passed in from the main `App` component to set the `user` state variable there. It then also triggers a snackbar to be shown indicating the successful login:

```
snack.enqueueSnackbar("Login succeeded!", {'variant': 'success'})
```

However, if the response returned from the REST server is indicated as being unauthorized, the modal state for the `Login` component is set back to `True` to show the login form again, and a snackbar is triggered to show the failed status.

Whenever the `Login` component is going to be shown, for security purposes, we reset the `username` and `password` displayed on the login form back to empty strings. The `clearUser()` function is called on any change to the `loginModal` state variable via the React `useEffect()` hook function.

To open the login form, we set the value of the `loginModal` state variable in the `onClick` event of the Login `Link` element. Once there is a valid session and the user is logged in, we hide that login link based on the login state so that it isn't triggered unnecessarily.

Finally, we add the modal `Login` component to the element tree in the same way we did for the `About` modal component earlier.

One last detail we need to take care of is the logout menu item in the `LandingPageMenu` component. We want it to be enabled anytime the user is logged in and disabled when they are not. This modification is on the existing **landingPageMenu.py** module in the **src/views/landingPage/** folder:

Listing 34-5 File: *landingPageMenu.py*

```
from common.pyreact import useState, createElement as el, Fragment
from common.pymui import Menu, MenuItem

lookup_tables = ['Categories', 'Publishers', 'Conditions', 'Formats']


def LandingPageMenu(props):
    mainMenu = props['mainMenu']
    mainMenuClose = props['mainMenuClose']
    aboutModalOpen = props['aboutModalOpen']
    logout = props['logout']
    isLoggedIn = props['isLoggedIn']
```

```python
lookupMenu, setLookupMenu = useState(None)

def lookupMenuOpen(event):
    setLookupMenu(event['currentTarget'])

def lookupMenuClose():
    setLookupMenu(None)
    mainMenuClose()

def handleLookup(event):
    value = event['currentTarget']['textContent']
    lookupMenuClose()
    print("Lookup Table:", value)

def handleAbout():
    mainMenuClose()
    aboutModalOpen()

def handleLogout():
    mainMenuClose()
    logout()

return el(Fragment, None,
        el(Menu, {'id': 'main-menu',
                  'anchorEl': mainMenu,
                  'keepMounted': True,
                  'open': bool(mainMenu),
                  'onClose': mainMenuClose,
                 },
            el(MenuItem, {'onClick': lookupMenuOpen}, "Lookup Tables"),
            el(MenuItem, {'onClick': handleAbout}, "About"),
            el(MenuItem, {'onClick': handleLogout,
                          'disabled': not isLoggedIn}, "Logout"),
        ),
        el(Menu, {'id': 'lookup-menu',
                  'anchorEl': lookupMenu,
                  'keepMounted': True,
                  'open': bool(lookupMenu),
                  'onClose': lookupMenuClose,
                  'transformOrigin': {'vertical': 'top',
                                      'horizontal': 'center'},
                 },
            [el(MenuItem, {'key': table,
                           'onClick': handleLookup
```

```
                }, table) for table in lookup_tables
        ],
    )
)
```

For the logout menu item to work, we need two more props to be passed in, an indicator of whether the user is logged in or not, and the function to actually do the logout. We call the `logout()` function when the user clicks the logout menu item obviously, and then use the `isLoggedIn` prop to determine whether or not the logout menu item should be disabled or not.

Now when the *Login* link is clicked, the `Login` modal form will be shown and we will be able to establish a client session:

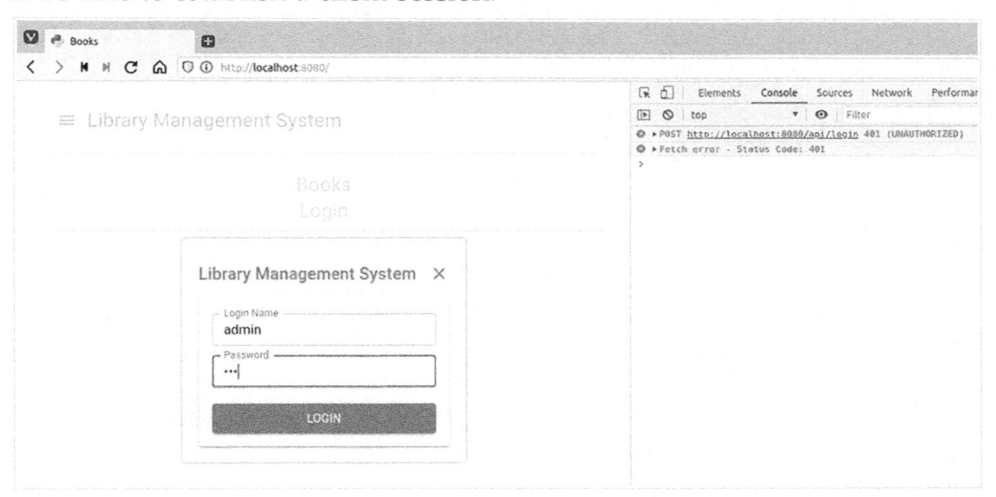

And again for your reference, here is our current file and folder structure for the client application:

```
client/
    ├── .git/
    ├── node_modules/
    ├── src/
    │   ├── common/
    │   │   ├── __init__.py
    │   │   ├── jsutils.py
    │   │   ├── pymui.py
    │   │   ├── pyreact.py
    │   │   └── urlutils.py
```

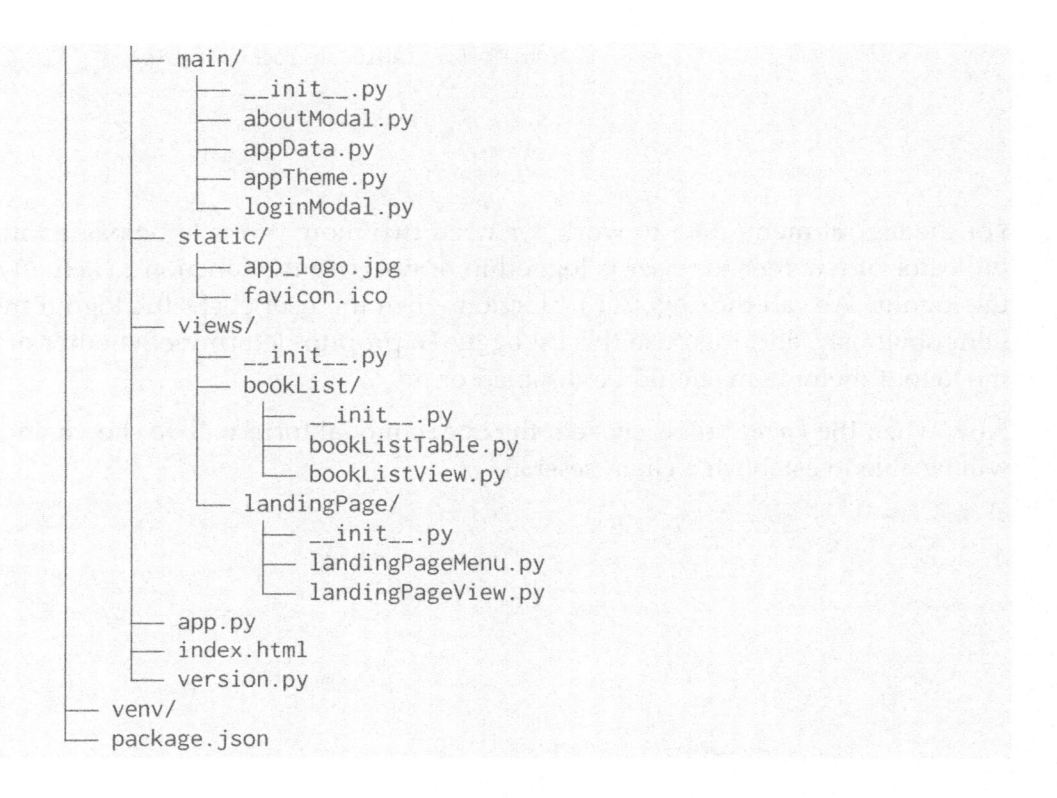

```
            ├── main/
            │   ├── __init__.py
            │   ├── aboutModal.py
            │   ├── appData.py
            │   ├── appTheme.py
            │   └── loginModal.py
            ├── static/
            │   ├── app_logo.jpg
            │   └── favicon.ico
            ├── views/
            │   ├── __init__.py
            │   ├── bookList/
            │   │   ├── __init__.py
            │   │   ├── bookListTable.py
            │   │   └── bookListView.py
            │   └── landingPage/
            │       ├── __init__.py
            │       ├── landingPageMenu.py
            │       └── landingPageView.py
            ├── app.py
            ├── index.html
            └── version.py
    ├── venv/
    └── package.json
```

Chapter Review:

1. Install Snackbar package:
   npm install notistack

2. Update source files:
   client/src/common/pymui.py
   client/src/app.py

3. Add source file:
   client/src/main/loginModal.py

4. Update source files:
   client/src/views/landingPage/landingPageView.py
   client/src/views/landingPage/landingPageMenu.py

5. Build the application for development with:
   npm run dev

6. Open the application:
   http://localhost:8080

7. Add and commit files to git (from the **src/client/** folder):
   ```
   git add .
   git commit -m "User Login"
   ```

8. Update version:
   ```
   npm version patch
   ```

References:

- Chapter code
  https://github.com/rtp-book/project/tree/step07

- Notistack JavaScript Library
  https://www.npmjs.com/package/notistack

Chapter 35 – Lookups

The lookup tables in our SQLite database are used to ensure consistency of the data that is entered in some of the fields in the *Books* table. These end up being foreign keys in the *Books* table, and we can use the records in these tables to populate lists in dropdown select boxes in our UI. So that we can view and eventually edit the data in these database lookup tables, we are going to create a generic view component that can be used for all of the tables rather than creating a view component that is specific to just one of them.

35.1 Container View

The first component we need is a modal view that has a title bar displaying the name of the table we are looking at and a close button. This component will be a container for the list of items in the lookup table as well. For this view, create a new folder under **src/views/** called **lookupTable/**, add an empty **__init__.py** file, then create the **lookupView.py** module:

Listing 35-1 File: *lookupView.py*

```python
from common.pyreact import Modal, useState, useEffect, createElement as el
from common.pymui import Typography, AppBar, Toolbar, Box, Paper
from common.pymui import IconButton, CloseIcon
from common.urlutils import fetch
from main.appTheme import modalStyles
from views.lookupTable.lookupList import ItemsList


lookup_tables = [
    {'name': 'Categories', 'fields': ['Category'], 'sort': 'Category'},
    {'name': 'Publishers', 'fields': ['Publisher'], 'sort': 'Publisher'},
    {'name': 'Conditions', 'fields': ['Code', 'Condition'], 'sort': 'ID}'},
    {'name': 'Formats', 'fields': ['Format'], 'sort': 'Format'}
]


def LookupTable(props):
    onClose = props['onClose']
    table_name = props['table']
```

```python
table_info = next(
    (table for table in lookup_tables if table['name'] == table_name),
    {})
table_fields = table_info['fields']
table_sort = table_info['sort']
modalState = bool(table_name)

items, setItems = useState([])

def getItems():
    def _getItems(data):
        item_list = data if data else []
        if len(item_list) > 0:
            item_list.sort(key=lambda item: item[table_sort])
            setItems(item_list)
        else:
            setItems([])

    if table_name:
        fetch(f"/api/lookup/{table_name}", _getItems)
    else:
        setItems([])

useEffect(getItems, [table_name])

return el(Modal, {'isOpen': modalState,
                  'style': modalStyles,
                  'ariaHideApp': False,
                  },
         el(AppBar, {'position': 'static',
                     'style': {'marginBottom': '0.5rem'}
                     },
            el(Toolbar, {'variant': 'dense'},
               el(Box, {'width': '100%'},
                  el(Typography, {'variant': 'h6'}, f"Table: {table_name}")
                  ),
               el(IconButton, {'edge': 'end',
                               'color': 'inherit',
                               'onClick': onClose
                               }, el(CloseIcon, None)
                  ),
               ),
            ),
         el(Paper, {'style': {'padding': '0.5rem', 'marginTop': '0.8rem'}},
            el(ItemsList, {'items': items,
```

Chapter 35 - Lookups | 293

```
                            'fields': table_fields}
                    )
                )
            )
```

The module-level variable `lookup_tables` is a list of our lookup tales containing the table name, the field names to display, and the field name to sort on for each table.

This module has one component `LookupTable` that takes two props: `onClose` which is the function used for hiding the modal form, and `table_name` which is the name of the table to view. The latter is important since we will be reusing this same component for editing all of our lookup tables.

The `table_info` variable holds the dictionary of values for the specific table we are going to display. We use a Python generator expression to pull the appropriate dictionary out of the `lookup_tables` list by returning the first one where the `name` key matches the `table_name` prop. Once we have that, we can break out the field list and sort field key values into `table_fields` and `table_sort` respectively.

The `modalState` value that indicates if the modal form should be shown, is determined by whether the `table_name` prop is empty or not. And as we did in the last chapter, we will grab a reference to the snackbar component so that we can display information about updates to the lookup table later on.

This component only has one state variable `items`, which stores the list of items from the lookup table.

The function `getItems()` pulls the list of records from the appropriate lookup table and sorts it based on the indicated sort field we previously saved in the `table_sort` local variable. The function is called via `useEffect()` when the modal form is opened, and the `table_name` prop is set to something other than None.

35.2 Table List

To show the list of values in the lookup table modal form, we use a separate component that we put into its own module since it has a bit of complexity on its own. You can put this **lookupList.py** component module in the **src/views/lookupTable/** folder along with the other one we just created:

Listing 35-2 File: *lookupList.py*

```python
from common.pyreact import useState, createElement as el, Fragment
from common.pymui import Box, AddIcon, IconButton
from common.pymui import TableContainer, Table
from common.pymui import TableHead, TableBody, TableRow, TableCell


def ItemCell(props):
    value = props['value']

    return el(TableCell, None,
              el(Box, {'width': '10rem', 'whiteSpace': 'nowrap'}, value)
              )


def ItemRowVu(props):
    item = props['item']
    fields = props['fields']

    return el(TableRow, None,
              [el(ItemCell, {'key': field,
                             'value': item[field],
                             }) for field in fields]
              )


def ItemRows(props):
    items = props['items']
    fields = props['fields']

    def itemToRow(item):
        return el(ItemRowVu, {'key': item['ID'],
                              'item': item,
                              'fields': fields,
                              }
                  )

    if len(items) > 0:
        return el(Fragment, None,
                  [itemToRow(item) for item in items if item]
                  )
    else:
        return el(TableRow, {'key': '0'})
```

```
def ItemsList(props):
    items = props['items']
    fields = props['fields']

    def HeaderCols():
        return el(TableRow, None,
                 [el(TableCell, {'key': field, 'fields': fields}, field)
                   for field in fields]
                 )
    return el(TableContainer, {'style': {'maxHeight': '10.5rem'}},
             el(Table, {'size': 'small', 'stickyHeader': True},
                el(TableHead, None,
                   el(HeaderCols, None),
                   ),
                el(TableBody, None,
                   el(ItemRows, {'items': items,
                                 'fields': fields}
                     )
                   )
                )
             )
```

This module consists of four separate components that build up a table of records. Starting at the bottom, we have the `ItemList` component that consists of the whole table container including the column headers. This component just needs two props passed into it, the list of `fields` to define the columns that are displayed, and the list of `items` in the lookup table. There is an encapsulated component definition `HeaderCols` that loops through the field names to build up the header cells using a Python list comprehension.

In the `TableBody`, we reference the second component in the module `ItemRows`, which returns a React `Fragment` consisting of a list containing all of the records in the lookup table. If there doesn't happen to be any records in the lookup table, we return a single empty `TableRow` just as a placeholder to keep the UI consistent. This component has the same `fields` and `items` props passed through to it from the `ItemList` component. To generate the actual table rows, we use a helper function `itemToRow()` that is called from a list comprehension that loops through each item in the `items` list. The `itemToRow()` function creates a single `ItemRowVu` component each time it is called.

The `ItemRowVu` component takes two props, the lookup `item` to render as a

TableRow, and the list of `fields` contained in the item. Using another Python list comprehension, we loop through the list of fields and add an `ItemCell` component with the item value for each field in the list.

Finally, the `ItemCell` component takes just the `value` of one field of the item as a prop and wraps it in a Material-UI `TableCell` component.

While several of the components we created in this module could actually be combined into one, we decomposed them into smaller chunks to maintain the readability of the code. If this was not done, the nesting of components (and indentation) starts to get pretty deep and more difficult to understand when you are reading through it.

35.3 Menu Control

Now that we have a way of displaying the lookup table data, we need to be able to control the visibility of it. We do that from the existing `landingPage` view by adding a few lines of code to access the functionality of the new `lookupTable` components. Starting with the **landingPageView.py** module in the **src/views/landingPage/** folder, we make several changes:

Listing 35-3 File: *landingPageView.py*

```
from common.pyreact import useState, createElement as el, useEffect
from common.pymui import Container, Paper, Typography, useSnackbar
from common.pymui import IconButton, MenuIcon, Link
from common.urlutils import fetch
from main.appTheme import Flexbox, FlexboxCenter
from main.aboutModal import About
from main.appData import appname
from main.loginModal import Login
from views.landingPage.landingPageMenu import LandingPageMenu
from views.lookupTable.lookupView import LookupTable


def LandingPage(props):
    setBooksShow = props['setBooksShow']
    login = props['login']
    logout = props['logout']
    isLoggedIn = props['isLoggedIn']

    mainMenu, setMainMenu = useState(None)
```

```
    aboutShow, setAboutShow = useState(False)
    lookupModal, setLookupModal = useState(None)
    loginModal, setLoginModal = useState(False)
    username, setUsername = useState("")
    password, setPassword = useState("")

...

    return el(Container, {'maxWidth': 'md'},
            el(Paper, {'style': {'padding': '1rem'}},
                el(Flexbox, {'alignItems': 'center'},
                    el(IconButton, {'edge': 'start',
                                    'color': 'inherit',
                                    'onClick': mainMenuOpen
                                   }, el(MenuIcon, None)
                    ),
                    el(Typography, {'variant': 'h5'}, appname)
                )
            ),
            el(LandingPageMenu, {'mainMenu': mainMenu,
                                 'mainMenuClose': mainMenuClose,
                                 'setLookupModal':
                                        lambda tbl: setLookupModal(tbl),
                                 'aboutModalOpen': aboutModalOpen,
                                 'logout': logout,
                                 'isLoggedIn': isLoggedIn}
            ),
            el(Paper, {'style': {'padding': '0.5rem',
                                 'marginTop': '1rem'}
                      },
              el(FlexboxCenter, None,
                el(Typography, {'variant': 'h5'},
                  el(Link, {'href': '#',
                            'variant': 'h5',
                            'onClick': lambda: setBooksShow(True)
                           }, "Books")
                ),
              ),
              el(FlexboxCenter, None,
                el(Typography, {'variant': 'h5'},
                  el(Link, {'href': '#',
                            'onClick': lambda: setLoginModal(True)
                           }, "Login")
                ) if not isLoggedIn else None
```

```
            ),
        ),
        el(Login, {'onClose': lambda: setLoginModal(False),
                   'onLogin': doLogin,
                   'password': password,
                   'username': username,
                   'setUsername': lambda usr: setUsername(usr),
                   'setPassword': lambda pwd: setPassword(pwd),
                   'modalState': loginModal,
                  }
        ),
        el(About, {'onClose': lambda: setAboutShow(False),
                   'modalState': aboutShow}
        ),
        el(LookupTable, {'table': lookupModal,
                         'onClose': lambda: setLookupModal(None)}
        ) if lookupModal else None
    )
```

Here, we just needed to import the new LookupTable component we created, and add lookupModal as a state variable to control when the modal view is shown.

Since opening the lookupTable view is done from the LandingPageMenu component, we pass a function to set that value:

```
setLookupModal': lambda tbl: setLookupModal(tbl)
```

Lastly, we add an attachment point for the LookupTable component as we did for the Login and About modal components, and make the rendering conditional on the value of the lookupModal state variable.

One more thing we need to do is update the action of the menu item that opens the lookupTable view. We change that in the existing **landingPageMenu.py** module:

Listing 35-4 File: *landingPageMenu.py*

```
from common.pyreact import useState, createElement as el, Fragment
from common.pymui import Menu, MenuItem
from views.lookupTable.lookupView import lookup_tables


def LandingPageMenu(props):
```

```
    mainMenu = props['mainMenu']
    mainMenuClose = props['mainMenuClose']
    setLookupModal = props['setLookupModal']
    aboutModalOpen = props['aboutModalOpen']
    logout = props['logout']
    isLoggedIn = props['isLoggedIn']

    lookupMenu, setLookupMenu = useState(None)

    def lookupMenuOpen(event):
        setLookupMenu(event['currentTarget'])

    def lookupMenuClose():
        setLookupMenu(None)
        mainMenuClose()

    def handleLookup(event):
        value = event['currentTarget']['textContent']
        lookupMenuClose()
        setLookupModal(value)

    def handleAbout():
        mainMenuClose()
        aboutModalOpen()

    def handleLogout():
        mainMenuClose()
        logout()

    return el(Fragment, None,
              el(Menu, {'id': 'main-menu',
                        'anchorEl': mainMenu,
                        'keepMounted': True,
                        'open': bool(mainMenu),
                        'onClose': mainMenuClose,
                        },
                 el(MenuItem, {'onClick': lookupMenuOpen}, "Lookup Tables"),
                 el(MenuItem, {'onClick': handleAbout}, "About"),
                 el(MenuItem, {'onClick': handleLogout,
                               'disabled': not isLoggedIn}, "Logout"),
                 ),
              el(Menu, {'id': 'lookup-menu',
                        'anchorEl': lookupMenu,
                        'keepMounted': True,
                        'open': bool(lookupMenu),
```

```
                    'onClose': lookupMenuClose,
                    'transformOrigin': {'vertical': 'top',
                                        'horizontal': 'center'},
                },
            [el(MenuItem, {'key': table['name'],
                           'onClick': handleLookup
                          }, table['name']) for table in lookup_tables
            ],
        )
    )
```

Here we add the new `setLookupModal` prop that will be used to open and close the `lookupTable` view. In the `handleLookup()` function, we replace the existing `print()` statement we had in there as a placeholder, with a call to that `setLookupModal()` function that will activate the `lookupTable` view.

One minor change we made in the menu items for the lookup tables is that since we are using a list of dictionaries for our lookup table information now instead of a simple list of names like we had before, we need to add the dictionary key `table['name']` that holds the name of each table when we generate each `MenuItem` component for the lookup tables.

Now when you select a lookup table to view from the menu, a modal form will be displayed showing the existing records from the selected table.

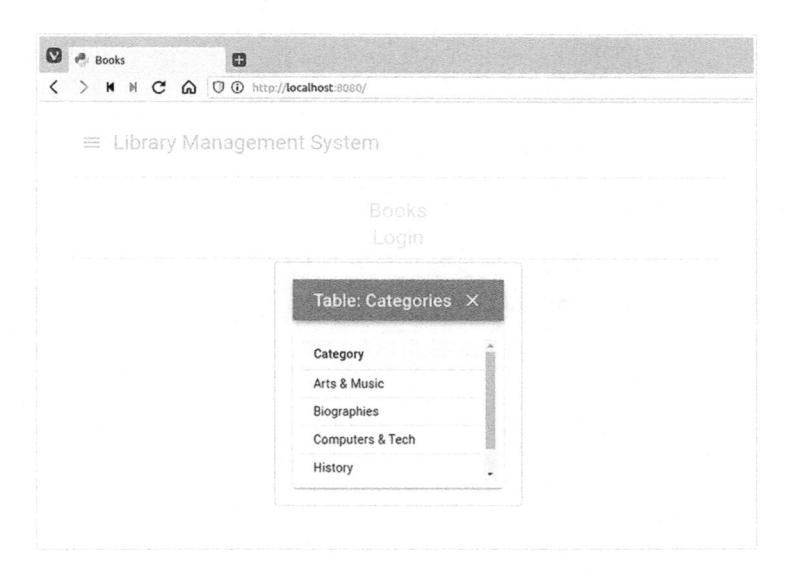

With the additional files we added in this chapter, our file and folder structure now looks like this:

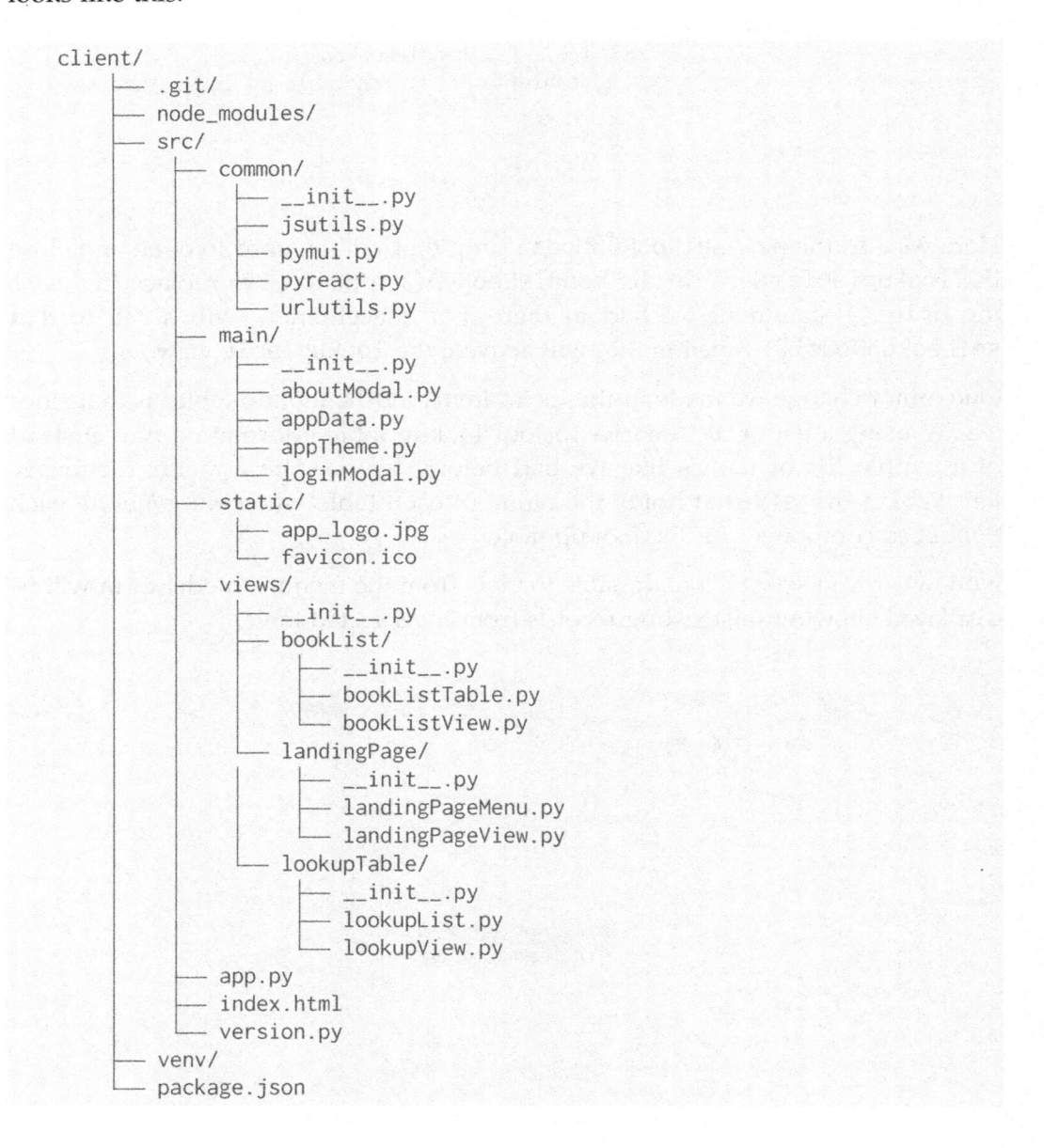

```
client/
    ├── .git/
    ├── node_modules/
    ├── src/
    │       ├── common/
    │       │       ├── __init__.py
    │       │       ├── jsutils.py
    │       │       ├── pymui.py
    │       │       ├── pyreact.py
    │       │       └── urlutils.py
    │       ├── main/
    │       │       ├── __init__.py
    │       │       ├── aboutModal.py
    │       │       ├── appData.py
    │       │       ├── appTheme.py
    │       │       └── loginModal.py
    │       ├── static/
    │       │       ├── app_logo.jpg
    │       │       └── favicon.ico
    │       ├── views/
    │       │       ├── __init__.py
    │       │       ├── bookList/
    │       │       │       ├── __init__.py
    │       │       │       ├── bookListTable.py
    │       │       │       └── bookListView.py
    │       │       ├── landingPage/
    │       │       │       ├── __init__.py
    │       │       │       ├── landingPageMenu.py
    │       │       │       └── landingPageView.py
    │       │       └── lookupTable/
    │       │               ├── __init__.py
    │       │               ├── lookupList.py
    │       │               └── lookupView.py
    │       ├── app.py
    │       ├── index.html
    │       └── version.py
    ├── venv/
    └── package.json
```

Chapter Review:

1. Create landingPage folder:
   client/src/views/lookupTable/

2. Add source files:
   client/src/views/lookupTable/__init__.py
   client/src/views/lookupTable/lookupView.py
   client/src/views/lookupTable/lookupList.py

3. Update source files:
   client/src/views/landingPage/landingPageView.py
   client/src/views/landingPage/landingPageMenu.py

4. Build the application for development with:
   npm run dev

5. Open the application:
   http://localhost:8080

6. Add and commit files to git (from the **src/client/** folder):
   git add .
   git commit -m "Lookups"

7. Update version:
   npm version patch

References:

- Chapter code
  https://github.com/rtp-book/project/tree/step08

Chapter 36 – User Context

To keep track of when we can allow a user to update data as opposed to just look at it, we need to know if the user is logged in or not. Because we might need this stateful information throughout our application, it is a good candidate for using React context variables.

As we talked about in the earlier chapter on React Context Hooks, a context component is kind of like a global prop variable that we can inject at the top of the component tree and then access it from anywhere in the tree without having to explicitly pass the value down through the tree as props.

36.1 Context Definition

To start with, we need to define a variable that will hold a reference to the context we create. This can generally be created in any module that can be imported where we need to use it. In this case, we don't really have a specific module for it, so let's just put it in the existing **__init__.py** module in the **src/main/** folder since it will be global to the entire application:

Listing 36-1 File: *__init__.py*

```
from common.pyreact import createContext

UserCtx = createContext()
```

The next step is to initialize the value property of the context and then inject it into the component tree, which we do in our main **app.py** entry point component:

Listing 36-2 File: *app.py*

```
from common.pyreact import render, createElement as el, ReactGA
from common.pyreact import useState, useEffect
from common.pymui import ThemeProvider, SnackbarProvider
from common.jsutils import setTitle, console
from common.urlutils import fetch
from main import UserCtx
from main.appTheme import theme
from main.appData import gaid
```

```
from views.bookList.bookListView import BookList
from views.landingPage.landingPageView import LandingPage

...

    useEffect(validateSession, [])

    user_ctx = {'user': user,
                'login': login,
                'logout': logout,
                'isLoggedIn': isLoggedIn
                }

    return el(ThemeProvider, {'theme': theme},
              el(SnackbarProvider, {'maxSnack': 3},
                el(UserCtx.Provider, {'value': user_ctx},
                  el(router[pathname], {'setBooksShow': setBooksShow}
                    )
                  )
                )
              )

render(App, {'title': "Books"}, 'root')
```

So here we import the UserCtx variable we created from main, then create a dictionary with the user information and the functions related to logging in and out.

```
user_ctx = {'user': user,
            'login': login,
            'logout': logout,
            'isLoggedIn': isLoggedIn
            }
```

Now, all that needs to be done is to inject the context variable into the component tree, which we do with the Provider method of the context component, passing value as a prop of the context object:

```
el(UserCtx.Provider, {'value': user_ctx}
```

Because we now have the login functionality available anywhere in the component tree, we no longer need to explicitly pass it to the lower level components as props.

36.2 Using the Context

In the places where we were passing the login functions as props, we can modify those to use the context variable instead. Let's start with the `landingPage` view:

Listing 36-3 File: *landingPageView.py*

```python
from common.pyreact import useState, createElement as el, useEffect, useContext
from common.pymui import Container, Paper, Typography, useSnackbar
from common.pymui import IconButton, MenuIcon, Link
from common.urlutils import fetch
from main import UserCtx
from main.appTheme import Flexbox, FlexboxCenter
from main.aboutModal import About
from main.appData import appname
from main.loginModal import Login
from views.landingPage.landingPageMenu import LandingPageMenu
from views.lookupTable.lookupView import LookupTable


def LandingPage(props):
    setBooksShow = props['setBooksShow']

    uCtx = useContext(UserCtx)
    isLoggedIn = uCtx['isLoggedIn']
    login = uCtx['login']

    mainMenu, setMainMenu = useState(None)
    aboutShow, setAboutShow = useState(False)
    lookupModal, setLookupModal = useState(None)
    loginModal, setLoginModal = useState(False)
    username, setUsername = useState("")
    password, setPassword = useState("")

    ...

    return el(Container, {'maxWidth': 'md'},
            el(Paper, {'style': {'padding': '1rem'}},
                el(Flexbox, {'alignItems': 'center'},
                    el(IconButton, {'edge': 'start',
                                    'color': 'inherit',
```

```
                            'onClick': mainMenuOpen
                        }, el(MenuIcon, None)
                    ),
                    el(Typography, {'variant': 'h5'}, appname)
                )
            ),
            el(LandingPageMenu, {'mainMenu': mainMenu,
                                 'mainMenuClose': mainMenuClose,
                                 'setLookupModal':
                                     lambda tbl: setLookupModal(tbl),
                                 'aboutModalOpen': aboutModalOpen}
            ),
...
```

To use the context variable, we just needed to import the context reference from `main`, and then utilize the React `useContext()` hook function to get the actual value from it, which in our case is a dictionary containing the login functionality that we had previously passed in as props. We can remove the `isLoggedIn` and `logout` props that we were explicitly passing to the `landingPageMenu` component as well, since we'll now be able to pull those out of the context variable right from within that component instead.

Speaking of which, let's do that same thing for the **landingPageMenu.py** module and have it utilize the context variable as well:

Listing 36-4 File: *landingPageMenu.py*

```
from common.pyreact import useState, createElement as el, Fragment, useContext
from common.pymui import Menu, MenuItem
from main import UserCtx
from views.lookupTable.lookupView import lookup_tables


def LandingPageMenu(props):
    mainMenu = props['mainMenu']
    mainMenuClose = props['mainMenuClose']
    setLookupModal = props['setLookupModal']
    aboutModalOpen = props['aboutModalOpen']

    ctx = useContext(UserCtx)
    logout = ctx['logout']
```

```
    isLoggedIn = ctx['isLoggedIn']
```
...

As before, we import the context reference variable from main, and then utilize the useContext() hook function to get the value from it. After that, we can pull out the specific dictionary items that we need to utilize in this particular component.

So far, the context variable hasn't saved us much typing over just passing props, but we will be using it in other places later on as we add more functionality to our application.

Chapter Review:

1. Update source files:
   client/src/main/__init__.py
   client/src/app.py
   client/src/views/landingPage/landingPageView.py
   client/src/views/landingPage/landingPageMenu.py

2. Build the application for development with:
   ```
   npm run dev
   ```

3. Open the application:
   http://localhost:8080

4. Add and commit files to git (from the **src/client/** folder):
   ```
   git add .
   git commit -m "User Context"
   ```

5. Update version:
   ```
   npm version patch
   ```

References:

- Chapter code
  https://github.com/rtp-book/project/tree/step09

Chapter 37 – Editing Lookups

Right now, we can only *view* the data in our lookup tables. In this chapter, we'll make it so you can add, edit, and delete entries in each table as well. We will add this functionality to the existing modules in the `lookupTable` view.

37.1 Saving Data

We'll start with the **lookupView.py** module in the **src/views/lookupTable/** folder and add a function that will allow us to save any changes that we make to items in the lookup table data.

Listing 37-1 File: *lookupView.py*

```
from common.pyreact import Modal, useState, useEffect, createElement as el
from common.pymui import Typography, AppBar, Toolbar, Box, Paper
from common.pymui import IconButton, CloseIcon, useSnackbar
from common.urlutils import fetch
from main.appTheme import modalStyles
from views.lookupTable.lookupList import ItemsList

lookup_tables = [
    {'name': 'Categories', 'fields': ['Category'], 'sort': 'Category'},
    {'name': 'Publishers', 'fields': ['Publisher'], 'sort': 'Publisher'},
    {'name': 'Conditions', 'fields': ['Code', 'Condition'], 'sort': 'ID}'},
    {'name': 'Formats', 'fields': ['Format'], 'sort': 'Format'}
]


def LookupTable(props):
    onClose = props['onClose']
    table_name = props['table']

    table_info = next(
        (table for table in lookup_tables if table['name'] == table_name),
        {})
    table_fields = table_info['fields']
    table_sort = table_info['sort']
    modalState = bool(table_name)

    items, setItems = useState([])
```

```python
    snack = useSnackbar()

    def on_update_error():
        snack.enqueueSnackbar("Error updating lookup table!",
                              {'variant': 'error'})
        getItems()

    def on_update_success():
        snack.enqueueSnackbar("Lookup table updated!", {'variant': 'success'})
        getItems()

    def saveItem(item):
        # If all non-ID values are empty, then delete record
        if len(''.join([val for key, val in item.items() if key != 'ID'])) == 0:
            if not item.get('ID', None):
                getItems()   # Probably an unmodified record so just refresh list
            else:
                fetch(f"/api/lookup/{table_name}", on_update_success,
                      method='DELETE', data=item, onError=on_update_error)
        else:
            fetch(f"/api/lookup/{table_name}", on_update_success,
                  method='POST', data=item, onError=on_update_error)

    def getItems():
        def _getItems(data):
            item_list = data if data else []
            if len(item_list) > 0:
                item_list.sort(key=lambda item: item[table_sort])
                setItems(item_list)
            else:
                setItems([])

        if table_name:
            fetch(f"/api/lookup/{table_name}", _getItems)
        else:
            setItems([])

    useEffect(getItems, [table_name])

    return el(Modal, {'isOpen': modalState,
                      'style': modalStyles,
                      'ariaHideApp': False,
                     },
            el(AppBar, {'position': 'static',
                        'style': {'marginBottom': '0.5rem'}
```

```
                    },
            el(Toolbar, {'variant': 'dense'},
                el(Box, {'width': '100%'},
                    el(Typography, {'variant': 'h6'}, f"Table: {table_name}")
                ),
                el(IconButton, {'edge': 'end',
                                'color': 'inherit',
                                'onClick': onClose
                                }, el(CloseIcon, None)
                ),
            ),
        ),
        el(Paper, {'style': {'padding': '0.5rem', 'marginTop': '0.8rem'}},
            el(ItemsList, {'items': items,
                           'fields': table_fields,
                           'saveItem': saveItem,
                           'setItems': setItems})
        )
    )
```

The saveItem() function that we added here performs the appropriate REST service call based on the state of the data, and is called any time a single item in the list is modified. If all of the fields in the item are blank, it will make an HTTP DELETE request to remove the item from the list. It does do a check to make sure there is a valid ID value before it tries to delete it. If the ID field doesn't exist, it means it is a new record anyway, so it just refreshes the list by calling the getItems() function.

If there is data in any of the item fields, it will use an HTTP POST request to send the updated record to the REST service. On the back-end server, if there is no ID field it will be treated as a new record and will use an INSERT to add the new record to the lookup table, otherwise it will be treated as a record UPDATE instead.

Once a call to saveItem() is made, it will display an appropriate snackbar to indicate a success or failure to the user once a response is received from the REST service. It will then refresh the list from the database by again using the getItems() function to pick up the changes that were just made.

37.2 Editing Items

The way we will enable editing the lookup list, is that if an item is double-clicked, it will switch to an editable text box. Clicking off the text box or pressing *Enter* will then trigger the edited item to be saved.

To allow for adding new items, we will append an *Add* icon button to the end of the list. Clicking that button will cause a new blank item to be appended to the list that can be edited. Clicking off the new item or pressing *Enter* will save the new item, just as it does when updating an item.

To delete an item from the list, you would double-click to put the item into edit mode, and then clear the fields in the row. When the item is saved, our saveItem() function in the **lookupView.py** module will detect that there is no data there and delete the item from the table.

To add the functionality for editing items and adding new items to the list will require a major refactoring of the **lookupList.py** module, so prepare yourself as there is quite a bit of code here to implement the described behavior:

Listing 37-2 File: *lookupList.py*

```python
from common.pyreact import useState, createElement as el, Fragment
from common.pymui import Box, AddIcon, IconButton
from common.pymui import TableContainer, Table
from common.pymui import TableHead, TableBody, TableRow, TableCell


def ItemEditCell(props):
    field = props['field']
    setEditValues = props['setEditValues']
    editValues = props['editValues']
    checkSaveItem = props['checkSaveItem']

    field_value = editValues[field]

    def handleChange(event):
        event.preventDefault()
        target = event['target']
        value = target['value']
        key = target['id']

        new_editValues = dict(editValues)
        new_editValues.update({key: value})
```

```python
            setEditValues(new_editValues)

    def handleKeyPress(event):
        key = event['key']
        if key == 'Enter':
            checkSaveItem()

    return el(TableCell, None,
            el('input', {'id': field,
                         'onKeyPress': handleKeyPress,
                         'onChange': handleChange,
                         'value': field_value,
                         'style': {'width': '10rem', 'margin': '-4px'}}
            )
        )


def ItemCell(props):
    value = props['value']

    return el(TableCell, None,
            el(Box, {'width': '10rem', 'whiteSpace': 'nowrap'}, value)
        )


def ItemRowVu(props):
    item = props['item']
    fields = props['fields']
    selected = props['selected']
    setSelected = props['setSelected']
    editValues = props['editValues']
    setEditValues = props['setEditValues']
    checkSaveItem = props['checkSaveItem']

    def handleClick():
        if selected:
            checkSaveItem()

    def handleDoubleClick():
        setEditValues(dict(item))
        setSelected(item['ID'])

    if item['ID'] == selected:
        return el(TableRow, None,
                [el(ItemEditCell, {'key': field,
```

```python
                            'field': field,
                            'setEditValues': setEditValues,
                            'editValues': editValues,
                            'checkSaveItem': checkSaveItem,
                        }) for field in fields]
            )
    else:
        return el(TableRow, {'onClick': handleClick,
                             'onDoubleClick': handleDoubleClick},
                [el(ItemCell, {'key': field,
                               'value': item[field],
                }) for field in fields]
            )


def ItemRows(props):
    items = props['items']
    fields = props['fields']
    setItems = props['setItems']
    saveItem = props['saveItem']

    selected, setSelected = useState(None)
    editValues, setEditValues = useState({})

    def checkSaveItem():
        old_item = next((item for item in items if item['ID'] == selected), {})
        new_item = dict(editValues)
        if new_item['ID'] == "NEW":
            new_item.pop("ID")
        # Transcrypt differs from CPython on object equality so check each value
        if len(new_item) != len(old_item) or \
                len([key for key, val in new_item.items()
                     if val != old_item[key]]) > 0:
            saveItem(new_item)
        setEditValues({})
        setSelected(None)

    def handleAdd():
        new_items = [dict(item) for item in items]
        new_item = {field: "" for field in fields}
        new_item['ID'] = "NEW"
        new_items.append(new_item)
        setItems(new_items)
        setEditValues(new_item)
        setSelected("NEW")
```

```python
    def itemToRow(item):
        return el(ItemRowVu, {'key': item['ID'],
                              'item': item,
                              'fields': fields,
                              'selected': selected,
                              'setSelected': setSelected,
                              'editValues': editValues,
                              'setEditValues': setEditValues,
                              'checkSaveItem': checkSaveItem,
                             }
                 )

    def AddItem():
        if selected == "NEW":
            return None
        else:
            return el(TableRow, {'key': 'ADD'},
                      el(TableCell, {'variant': 'footer',
                                     'align': 'center',
                                     'colSpan': len(fields)},
                         el(IconButton, {'edge': 'end',
                                         'color': 'primary',
                                         'size': 'small',
                                         'padding': 'none',
                                         'onClick': handleAdd
                                        }, el(AddIcon, None)
                           )
                        )
                     )

    if len(items) > 0:
        return el(Fragment, None,
                  [itemToRow(item) for item in items if item],
                  el(AddItem, None)
                 )
    else:
        return el(AddItem, None)

def ItemsList(props):
    items = props['items']
    fields = props['fields']
    saveItem = props['saveItem']
    setItems = props['setItems']
```

```
def HeaderCols():
    return el(TableRow, None,
            [el(TableCell, {'key': field, 'fields': fields}, field)
              for field in fields]
            )

return el(TableContainer, {'style': {'maxHeight': '10.5rem'}},
        el(Table, {'size': 'small', 'stickyHeader': True},
            el(TableHead, None,
                el(HeaderCols, None),
            ),
            el(TableBody, None,
                el(ItemRows, {'items': items,
                            'fields': fields,
                            'setItems': setItems,
                            'saveItem': saveItem}),
            )
        )
    )
```

We now have five components defined in this module instead of four, where we added one that we'll use for an editable table cell. So starting again at the bottom of the module with the `ItemList` component since that is our entry point for the component, we only added two new props, `saveItem` and `setItems`, which we don't use here but will just pass on to the next component in the tree.

The `ItemRows` component gets a much bigger makeover since it is now responsible for adding new rows and determining if an item needs to be saved or not. We introduce two state variables to this component that we didn't have before. The `selected` state variable stores the ID value of an item that is currently being edited. If the item being edited is a new item, it will have the value "NEW" instead of an ID number. The `editValues` state variable is a dictionary containing the current values of an item being edited.

The returned React Fragment is pretty much the same as before. We just append an extra row that has the `AddItem` component that displays an Add button. If there is already a new item being added, then the *Add* button will not be rendered by React since the `AddItem` component will return a value of None if that is the case.

When the *Add* button is clicked, it makes a copy of the current item list (since the list of items is immutable at run time), and adds a new item to it with blank values for each of the item fields. The ID field of the new item is set to "NEW" to identify it as a new row (obviously). The selected and editValues state variables are updated to reflect the new item that is now being edited.

The checkSaveItem() function determines if an item that was being edited needs to be saved. It does this by making a copy of the original item dictionary from the items list, and then comparing the values in that to the values in the editValues dictionary. If the edited item is new, we remove the ID field since that's how the REST service differentiates between a record that needs to be added versus one that needs to be updated. If the length of the dictionaries are different, or if any of the values of the fields are different, then the item gets saved via a call to the saveItem() function defined in the **lookupView.py** module. Regardless if the item needs to be saved or not, at this point the two state variables also get reset to a non-editing status.

This leads us to the itemToRow() function that works the same as it did before, but we pass in several more props for the ItemRowVu component to utilize. This includes the two state variables with their set functions, and the checkSaveItem() function that will be called after an item leaves an editing mode.

The ItemRowVu component adds two new functions. One to handle a single-click that will call the checkSaveItem() function if there is an item currently being edited, and another that handles a double-click. In the latter case, the item is put into an edit mode by setting the selected and editValues state variables with the value of the ID field and a copy of the current item values respectively.

What the ItemRowVu component returns, is based on if it is currently an item being edited or not. If it isn't being edited, it works just the way it did before, returning a TableRow consisting of a list of ItemCell components. On the other hand, if it is being edited, it returns a TableRow consisting of a list of our new ItemEditCell components instead.

Instead of using a simple Material-UI Box component (which eventually gets turned into an HTML div element by React) to hold the item values, the ItemEditCell component wraps the values in an HTML input element instead. We have a handleChange() function that keeps our editValues state variable synchronized with what is in the input boxes, and is bound to the onChange event of the input box. And again, since the editValues dictionary is going to be immutable at run time, we first make a copy of it, update the copy, then call the setEditValues() function to update the state.

We also have a `handleKeyPress()` function that saves the item if there is an *Enter* keypress event.

37.3 Menu Control

Since it now allows edits, one last thing we'll take care of in this chapter is to not allow access to the lookup table view if the user is not logged in. This just requires a minor change in the **landingPageMenu.py** module:

Listing 37-3 File: *landingPageMenu.py*

```python
from common.pyreact import useState, createElement as el, Fragment, useContext
from common.pymui import Menu, MenuItem
from main import UserCtx
from views.lookupTable.lookupView import lookup_tables

...

    return el(Fragment, None,
            el(Menu, {'id': 'main-menu',
                      'anchorEl': mainMenu,
                      'keepMounted': True,
                      'open': bool(mainMenu),
                      'onClose': mainMenuClose,
                    },
                el(MenuItem, {'onClick': lookupMenuOpen,
                              'disabled': not isLoggedIn}, "Lookup Tables"),
                el(MenuItem, {'onClick': handleAbout}, "About"),
                el(MenuItem, {'onClick': handleLogout,
                              'disabled': not isLoggedIn}, "Logout"),
            ),
            el(Menu, {'id': 'lookup-menu',
                      'anchorEl': lookupMenu,
                      'keepMounted': True,
                      'open': bool(lookupMenu),
                      'onClose': lookupMenuClose,
                      'transformOrigin': {'vertical': 'top',
                                          'horizontal': 'center'},
                    },
                [el(MenuItem, {'key': table['name'],
                               'onClick': handleLookup
                             }, table['name']) for table in lookup_tables
                ],
```

)
)

The only thing we did here was to make the availability of the *Lookup Table* menu item dependent on whether or not the user is logged in, the same way we did it for the *Logout* menu item. So if the user is not logged in, the menu item will be disabled.

So now, if you are logged in, you can view, add, update, and delete entries in lookup tables. To add an entry, you click the plus icon at the end of the list. To edit an item in the list, you double-click the item. And to delete an item from the list, you just have to delete the contents in the row.

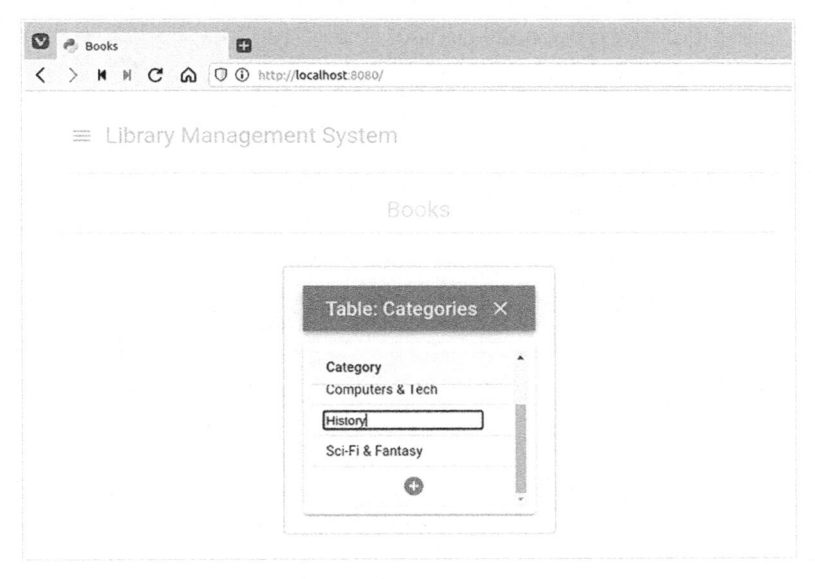

Chapter Review:

1. Update source files:
   client/src/views/lookupTable/lookupView.py
   client/src/views/lookupTable/lookupList.py
   client/src/views/landingPage/landingPageMenu.py

2. Build the application for development with:
   npm run dev

3. Open the application:
   http://localhost:8080

4. Add and commit files to git (from the **src/client/** folder):
   git add .
   git commit -m "Editing Lookups"

5. Update version:
   npm version patch

References:

- Chapter code
  https://github.com/rtp-book/project/tree/step10

Chapter 38 – Filtering Data

Let's go back to our book list view and add a mechanism to filter the records that are returned from the REST API. Instead of only being able to show the full list of books, we will add the ability to selectively query the database to only display books that meet the search criteria.

38.1 Filter Form

What we are going to do is create a new component that we will add to the `BookListView` component, which will then add a section of `TextField` components to enter filter criteria into.

This **bookListFilter.py** module will go with the other bookList view modules in the **src/views/bookList/** folder:

Listing 38-1 File: *bookListFilter.py*

```python
from common.pyreact import useState, createElement as el
from common.pymui import TextField, Button, Paper
from main.appTheme import Flexbox


def CategoriesList(props):
    categories = props['categories']

    def categoryToRow(author):
        category_id = author['ID']
        category_name = author['Category']

        return el('option', {'key': category_id,
                             'value': category_name
                             }, category_name)

    return [categoryToRow(category) for category in categories]


def BooksFilterVu(props):
    categories = props['categories']
    setFilterParams = props['setFilterParams']
```

```python
Title, setTitle = useState("")
Author, setAuthor = useState("")
IsFiction, setIsFiction = useState("")
Category, setCategory = useState("")
ISBN, setISBN = useState("")

def setState(field, value):
    switch = dict(Title=setTitle,
                  Author=setAuthor,
                  IsFiction=setIsFiction,
                  Category=setCategory,
                  ISBN=setISBN
                  )
    switch[field](value)

def handleInputChange(event):
    event.preventDefault()
    target = event['target']
    value = target['value']
    key = target['name']
    setState(key, value)

def handleFilter():
    params = dict(Title=Title,
                  Author=Author,
                  IsFiction=IsFiction,
                  Category=Category,
                  ISBN=ISBN
                  )
    filters = {key: val for key, val in params.items() if len(val) > 0}
    setFilterParams(filters)

filter_width = '17%'

return el(Paper, None,
          el(Flexbox, {'flexWrap': 'wrap', 'style': {'margin': '0.5rem'}},
             el(TextField, {'label': "Title",
                            'name': 'Title',
                            'style': {'width': filter_width},
                            'value': Title,
                            'onChange': handleInputChange,
                            }
                ),
             el(TextField, {'label': "Author",
                            'name': 'Author',
```

```
                        'style': {'width': filter_width},
                        'value': Author,
                        'onChange': handleInputChange,
                    }
            ),
            el(TextField, {'label': "Genre",
                        'name': 'IsFiction',
                        'style': {'width': filter_width},
                        'value': IsFiction,
                        'onChange': handleInputChange,
                        'select': True,
                        'SelectProps': {'native': True},
                    },
                el('option', {'value': ''}, ""),
                el('option', {'value': '1'}, "Fiction"),
                el('option', {'value': '0'}, "Non-Fiction"),
            ),
            el(TextField, {'label': "Category",
                        'name': 'Category',
                        'style': {'width': filter_width},
                        'value': Category,
                        'onChange': handleInputChange,
                        'select': True,
                        'SelectProps': {'native': True},
                    },
                el('option', {'value': ''}),
                el(CategoriesList, {'categories': categories}),
            ),
            el(TextField, {'label': "ISBN",
                        'name': 'ISBN',
                        'style': {'width': filter_width},
                        'value': ISBN,
                        'onChange': handleInputChange,
                    }
            ),
            el(Button, {'type': 'button',
                        'color': 'primary',
                        'size': 'small',
                        'style': {'minWidth': '7rem', 'margin': '0.5rem'},
                        'onClick': handleFilter
                    }, "Filter"
            ),
        )
    )
```

The `BooksFilterVu` component takes two parameters: the `setFilterParams()` function that we use to set the filter criteria, and the list of `categories` from the lookup table that we use to fill the *Category* select list filter.

We will have five different criteria that we will be able to filter on, and we set up a state variable for each one:

- Title
- Author
- Genre (aka *IsFiction* field)
- Category
- ISBN

To set state for the five variables, we created a single `setState()` function that does a dictionary lookup based on the field name to determine the appropriate field-specific state variable update function to use:

```
def setState(field, value):
    switch = dict(Title=setTitle,
                  Author=setAuthor,
                  IsFiction=setIsFiction,
                  Category=setCategory,
                  ISBN=setISBN
                  )
    switch[field](value)
```

It then passes the new value to that particular update function. For example, if the field name is "Category" and the value is "History", `switch["Category"]` would evaluate to `setCategory` based on the `switch` dictionary, and it would ultimately get called as `setCategory("History")`. This is one way to efficiently emulate in Python, what would normally be a switch or select statement in other programming languages.

The returned element tree of this component consists of five `TextField` components and a `Button` component. Each of the `TextField` components has the `handleInputChange()` function tied to its onChange event to keep the state variables synchronized with what is shown in the UI. Two of the `TextField` components are set up as select boxes. The *Genre* `TextField` uses a static option list, and the *Category* `TextField` uses the `CategoriesList` component, where we pass the `categories` prop that has the list of categories on through to that component to generate the list of `option` elements.

The CategoriesList component at the top of the module simply takes the list of categories that is passed into it and returns a list of HTML option elements, one for each category.

The Button component onClick event triggers the handleFilter() function that converts the five state variables to a Python dictionary. It then filters that dictionary to include only non-empty values using a Python dictionary comprehension. We then call the setFilterParams() function with the result of that filtered dictionary to set the filterParams state in the BookList parent component.

38.2 Lookup Data

In addition to using the filter parameters that we collect in the BookFilterVu component, we also need to get the lookup table data so we can populate any select lists that we may have. We will add that capability to the existing **bookListView.py** module:

Listing 38-2 File: *bookListView.py*

```
from common.pyreact import useState, useEffect, createElement as el
from common.pymui import Typography, AppBar, Toolbar, IconButton, CloseIcon
from common.pymui import Container, Box, Paper, CircularProgress
from common.urlutils import fetch
from views.bookList.bookListFilter import BooksFilterVu
from views.bookList.bookListTable import BooksTable


def BookList(props):
    setBooksShow = props['setBooksShow']

    books, setBooks = useState([])
    sortKey, setSortKey = useState('Title')
    showProgress, setShowProgress = useState(False)
    filterParams, setFilterParams = useState({})

    categories, setCategories = useState([])
    publishers, setPublishers = useState([])
    formats, setFormats = useState([])
    conditions, setConditions = useState([])

    def sortBooks():
        book_list = [dict(tmp_book) for tmp_book in books]
```

```python
        if len(book_list) > 0:
            setBooks(sorted(book_list, key=lambda k: k[sortKey] or ""))

    def on_fetch_error():
        setShowProgress(False)

    def getBooks():
        isPending = True

        def _getBooks(data):
            book_list = data if data else []
            if isPending:
                if len(book_list) > 0:
                    setBooks(sorted(book_list, key=lambda k: k[sortKey]))
                else:
                    setBooks([])
                setShowProgress(False)

        def abort():
            nonlocal isPending
            isPending = False

        setShowProgress(True)
        fetch("/api/books", _getBooks,
            params=filterParams,
            onError=on_fetch_error
            )
        return abort

    def getLookup(table_name, setState):
        isPending = True

        def _getLookup(data):
            if isPending:
                if data:
                    setState(data)
                else:
                    setState([])

        def abort():
            nonlocal isPending
            isPending = False

        fetch(f"/api/lookup/{table_name}", _getLookup)
        return abort
```

```
def getLookups():
    getLookup('Categories', setCategories)
    getLookup('Publishers', setPublishers)
    getLookup('Formats', setFormats)
    getLookup('Conditions', setConditions)

useEffect(getLookups, [])
useEffect(getBooks, [filterParams])
useEffect(sortBooks, [sortKey])

return el(Container, None,
          el(AppBar, {'position': 'static',
                      'style': {'marginBottom': '0.5rem'}
                     },
             el(Toolbar, {'variant': 'dense'},
                el(Box, {'width': '100%'},
                   el(Typography, {'variant': 'h6'}, "Books")
                   ),
                el(IconButton, {'edge': 'end',
                                'color': 'inherit',
                                'onClick': lambda: setBooksShow(False)
                               }, el(CloseIcon, None)
                   ),
                ),
             ),
          el(BooksFilterVu, {'categories': categories,
                             'setFilterParams': setFilterParams}
             ),
          el(Paper, {'style': {'padding': '0.5rem', 'marginTop': '0.8rem'}},
             el(BooksTable, {'books': books, 'setSortKey': setSortKey})
             ),
          el(CircularProgress,
             {'style': {'position': 'absolute',
                        'top': '30%',
                        'left': '50%',
                        'marginLeft': -12}
             }) if showProgress else None
          )
```

Here we added a new state variable `filterParams` to hold the filter criteria in the form of a Python dictionary. We also add state variables for each of the lookup tables: categories, publishers, formats, and conditions.

The lookup table data gets loaded after the `BookList` component loads by using a `useEffect()` hook function with an empty list as the watch criteria. This calls the `getLookups()` function, which in turn then calls `getLookup()` for each of the lookup tables we need to load. The `getLookup()` function works just like the `getItems()` function we used earlier for loading the `LookupView` component. Technically, we could even reuse this version in both places, but for this application, we'll use both and keep the components more modular.

To apply the filter criteria, the only thing we need to do is send the `filterParams` dictionary state variable as a parameter to the `fetch()` function call. The `fetch()` function will take care of turning the dictionary into a properly formatted and URL encoded query string for us.

From there, the Flask REST service takes care of retrieving the matching book records. Note that while the Category, Genre, and ISBN fields filter on exact matches, the Title and Author filters will do partial matches because of how the Flask REST route is designed.

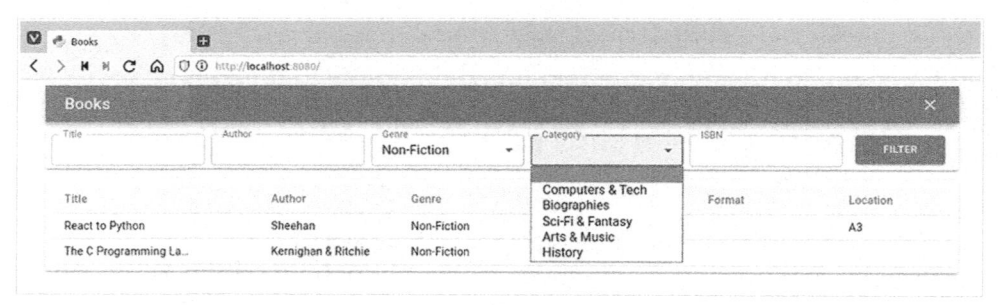

Chapter Review:

1. Add source file:
   client/src/views/bookList/bookListFilter.py

2. Update source file:
   client/src/views/bookList/bookListView.py

3. Build the application for development with:
   `npm run dev`

4. Open the application:
   http://localhost:8080

5. Add and commit files to git (from the **src/client/** folder):
   ```
   git add .
   git commit -m "Filtering Data"
   ```

6. Update version:
   ```
   npm version patch
   ```

References:

- Chapter code
  https://github.com/rtp-book/project/tree/step11

- Material-UI TextField Component
  https://material-ui.com/components/text-fields/

Chapter 39 – Editing Books

The last view that we still need to implement, is one that allows us to add and edit the books in our database. This is implicitly the purpose of the entire application, and a lot of what we've done up to this point is in support of it. We will include logic in this view that will only allow modifications to the data if the user is logged in. If not logged in, the data will be viewable but will be displayed as read-only.

39.1 View Container

We will start by creating the main view container that will hold, among other things, the title bar, close button, and a separate form component that displays all of the fields of the book record. For this view, we will create a new view folder in **src/views/** called **bookEdit/**, and once again add an empty **__init__.py** file to that folder so that it gets treated as a Python package. Next, create the **bookEditView.py** module in that folder:

Listing 39-1 File: *bookEditView.py*

```
from common.jsutils import confirm
from common.pyreact import useState, useEffect, createElement as el, Modal
from common.pymui import Typography, AppBar, Toolbar, Box, useSnackbar
from common.pymui import IconButton, CloseIcon
from common.urlutils import fetch
from main.appTheme import modalStyles
from views.bookEdit.bookEditForm import BookEditForm


book_template = dict(
    ID=None,
    Title="",
    Author=None,
    Publisher=None,
    IsFiction=0,
    Category=None,
    Edition=None,
    DatePublished=None,
    ISBN=None,
    Pages=None,
    DateAcquired=None,
```

```
        Condition=None,
        Format=None,
        Location=None,
        Notes=None
)


def BookEdit(props):
    bookId = props['bookId']
    categories = props['categories']
    publishers = props['publishers']
    formats = props['formats']
    conditions = props['conditions']
    getBooks = props['getBooks']
    onClose = props['onClose']

    book, setBook = useState(book_template)
    bookInitial, setBookInitial = useState(book_template)
    modalState = bool(bookId)

    snack = useSnackbar()

    def handleInputChange(event):
        event.preventDefault()
        target = event['target']
        value = target['value']
        key = target['name']

        if key == "IsFiction":   # RadioGroup sends str instead of int
            value = int(value)

        tmp_book = dict(book)
        tmp_book.update({key: value})
        setBook(tmp_book)

    def isDirty():
        changed = [key for key, val in book.items() if val != bookInitial[key]]
        return len(changed) > 0

    def saveBook():
        tmp_book = dict(book)
        if tmp_book['ID'] == "NEW":
            tmp_book.pop('ID')

        fetch(f"/api/book", on_update_success,
```

```
                method='POST', data=tmp_book, onError=on_update_error)

    def deleteBook():
        if confirm(f"Are you sure you want to delete {book.Title}?"):
            fetch(f"/api/book", on_update_success,
                method='DELETE', data=book, onError=on_update_error)

    def on_update_success():
        getBooks()
        snack.enqueueSnackbar("Book was updated!", {'variant': 'success'})
        onClose()

    def on_update_error():
        snack.enqueueSnackbar("Error updating data!", {'variant': 'error'})

    def on_fetch_error():
        snack.enqueueSnackbar("Error retrieving data!", {'variant': 'error'})

    def getBook():
        def _getBook(data):
            if data:
                tmp_book = dict(book)
                tmp_book.update(**data)
                setBookInitial(tmp_book)
            else:
                setBookInitial(book_template)

        if bookId == "NEW":
            new_book = dict(book_template)
            new_book.update(ID=bookId)
            setBookInitial(new_book)
        elif bookId:
            fetch(f"/api/book", _getBook,
                params={'id': bookId},
                onError=on_fetch_error
                )

    def update_book():
        tmp_book = dict(bookInitial)
        setBook(tmp_book)

    useEffect(getBook, [bookId])
    useEffect(update_book, [bookInitial])

    return el(Modal, {'isOpen': modalState,
```

```
                    'style': modalStyles,
                    'ariaHideApp': False,
                },
            el(AppBar, {'position': 'static',
                        'style': {'marginBottom': '0.5rem'}
                    },
                el(Toolbar, {'variant': 'dense'},
                    el(Box, {'width': '100%'},
                        el(Typography, {'variant': 'h6'}, book.Title)
                    ),
                    el(IconButton, {'edge': 'end',
                                    'color': 'inherit',
                                    'onClick': onClose
                                }, el(CloseIcon, None)
                    ),
                ),
            ),
            el(BookEditForm, {'book': book,
                              'handleInputChange': handleInputChange,
                              'categories': categories,
                              'publishers': publishers,
                              'formats': formats,
                              'conditions': conditions,
                              'isDirty': isDirty,
                              'saveBook': saveBook,
                              'deleteBook': deleteBook
                            }),
        )
```

This module starts by defining a dictionary that represents the contents of a new book record, and contains a key for each of the fields in the Books table. This gets used whenever we need to initialize the state variable that holds information about a selected book.

The module has one top-level component called BookEdit that is a modal view container. It holds most of the functionality required to view, add, and edit a single book. From a UI perspective, it only holds the title bar and another component BookEditForm, that actually contains all of the UI edit fields. It has several props passed into it, including the four lookup table lists that we added to the BookList component in the last chapter, the ID number of the book currently being edited, the function to refresh the list of books showing in the BookList component, and a function to close the modal BookEdit view.

This component manages two state variables: one representing the current field values of the book being edited, and one representing the original field values of the book being edited. The modal state is determined by the value of the bookId prop. If it is a value other than None, then the BookEdit modal view will be shown, otherwise it will be hidden.

The handleInputChange() function keeps the book state variable synchronized with the UI, and will be bound to the onChange event on each of the edit fields. The isDirty() function determines if any changes have been made to the book being edited, by doing a field-by-field comparison between the book state variable and the bookInitial state variable. If the value of any field is different from the original value, it will return True.

Whenever the bookId prop changes, a useEffect() hook function triggers the getBook() function to be called, which retrieves the record for the book with that ID number. The bookInitial state variable is then updated with the field data that was received from the REST service response. When that happens, there is another useEffect() function watching the bookInitial state variable, that updates the book state variable to match the values in bookInitial. This gives us the starting point for the field values to be edited from.

The saveBook() function does just what it says. If it is a new record being added, the ID field is removed before making the POST request so that the REST API knows that it is a new record. In the request, the book state variable dictionary is just sent in the body of the HTTP POST. The deleteBook() function works the same way, but it sends an HTTP DELETE request and uses the original values in the bookInitial state variable instead. Technically either state variable could be used for deleting the record since the only value it really needs is the ID number. We also make liberal use of the snackbar on calls to the REST service to let the user know if the requests were successful or not.

The onClose() function that is passed in as a prop just sets the bookId to None, which causes the modalState to be False and hides the modal BookEdit view.

39.2 Select Lists

Since we will be using select lists for all four of the lookup tables this time, we will need components that build up the option element lists just like we did for the CategoriesList component in the **bookListFilter.py** module that we created in the last chapter. To keep things tidy, we can put all of those list building components into one module. This can go in the same **src/views/bookEdit/** folder that we recently created:

Listing 39-2 File: *bookEditLookups.py*

```python
from common.pyreact import createElement as el


def CategoriesList(props):
    categories = props['categories']

    def categoryToRow(author):
        category_id = author['ID']
        category_name = author['Category']

        return el('option', {'key': category_id,
                             'value': category_name}, category_name)

    return [categoryToRow(category) for category in categories]


def PublishersList(props):
    publishers = props['publishers']

    def publisherToRow(publisher):
        publisher_id = publisher['ID']
        publisher_name = publisher['Publisher']

        return el('option', {'key': publisher_id,
                             'value': publisher_name}, publisher_name)

    return [publisherToRow(publisher) for publisher in publishers]


def ConditionsList(props):
    conditions = props['conditions']

    def conditionToRow(condition):
        condition_id = condition['ID']
        condition_code = condition['Code']
        condition_name = condition['Condition']

        return el('option', {'key': condition_id,
                             'value': condition_code}, condition_name)
```

```
    return [conditionToRow(condition) for condition in conditions]


def FormatsList(props):
    formats = props['formats']

    def formatToRow(publisher):
        format_id = publisher['ID']
        format_name = publisher['Format']

        return el('option', {'key': format_id,
                             'value': format_name}, format_name)

    return [formatToRow(format_) for format_ in formats]
```

These four components work exactly the same way as the one we did for the `CategoriesList` component. Each one takes the list of lookup table items that is passed into it as a prop, and returns a list of HTML `option` elements, one for each item in the list. Because each lookup table has different field names, we created a separate component for each one. These will all be used to populate the select lists in the `BookEditForm` component that we will create in just a bit.

Because we now have these option list generation components in one centralized location, we should refactor the **bookListFilter.py** module from the last chapter to utilize this new version as well so that we don't have duplicated code:

Listing 39-3 File: *bookListFilter.py*

```
from common.pyreact import useState, createElement as el
from common.pymui import TextField, Button, Paper
from main.appTheme import Flexbox
from views.bookEdit.bookEditLookups import CategoriesList


def BooksFilterVu(props):
    categories = props['categories']
    setFilterParams = props['setFilterParams']

...
```

Here, we removed the `CategoriesList` component that was previously there, and then added an import for it from the new **bookEditLookups.py** module instead.

39.3 Data Entry

This next module holds all of the edit fields that will be used for displaying and editing all of the book fields. Because defining those text fields is a little chatty in terms of the code required, combined with organizing the layout of those fields, it gets a bit long. The good news is that a lot of that code is repetitive, and not as complex as it may first look. All of the logic required for this component is passed in from its parent component, and this one contains only UI elements. That said, we can go ahead and add the **bookEditForm.py** module to the **src/views/bookEdit/** folder:

Listing 39-4 File: *bookEditForm.py*

```
from common.pyreact import createElement as el, useContext
from common.pymui import TextField, RadioGroup, FormControlLabel, Radio, Button
from common.pymui import Paper, Divider, Typography
from main import UserCtx
from main.appTheme import Flexbox
from views.bookEdit.bookEditLookups import CategoriesList, PublishersList
from views.bookEdit.bookEditLookups import  FormatsList, ConditionsList


def BookEditForm(props):
    book = props['book']
    handleInputChange = props['handleInputChange']
    categories = props['categories']
    publishers = props['publishers']
    formats = props['formats']
    conditions = props['conditions']
    isDirty = props['isDirty']
    saveBook = props['saveBook']
    deleteBook = props['deleteBook']

    ctx = useContext(UserCtx)
    isLoggedIn = ctx['isLoggedIn']

    read_only = not isLoggedIn

    return el(Paper, {'style': {'padding': '0.5rem', 'marginTop': '0.8rem'}},
              el(Flexbox, None,
                 el(Flexbox, {'style': {'width': '40%',
                                        'flexDirection': 'column'}
                             },
                    el(TextField, {'label': "Title",
```

```python
                            'name': 'Title',
                            'value': book.Title,
                            'onChange': handleInputChange,
                            'required': True,
                            'autoFocus': True,
                            'disabled': read_only
                        }
                    ),
                    el(TextField, {'label': "Author",
                                   'name': 'Author',
                                   'value': book.Author or "",
                                   'onChange': handleInputChange,
                                   'disabled': read_only
                        }
                    ),
                    el(TextField, {'select': True,
                                   'label': "Publisher",
                                   'name': 'Publisher',
                                   'value': book.Publisher or "",
                                   'onChange': handleInputChange,
                                   'SelectProps': {'native': True},
                                   'disabled': read_only
                        },
                        el('option', {'value': ''}),
                        el(PublishersList, {'publishers': publishers}),
                    ),
                ),
                el(Divider, {'orientation': 'vertical', 'flexItem': True}),
                el(Flexbox, {'flexWrap': 'wrap',
                             'style': {'width': '60%',
                                       'flexDirection': 'column'}
                    },
                    el(Flexbox, {'flexWrap': 'wrap'},
                        el(Flexbox, {'style': {'width': '70%'},
                                     'flexDirection': 'column'},
                            el(Flexbox, None,
                                el(TextField, {'select': True,
                                               'label': "Category",
                                               'name': 'Category',
                                               'value': book.Category or "",
                                               'onChange': handleInputChange,
                                               'SelectProps': {'native': True},
                                               'disabled': read_only
                                    },
                                    el('option', {'value': ''}),
```

```
                    el(CategoriesList, {'categories': categories}),
                ),

            ),
            el(Flexbox, None,
                el(TextField, {'label': "Edition",
                               'name': 'Edition',
                               'value': book.Edition or "",
                               'onChange': handleInputChange,
                               'disabled': read_only
                              }
                ),
                el(TextField, {'label': "DatePublished",
                               'name': 'DatePublished',
                               'value': book.DatePublished or "",
                               'onChange': handleInputChange,
                               'disabled': read_only
                              }
                ),
            ),
        ),
        el(Flexbox, {'style': {'width': '30%'}},
            el(RadioGroup, {'name': 'IsFiction',
                            'style': {'margin': '0.7rem'},
                            'value': book.IsFiction,
                            'onChange': handleInputChange,
                           },
                el(FormControlLabel,
                    {'control': el(Radio, {'color': 'primary',
                                           'size': 'small'}
                                  ),
                     'value': 1,
                     'label': 'Fiction',
                     'disabled': read_only}
                ),
                el(FormControlLabel,
                    {'control': el(Radio, {'color': 'primary',
                                           'size': 'small'}
                                  ),
                     'value': 0,
                     'label': 'Non-Fiction',
                     'disabled': read_only}
                ),
            ),
        ),
```

```
                ),
                el(Flexbox, {'flexWrap': 'wrap'},
                    el(TextField, {'select': True,
                                   'label': "Format",
                                   'name': 'Format',
                                   'style': {'width': '45%'},
                                   'value': book.Format or "",
                                   'onChange': handleInputChange,
                                   'SelectProps': {'native': True},
                                   'disabled': read_only
                                  },
                        el('option', {'value': ''}),
                        el(FormatsList, {'formats': formats}),
                    ),
                    el(TextField, {'label': "ISBN",
                                   'name': 'ISBN',
                                   'style': {'width': '36%'},
                                   'value': book.ISBN or "",
                                   'onChange': handleInputChange,
                                   'disabled': read_only
                                  }
                    ),
                    el(TextField, {'label': "Pages",
                                   'name': 'Pages',
                                   'style': {'width': '15%',
                                             'marginRight': 0},
                                   'value': book.Pages or "",
                                   'onChange': handleInputChange,
                                   'disabled': read_only
                                  }
                    ),
                ),
            ),
        ),
        el(Divider, None),
        el(Flexbox, None,
            el(Flexbox, {'style': {'width': '30%',
                                   'flexDirection': 'column'}
                        },
                el(TextField, {'label': "DateAcquired",
                               'name': 'DateAcquired',
                               'type': 'date',
                               'style': {'marginBottom': '0.7rem'},
                               'value': book.DateAcquired or "",
                               'onChange': handleInputChange,
```

```
                        'disabled': read_only
                    }
            ),
        el(TextField, {'select': True,
                      'label': "Condition",
                      'name': 'Condition',
                      'value': book.Condition or "",
                      'onChange': handleInputChange,
                      'SelectProps': {'native': True},
                      'disabled': read_only
                  },
            el('option', {'value': ''}),
            el(ConditionsList, {'conditions': conditions}),
        ),
        el(TextField, {'label': "Location",
                      'name': 'Location',
                      'style': {'marginTop': '0.7rem'},
                      'value': book.Location or "",
                      'onChange': handleInputChange,
                      'disabled': read_only
                  }
        ),
    ),
    el(Divider, {'orientation': 'vertical', 'flexItem': True}),
    el(Flexbox, {'style': {'width': '70%',
                          'flexDirection': 'column'}
                },
        el(Flexbox, None,
            el(TextField, {'label': "Notes",
                          'name': 'Notes',
                          'multiline': True,
                          'rows': 4,
                          'rowsMax': 4,
                          'style': {'marginRight': 0},
                          'value': book.Notes or "",
                          'onChange': handleInputChange,
                          'disabled': read_only
                      }
            ),
        ),
        el(Flexbox, {'justifyContent': 'flex-end',
                    'style': {'marginTop': '0.7rem'}
                },
            el(Flexbox, {'justifyContent': 'center',
                        'alignItems': 'center',
```

```
                                'width': '100%'},
                    el(Typography, {'color': 'secondary'},
                       "A book title is required!"
                    ) if len(book.Title or "") == 0 else None
                ),
                el(Button, {'type': 'button',
                            'color': 'secondary',
                            'style': {'minWidth': '8rem'},
                            'disabled': not isLoggedIn or
                                        book.ID == "NEW",
                            'onClick': deleteBook
                         }, "Delete"
                ),
                el(Button, {'type': 'button',
                            'color': 'primary',
                            'style': {'minWidth': '8rem',
                                      'marginLeft': '1rem'},
                            'disabled': not (isLoggedIn and isDirty() and
                                        len(book.Title or "") > 0),
                            'onClick': saveBook
                         }, "Save"
                ),
            ),
        ),
    ),
)
```

Most of this module consists of `Flexbox` components (essentially HTML div elements) for defining the layout, and `TextField` components for editing the data. We also added a few `Divider` components (which end up as HTML hr elements) as well that help to better define the UI visually. We could have broken some of these sections out into separate components which would help to reduce the nesting somewhat, but we'll leave that for a future optimization.

As we mentioned earlier, the functionality for this modal view is mostly contained in the `BookEditView` component since that is where the state is being managed. The downside to that is we have to pass all that functionality into lower-level components as props as we did here. The book prop is a dictionary that has the current field values for the book being edited. Then the `handleInputChange()` function is used to keep those values synchronized with what is shown in the fields of the UI.

The list of items from each of the four lookup tables is also passed in as props.

While this data could have been loaded from the BookEdit component itself, it would have to reload that same data from the REST server each time a different book was loaded into the BookEditView. By loading the lookup table data in the BookList component instead, we only have to make those four REST calls one time. As long as the BookList stays open, we can then just pass that data that is already loaded to the BookEdit component as props each time a different book row is clicked.

The isDirty() prop is used to determine if the *Save* button on the form should be enabled. If no changes have been made, the *Save* button is disabled. We also have a condition on the *Save* button that requires a book title to be entered in order to save any changes. We use the isLoggedIn value out of the React context variable to determine if the fields should be editable or read-only. This also affects the *Delete* and *Save* buttons as well.

The saveBook() and deleteBook() functions that are passed in as props are what make the calls back to the REST server to update the back-end database.

39.4 Edit Control

Now that we have a view to edit book records in, we need a way to open that view. To edit a book record, the user just needs to single-click a row in the list of books. This will open up the modal BookEditView component with the fields of the form filled in with the appropriate information based on the book row that was clicked on. To add a new book, we will put an icon button on the left side of the title bar that will open the modal form with all of the fields blank. This icon button to add a new record will only be visible if the user is logged in.

To add this functionality, we'll start by making some updates to the existing **bookListView.py** module:

Listing 39-5 File: *bookListView.py*

```
from common.pyreact import useState, useEffect, createElement as el, useContext
from common.pymui import Typography, AppBar, Toolbar, Tooltip, useSnackbar
from common.pymui import Container, Box, Paper, CircularProgress
from common.pymui import IconButton, CloseIcon, AddIcon
from common.urlutils import fetch
from main import UserCtx
from views.bookEdit.bookEditView import BookEdit
```

```python
from views.bookList.bookListFilter import BooksFilterVu
from views.bookList.bookListTable import BooksTable

def BockList(props):
    setBooksShow = props['setBooksShow']

    books, setBooks = useState([])
    sortKey, setSortKey = useState('Title')
    showProgress, setShowProgress = useState(False)
    filterParams, setFilterParams = useState({})
    bookModal, setBookModal = useState(None)

    categories, setCategories = useState([])
    publishers, setPublishers = useState([])
    formats, setFormats = useState([])
    conditions, setConditions = useState([])

    ctx = useContext(UserCtx)
    isLoggedIn = ctx['isLoggedIn']

    snack = useSnackbar()

    def setEdit(book_id):
        if book_id:
            setBookModal(book_id)
        else:
            setBookModal(None)

    def sortBooks():
        book_list = [dict(tmp_book) for tmp_book in books]
        if len(book_list) > 0:
            setBooks(sorted(book_list, key=lambda k: k[sortKey] or ""))

    def on_fetch_error():
        snack.enqueueSnackbar("Error retrieving data!",
                              {'variant': 'error'}
                              )
        setShowProgress(False)

    def getBooks():
...

    return el(Container, None,
            el(AppBar, {'position': 'static',
```

Part III - Putting it all Together

```
                    'style': {'marginBottom': '0.5rem'}
                },
            el(Toolbar, {'variant': 'dense'},
                el(Tooltip, {'title': 'Add new book'},
                    el(IconButton, {'edge': 'start',
                                    'color': 'inherit',
                                    'padding': 'none',
                                    'onClick': lambda: setEdit("NEW")
                        }, el(AddIcon, None)
                    )
                ) if isLoggedIn else None,
                el(Box, {'width': '100%'},
                    el(Typography, {'variant': 'h6'}, "Books")
                ),
                el(IconButton, {'edge': 'end',
                                'color': 'inherit',
                                'onClick': lambda: setBooksShow(False)
                        }, el(CloseIcon, None)
                ),
            ),
        ),
        el(BooksFilterVu, {'categories': categories,
                           'setFilterParams': setFilterParams}
        ),
        el(Paper, {'style': {'padding': '0.5rem', 'marginTop': '0.8rem'}},
            el(BooksTable, {'books': books,
                            'setSortKey': setSortKey,
                            'setEdit': setEdit}
            )
        ),
        el(BookEdit, {'bookId': bookModal,
                      'categories': categories,
                      'publishers': publishers,
                      'formats': formats,
                      'conditions': conditions,
                      'getBooks': getBooks,
                      'onClose': lambda: setBookModal(None)
                    }),
        el(CircularProgress,
            {'style': {'position': 'absolute',
                       'top': '30%',
                       'left': '50%',
                       'marginLeft': -12}
        }) if showProgress else None
    )
```

Chapter 39 - Editing Books | 345

We started here by adding imports for the `BookEdit` component and the `UserCtx` context variable. Then we add the `bookModal` state variable that will be used to indicate when the `BookEdit` component should be shown.

The `isLoggedIn` value from the context variable will let us know when we should be in read-only mode. If we are, then the icon button for adding new book records will not be shown. The `AddIcon` appears on the left side of the title bar in front of the window title, and we wrapped it in a `Tooltip` component to make it clear what that button is for. By adding an inline conditional statement to that particular `createElement()` function call, we can control the visibility of that element on the fly without having to introduce any additional external logic. We've used this method several times already for controlling modal views, but keep in mind that it works for individual nested elements as well.

One helper function we added is `setEdit()`, which is used to set the value of the `bookModal` state variable that determines when the `BookEdit` modal component is shown. If `bookModal` has an ID value assigned to it, the modal view will be visible. We need to pass this function to the `BookTable` component so that the `bookModal` state variable can be updated when a row in the table is clicked, which then causes the modal `BookEdit` component to be shown for editing that particular book record.

Lastly, we attach the `BookEdit` component itself to the element tree and pass in all of the props that it requires.

This brings us to the last existing module we need to update, and that is the **bookListTable.py** module. Here, we just need to add the functionality that shows the modal `BookEdit` view whenever a row is clicked:

Listing 39-6 File: *bookListTable.py*

```
from common.pyreact import createElement as el
from common.pymui import Box, Link, Tooltip
from common.pymui import TableContainer, Table
from common.pymui import TableHead, TableBody, TableRow, TableCell

def BookRowVu(props):
    book = props['book']
    setEdit = props['setEdit']

    book_id = book['ID']
    title = book['Title']
```

```python
    author = book['Author']
    book_type = "Fiction" if book['IsFiction'] else "Non-Fiction"
    category = book['Category']
    book_fmt = book['Format']
    location = book['Location']

    def handleEdit():
        setEdit(book_id)

    return el(TableRow, {'onClick': handleEdit},
              el(TableCell, None,
                 el(Tooltip, {'title': title if title else ''},
                    el(Box, {'width': '10rem',
                             'textOverflow': 'ellipsis',
                             'overflow': 'hidden',
                             'whiteSpace': 'nowrap'}, title),
                    )
                 ),
              el(TableCell, None,
                 el(Box, {'width': '6rem', 'whiteSpace': 'nowrap'}, author)),
              el(TableCell, None,
                 el(Box, {'width': '5rem'}, book_type)),
              el(TableCell, None,
                 el(Box, {'width': '8rem'}, category)),
              el(TableCell, None,
                 el(Box, {'width': '6rem'}, book_fmt)),
              el(TableCell, None,
                 el(Box, {'width': '5rem'}, location)),
              )

def BooksTable(props):
    books = props['books']
    setSortKey = props['setSortKey']
    setEdit = props['setEdit']

    def bookToRow(book):
        return el(BookRowVu, {'key': book['ID'],
                              'book': book,
                              'setEdit': setEdit}
                  )

    def BookRows():
...
```

React to Python

We added the `setEdit()` function as a prop that is passed into this `BooksTable` component from the parent `BookList` component. We destructure that prop, creating a local variable for it, and then pass it on through to the `BookRowVu` component, which is where we actually need to use it.

In the BookRowVu component, we destructure the `setEdit()` function prop there as well, and also extract the ID value from the book dictionary. We then add an `onClick` event handler to each `TableRow` that calls the encapsulated `handleEdit()` function. When that function is called, it sets the value of the bookModal state variable in the `BookList` component, which will then result in the modal `BookEdit` component being visible when the row is clicked.

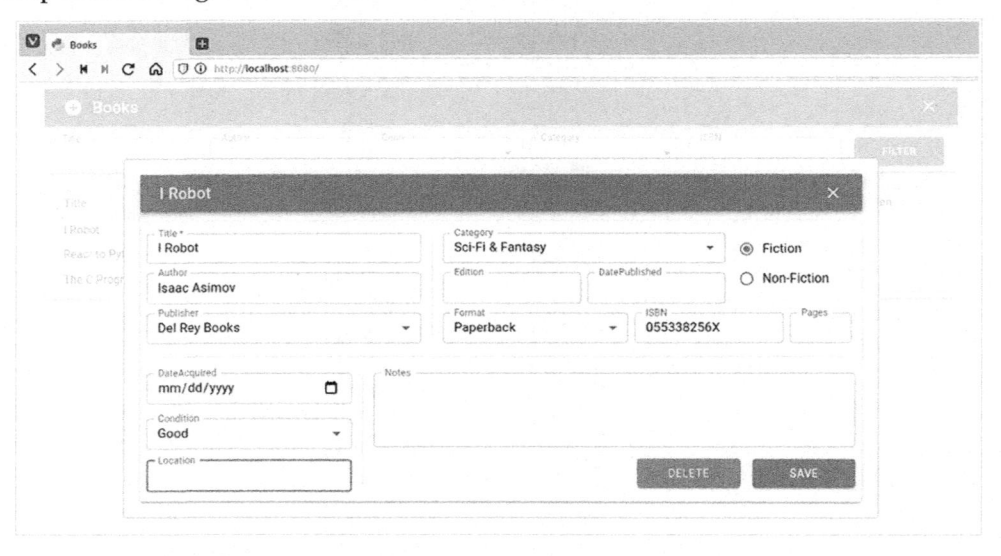

The final file and folder structure of our client application looks like this:

```
client/
├── .git/
├── node_modules/
├── src/
│   ├── common/
│   │   ├── __init__.py
│   │   ├── jsutils.py
│   │   ├── pymui.py
│   │   ├── pyreact.py
│   │   └── urlutils.py
│   ├── main/
│   │   ├── __init__.py
```

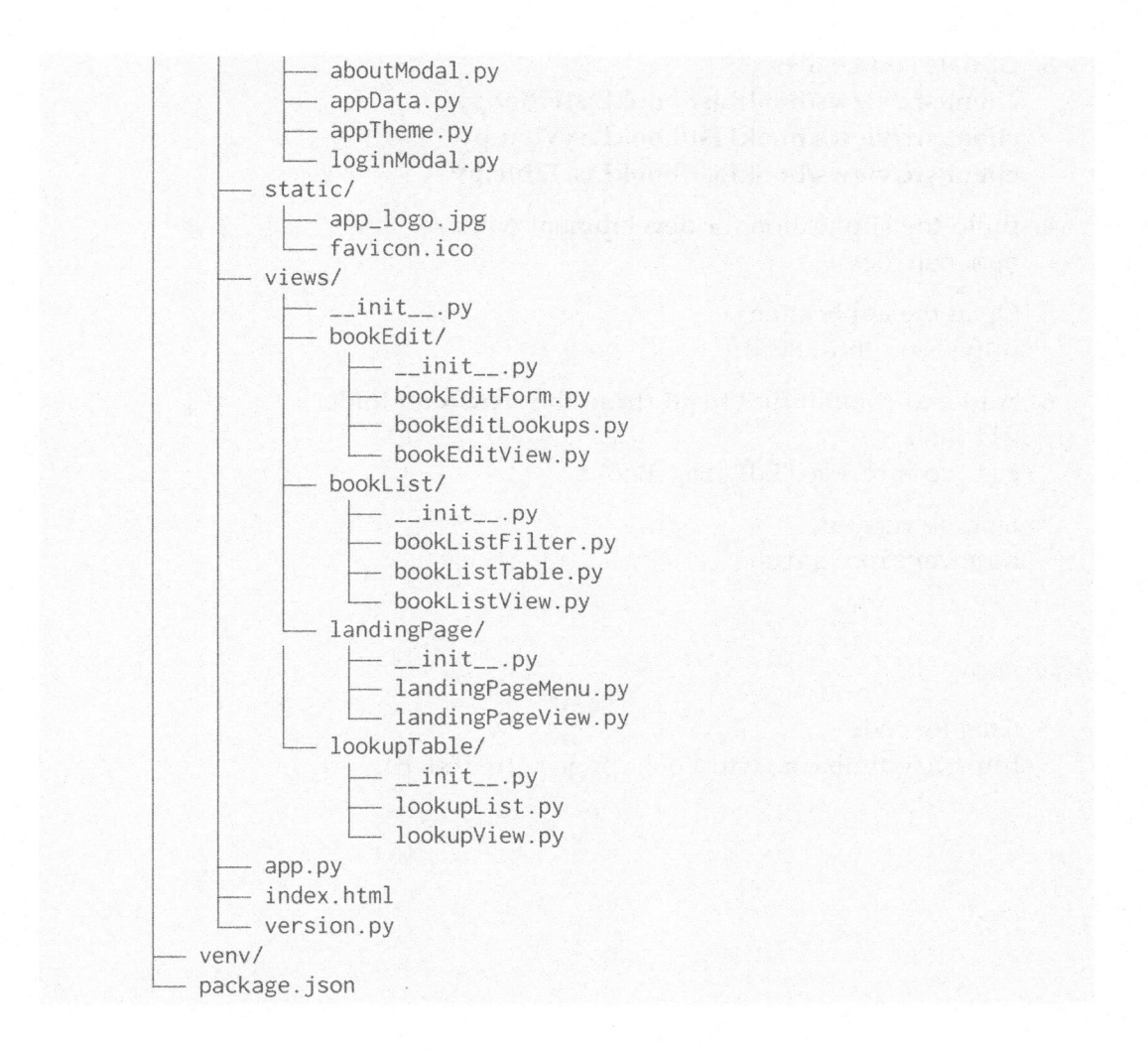

```
            ├── aboutModal.py
            ├── appData.py
            ├── appTheme.py
            └── loginModal.py
        ├── static/
        │   ├── app_logo.jpg
        │   └── favicon.ico
        ├── views/
        │   ├── __init__.py
        │   ├── bookEdit/
        │   │   ├── __init__.py
        │   │   ├── bookEditForm.py
        │   │   ├── bookEditLookups.py
        │   │   └── bookEditView.py
        │   ├── bookList/
        │   │   ├── __init__.py
        │   │   ├── bookListFilter.py
        │   │   ├── bookListTable.py
        │   │   └── bookListView.py
        │   ├── landingPage/
        │   │   ├── __init__.py
        │   │   ├── landingPageMenu.py
        │   │   └── landingPageView.py
        │   └── lookupTable/
        │       ├── __init__.py
        │       ├── lookupList.py
        │       └── lookupView.py
        ├── app.py
        ├── index.html
        └── version.py
    ├── venv/
    └── package.json
```

Chapter Review:

1. Create bookEdit folder:
   client/src/views/bookEdit/

2. Add source files:
   client/src/views/bookEdit/__init__.py
   client/src/views/bookEdit/bookEditView.py
   client/src/views/bookEdit/bookEditLookups.py
   client/src/views/bookEdit/bookEditForm.py

3. Update source files:
client/src/views/bookList/bookListFilter.py
client/src/views/bookList/bookListView.py
client/src/views/bookList/bookListTable.py

4. Build the application for development with:
```
npm run dev
```

5. Open the application:
http://localhost:8080

6. Add and commit files to git (from the **src/client/** folder):
```
git add .
git commit -m "Editing Books"
```

7. Update version:
```
npm version patch
```

References:

- Chapter code
  https://github.com/rtp-book/project/tree/step12

Chapter 40 – SPA Redirect

One problem with single-page applications, is that because the application loads all at once at the beginning of a session, the browser URL never changes. This makes it difficult to get back to a particular screen in the application, and also makes it impossible to bookmark specific views. To work around this limitation of single-page applications, by using some built-in JavaScript function calls, we can manually set the browser URL ourselves without causing the application itself to reload.

Once we have this capability in place, we will be able to bookmark views, and jump directly to specific screens in our application, even if the application gets reloaded into the web browser. It will also give us the ability to use the web browser's forward and back buttons to move through our application.

40.1 Redirect Functionality

The first step is to add the functionality that allows us to modify the web browser URL without reloading the application, and to re-render our application if the URL changes. We start by modifying the render() function in the **pyreact.py** module to inject the current URL path and query parameters into the component props. With this information available, we will be able to perform view routing in the main App component using the URL in the web browser. The minor changes we make to this module are the key to the redirect framework we will be implementing in this chapter.

Listing 40-1 File: *pyreact.py*

```
# __pragma__ ('skip')
from common import require, document, window, __new__
# __pragma__ ('noskip')

...

def render(root_component, props, container):
    def main():
        querystring = window.location.search
        params = __new__(window.URLSearchParams(querystring)).entries()
        new_props = {'pathname': window.location.pathname,
```

```
                    'params': {p[0]: p[1] for p in params if p}}
        new_props.update(props)
        ReactDOM.render(
            React.createElement(root_component, new_props),
            document.getElementById(container)
        )
    document.addEventListener('DOMContentLoaded', main)
    window.addEventListener('popstate', main)
```

Here, we use some built-in JavaScript window methods to get the URL path (`location.pathname`) and querystring parameters (`location.search`), and add those as two additional props that get sent to the main entry point App component. To turn the querystring parameters into a proper Python dictionary requires a few extra steps. We first get an iterator by passing the querystring to the `window.URLSearchParams()` method. Because Python doesn't have the keyword "new", we need to use the Transcrypt `__new__()` constructor function here since we are explicitly creating a JavaScript object. During transpilation, Transcrypt will convert this expression into the proper JavaScript format:

```
var params = new window.URLSearchParams (window.location.search).entries ();
```

Then, once we have that iterator, we use a Python dictionary comprehension to loop through the iterator object and create the parameter dictionary.

We also added a browser event listener for `popstate` that calls the functional part of our `render()` function to refresh the application whenever the web browser back button is pressed.

Now that our application has the ability to work with the web browser URL, we can add some additional functionality to the existing **urlutils.py** module to perform page redirects based on the URL.

Listing 40-2 File: *urlutils.py*

```
import time
from common.pyreact import ReactGA, createElement as el
from common.pymui import Link as MuiLink
from common.jsutils import console

# __pragma__ ('skip')
```

React to Python

```python
from common import require, window, JSON, __new__
# __pragma__ ('noskip')


polyfill = require("@babel/polyfill")  # required by async/await


# __pragma__ ('kwargs')
async def fetch(url, callback=None, **kwargs):
    ReactGA.event({'category': 'api', 'action': 'request', 'label': url})
    t_start = time.time()
    on_error = kwargs.pop('onError', None)
    redirect = kwargs.pop('redirect', True)
    method = kwargs.pop('method', 'GET')
    try:
        if method == 'POST' or method == 'DELETE':
            data = kwargs.pop('data', None)
            # headers needs to be a plain JS object
            headers = {'Content-Type': 'application/json;'}  # __:jsiter
            response = await window.fetch(url, {'method': method,
                                                'headers': headers,
                                                'body': JSON.stringify(data)
                                                }
                                          )
        else:
            kw_params = kwargs.pop('params', {})
            params = buildParams(kw_params)
            response = await window.fetch(f"{url}{params}")

        if response.status == 401:
            console.error("401 - Session Expired")
            if redirect:
                redirToLoginPage()
            raise Exception("Unauthorized")
        elif response.status != 200:
            console.error('Fetch error - Status Code: ' + response.status)
            if on_error:
                on_error()
        else:
            json_data = await response.json()
            t_elapsed = time.time() - t_start
            ReactGA.timing({'category': 'API',
                            'variable': 'fetch',
                            'value': int(t_elapsed * 1000),
                            'label': url}
```

Chapter 40 - SPA Redirect | 353

```python
                )
            error = dict(json_data).get('error', None)
            if error:
                raise Exception(error)
            else:
                result = dict(json_data).get('success', None)
                if callback:
                    callback(result)
    except object as e:
        console.error(str(e))
        if on_error:
            on_error()

# __pragma__ ('nokwargs')


def buildParams(param_dict: dict):
    param_list = [f"&{key}={window.encodeURIComponent(val)}"
                    for key, val in param_dict.items() if val]
    params = ''.join(param_list)
    return f"?{params[1:]}" if len(params) > 0 else ''


def spaRedirect(url):
    window.history.pushState(None, '', url)
    window.dispatchEvent(__new__(window.PopStateEvent('popstate')))


def redirToLoginPage():
    # Check if redir is already in params
    params = __new__(window.URLSearchParams(window.location.search)).entries()
    param_dict = {p[0]: p[1] for p in params if p}
    redir = param_dict.get('redir', None)

    if redir:
        hrefNew = f"/?login=show&redir={window.encodeURIComponent(redir)}"
    else:
        hrefCurrent = window.location.href
        if hrefCurrent:
            encoded_href = window.encodeURIComponent(hrefCurrent)
            hrefNew = f"/?login=show&redir={encoded_href}"
        else:
            hrefNew = '/?login=show'
```

```
    window.location.href = hrefNew


def Link(props):
    """Internal SPA link with browser history"""

    def onClick(event):
        event.preventDefault()
        spaRedirect(props['to'])

    def onClickAlt(event):
        event.preventDefault()
        props['onClick']()

    if props['onClick']:
        return el(MuiLink, {'href': props['to'],
                           'onClick': onClickAlt}, props['children'])
    else:
        return el(MuiLink, {'href': props['to'],
                           'onClick': onClick}, props['children'])
```

There are several things we added here, the first being the ability to automatically redirect to the Login modal view if we receive an HTTP 401 *Unauthorized* response from the back-end server. This option is facilitated by looking for a "redirect" keyword argument that is sent to our fetch() function, which defaults to True if not supplied. If the redirect option is enabled, the redirToLoginPage() function will be called if the request receives a 401 response. We raise an error here just so that the calling function knows something went wrong and can do things like show an error snackbar to the user.

The redirToLoginPage() function keeps track of what the current URL is by adding it to the URL querystring as a parameter called "redir", after checking to make sure that there isn't already one there. If the "redir" parameter *is* already part of the querystring, it will keep the one that is there. It then sets the current web browser URL to the landingPage view with an extra querystring parameter login=show that lets the LandingPage component know that the modal Login component should be shown when the view is loaded.

The key function that allows our application to change views based on the URL is spaRedirect(). It makes calls to two JavaScript window methods. The first one pushes the specified URL onto the web browser's history stack using the pushState() method. It then fires a browser event that pops that URL off the stack with the `PopStateEvent()` method. When this happens, it triggers the web browser event listener for `popstate` that we just added to the `render()` function in the **pyreact.py** module, which causes our application to re-render.

The last item we added to this module is a wrapper for the Material-UI `Link` component that we currently use on the `landingPage` view. We added some conditional logic to it where if an `onClick` event handler is supplied, it will just behave normally and call whatever function is supplied. If an `onClick` handler is not supplied and there is just a destination URL, then it will use the `spaRedirect()` function to process the supplied URL. In both cases, it is still the Material-UI `Link` component that gets rendered in the UI by React. Our wrapper component just modifies the behavior of it when a URL is supplied. Note that to avoid namespace collisions, we imported the Material-UI `Link` component using the `MuiLink` alias.

One benefit of using the SPA redirect functionality, is that it actually makes our code a little cleaner when we need to move between views. Rather than passing view logic around using props, we can instead use the `spaRedirect()` function to directly update the URL in the web browser. Each of our view components can then adjust its behavior based on the current URL and querystring parameters.

40.2 Page Routing

Now that our application has the ability to update the URL, let's factor that into our application routing mechanism. Instead of using state variables to keep track of what view component needs to be shown, we can now use the URL in the web browser to route views. We change that routing functionality in our main **app.py** module:

Listing 40-3 File: *app.py*

```
from common.pyreact import render, createElement as el, ReactGA
from common.pyreact import useState, useEffect
from common.pymui import ThemeProvider, SnackbarProvider
from common.jsutils import setTitle, console
from common.urlutils import fetch, spaRedirect
from main import UserCtx
from main.appTheme import theme
from main.appData import gaid
from views.bookList.bookListView import BookList
from views.landingPage.landingPageView import LandingPage
```

React to Python

```python
ReactGA.initialize(gaid, {'titleCase': False, 'debug': False,
                    'gaOptions': {'siteSpeedSampleRate': 100}}
                )


def App(props):
    title = props['title']
    pathname = props['pathname']

    user, setUser = useState("")

    setTitle(title)

    router = {
        '/': LandingPage,
        '/books': BookList,
    }

    route_is_valid = pathname in router
    isLoggedIn = len(user) > 0

    def login(username):
        setUser(username)

    def logout():
        setUser("")
        fetch('/api/logout', lambda: spaRedirect('/'))

    def validateSession():
        def validated():
            def _setuser(data):
                login(data['user'])

            if not isLoggedIn:
                fetch('/api/whoami', _setuser,
                    onError=console.error,
                    redirect=False
                    )

        def notValidated(error):
            if len(user) > 0:
                setUser("")
```

```
        if route_is_valid:
            fetch('/api/ping', validated, onError=notValidated, redirect=False)

    user_ctx = {'user': user,
                'login': login,
                'logout': logout,
                'isLoggedIn': isLoggedIn
                }

    useEffect(validateSession, [])
    useEffect(lambda: ReactGA.pageview(pathname), [pathname])

    if route_is_valid:
        return el(ThemeProvider, {'theme': theme},
                  el(SnackbarProvider, {'maxSnack': 3},
                     el(UserCtx.Provider, {'value': user_ctx},
                        el(router[pathname], props)
                        )
                     )
                  )
    else:
        console.error(f"ERROR - Bad pathname for route: {props['pathname']}")
        return el('div', None,
                  el('h1', None, "Page Not Found"),
                  el('p', None, f"Bad pathname: {props['pathname']}"),
                  el('div', None, el('a', {'href': "/"}, "Back to Home"))
                  )

render(App, {'title': "Books"}, 'root')
```

Instead of using the booksShow state variable to indicate whether the LandingPage or BookList view component should be shown, we now use the pathname prop that is based on the web browser URL to determine the view. Because the URL can be manually manipulated by the user, we will need to do some data validation to make sure the URL is something we are expecting.

The route_is_valid local variable is based on whether or not the URL that was passed in is a valid route in our router dictionary, which we do with a simple dictionary key check. When validating the user session, we now avoid making the call to the REST service to check the login status if the requested view route is not valid. When logging out, we also set the web browser URL to the default route using the spaRedirect() function, which will take the user back to the landingPage view when the logout is complete.

If the URL route is valid, we render the application just as we did before, with the exception that instead of passing the booksShow state variable set function that we used to have before, we now just forward the props that were passed into the App component. This way, the view we are rendering can utilize any URL querystring parameters that may exist. If the route is not valid, we render a raw HTML error page indicating the bad URL, and provide a link to get back to the default landingPage view.

One last extra thing we did here was to add another call to Google Analytics that logs a page view any time the URL we are processing changes. This is accomplished with the useEffect() hook function that monitors the pathname prop.

40.3 Redirecting Pages

Now we need to update all of our application views to utilize the new SPA redirect functionality. We will need to consider both using the spaRedirect() function to facilitate a view change, and also factor in utilizing the URL parameters to possibly initialize state when view components are loaded. We'll start by updating the **landingPageView.py** module:

Listing 40-4 File: *landingPageView.py*

```
from common.pyreact import useState, createElement as el, useEffect, useContext
from common.pymui import Container, Paper, Typography, useSnackbar
from common.pymui import IconButton, MenuIcon
from common.urlutils import fetch, Link, buildParams, spaRedirect
from main import UserCtx
from main.appTheme import Flexbox, FlexboxCenter
from main.aboutModal import About
from main.appData import appname
from main.loginModal import Login
from views.landingPage.landingPageMenu import LandingPageMenu
from views.lookupTable.lookupView import LookupTable


def LandingPage(props):
    params = dict(props['params'])
    pathname = props['pathname']

    show_login = params.get('login', 'hide') == 'show'
```

```python
uCtx = useContext(UserCtx)
isLoggedIn = uCtx['isLoggedIn']
login = uCtx['login']

mainMenu, setMainMenu = useState(None)
aboutShow, setAboutShow = useState(False)
lockupModal, setLookupModal = useState(None)
loginModal, setLoginModal = useState(False)
username, setUsername = useState("")
password, setPassword = useState("")

snack = useSnackbar()

def doLogin():
    def _login():
        login(username)
        snack.enqueueSnackbar("Login succeeded!", {'variant': 'success'})
        spaRedirect(redir)

    def _loginFailed():
        setLoginModal(True)
        snack.enqueueSnackbar("Login failed, please try again",
                              {'variant': 'error'}
                              )

    redir = params.get('redir', f"{pathname}{buildParams(params)}")
    fetch("/api/login", _login,
          data={'username': username, 'password': password},
          method='POST',
          onError=_loginFailed
          )

    setLoginModal(False)

def clearUser():
    if loginModal:
        setUsername("")
        setPassword("")

def mainMenuOpen(event):
    setMainMenu(event['currentTarget'])

def mainMenuClose():
    setMainMenu(None)
```

React to Python

```python
def aboutModalOpen():
    setAboutShow(True)

useEffect(lambda: setLoginModal(show_login), [show_login])
useEffect(clearUser, [loginModal])

return el(Container, {'maxWidth': 'md'},
        el(Paper, {'style': {'padding': '1rem'}},
            el(Flexbox, {'alignItems': 'center'},
                el(IconButton, {'edge': 'start',
                                'color': 'inherit',
                                'onClick': mainMenuOpen
                               }, el(MenuIcon, None)
                  ),
                el(Typography, {'variant': 'h5'}, appname)
            )
        ),
        el(LandingPageMenu, {'mainMenu': mainMenu,
                             'mainMenuClose': mainMenuClose,
                             'setLookupModal':
                                 lambda tbl: setLookupModal(tbl),
                             'aboutModalOpen': aboutModalOpen}
        ),
        el(Paper, {'style': {'padding': '0.5rem',
                             'marginTop': '1rem'}
                  },
            el(FlexboxCenter, None,
                el(Typography, {'variant': 'h5'},
                    el(Link, {'to': '/books'}, "Books")
                ),
            ),
            el(FlexboxCenter, None,
                el(Typography, {'variant': 'h5'},
                    el(Link, {'to': '#',
                              'onClick': lambda: setLoginModal(True)
                             }, "Login")
                ) if not isLoggedIn else None
            ),
        ),
        el(Login, {'onClose': lambda: setLoginModal(False),
                   'onLogin': doLogin,
                   'password': password,
                   'username': username,
                   'setUsername': lambda usr: setUsername(usr),
```

```
                    'setPassword': lambda pwd: setPassword(pwd),
                    'modalState': loginModal,
                }
        ),
        el(About, {'onClose': lambda: setAboutShow(False),
                   'modalState': aboutShow}
        ),
        el(LookupTable, {'table': lookupModal,
                         'onClose': lambda: setLookupModal(None)}
        ) if lookupModal else None
    )
```

For the `LandingPage` component, instead of using the `setBooksShow()` function that was previously passed in as a prop to change views, we now use the `params` and `pathname` props and the `spaRedirect()` function to control the view. One of the keys that may be included in the `params` dictionary is "login", that when set to a value of "show", will trigger the modal `Login` view to be visible. This is accomplished with a `useEffect()` hook function that monitors the local variable `show_login` and will set the `loginModal` state variable when it changes.

In the `doLogin()` function, we check and see if there is a "redir" key in the `params` dictionary. This may have been set if the user session had been invalidated at some point, and the `fetch()` function redirected to the login form after receiving an HTTP 401 response. If there is a "redir" key present, after a successful login, `spaRedirect()` will be called with the URL value that was specified in that key. This will take the user back to the view they were in before being redirected to the login form.

Notice that we changed the module that we import the `Link` component from. Instead of using the Material-UI Link component like we were using before, we now import the wrapped version of the `Link` component from the **urlutils.py** module that allows us to take advantage of the SPA redirect functionality.

So for the link to the `bookList` view, instead of having an `onClick` event handler, we can now just directly provide the routing URL for the `bookList` view in the `to` prop. Our wrapped `Link` component will then take care of executing the `spaRedirect()` function using the provided URL. For the login link, we keep the same `onClick` event handler since we are still executing a function without changing the current view. The wrapped `Link` component does have a slightly different prop signature, so we do need to change the href prop and use the to prop instead.

Next, let's give the same treatment to the bookList view:

Listing 40-5 File: *bookListView.py*

```python
from common.pyreact import useState, useEffect, createElement as el, useContext
from common.pymui import Typography, AppBar, Toolbar, Tooltip, useSnackbar
from common.pymui import Container, Box, Paper, CircularProgress
from common.pymui import IconButton, CloseIcon, AddIcon
from common.urlutils import fetch, spaRedirect, buildParams
from main import UserCtx
from views.bookEdit.bookEditView import BookEdit
from views.bookList.bookListFilter import BooksFilterVu
from views.bookList.bookListTable import BooksTable


def BookList(props):
    params = props['params']

    book_id = params['id']

    books, setBooks = useState([])
    sortKey, setSortKey = useState('Title')
    showProgress, setShowProgress = useState(False)
    filterParams, setFilterParams = useState({})
    bookModal, setBookModal = useState(None)

    categories, setCategories = useState([])
    publishers, setPublishers = useState([])
    formats, setFormats = useState([])
    conditions, setConditions = useState([])

    ctx = useContext(UserCtx)
    isLoggedIn = ctx['isLoggedIn']

    snack = useSnackbar()

    def handleAdd():
        new_params = buildParams({'id': "NEW"})
        spaRedirect(f'/books{new_params}')

    def setEdit():
```

```python
        if book_id:
            setBookModal(book_id)
        else:
            setBookModal(None)

    def sortBooks():
        book_list = [dict(tmp_book) for tmp_book in books]
        if len(book_list) > 0:
            setBooks(sorted(book_list, key=lambda k: k[sortKey] or ""))

    def on_fetch_error():
        snack.enqueueSnackbar("Error retrieving data!",
                              {'variant': 'error'}
                              )
        setShowProgress(False)

    def getBooks():
        isPending = True

        def _getBooks(data):
            book_list = data if data else []
            if isPending:
                if len(book_list) > 0:
                    setBooks(sorted(book_list, key=lambda k: k[sortKey]))
                else:
                    setBooks([])
                setShowProgress(False)

        def abort():
            nonlocal isPending
            isPending = False

        setShowProgress(True)
        fetch("/api/books", _getBooks,
            params=filterParams,
            onError=on_fetch_error
            )
        return abort

    def getLookup(table_name, setState):
        isPending = True

        def _getLookup(data):
            if isPending:
                if data:
```

```python
                setState(data)
            else:
                setState([])
        
        def abort():
            nonlocal isPending
            isPending = False
        
        fetch(f"/api/lookup/{table_name}", _getLookup)
        return abort
    
    def getLookups():
        getLookup('Categories', setCategories)
        getLookup('Publishers', setPublishers)
        getLookup('Formats', setFormats)
        getLookup('Conditions', setConditions)
    
    useEffect(getBooks, [filterParams])
    useEffect(sortBooks, [sortKey])
    useEffect(setEdit, [book_id])
    useEffect(getLookups, [])
    
    return el(Container, None,
            el(AppBar, {'position': 'static',
                        'style': {'marginBottom': '0.5rem'}
                       },
                el(Toolbar, {'variant': 'dense'},
                    el(Tooltip, {'title': 'Add new book'},
                        el(IconButton, {'edge': 'start',
                                        'color': 'inherit',
                                        'padding': 'none',
                                        'onClick': handleAdd
                                       }, el(AddIcon, None)
                        )
                    ) if isLoggedIn else None,
                    el(Box, {'width': '100%'},
                      el(Typography, {'variant': 'h6'}, "Books")
                    ),
                    el(IconButton, {'edge': 'end',
                                    'color': 'inherit',
                                    'onClick': lambda: spaRedirect('/')
                                   }, el(CloseIcon, None)
                    ),
                ),
            ),
```

```
        el(BooksFilterVu, {'categories': categories,
                          'setFilterParams': setFilterParams}
        ),
        el(Paper, {'style': {'padding': '0.5rem', 'marginTop': '0.8rem'}},
            el(BooksTable, {'books': books, 'setSortKey': setSortKey})
        ),
        el(BookEdit, {'bookId': bookModal,
                      'categories': categories,
                      'publishers': publishers,
                      'formats': formats,
                      'conditions': conditions,
                      'getBooks': getBooks
                     }),
        el(CircularProgress,
            {'style': {'position': 'absolute',
                       'top': '30%',
                       'left': '50%',
                       'marginLeft': -12}
        }) if showProgress else None
    )
```

Just like in the `LandingPage` component, we swap out the `setBooksShow()` function that was previously passed in as a prop to change views, and we now use the `params` prop and the `spaRedirect()` function to control the view.

To control the visibility of the modal `BookEdit` view, instead of setting the `bookModal` state variable directly, we can add the ID of the book record that we want to edit as a URL querystring parameter. We then update the `bookModal` state variable indirectly by utilizing a `useEffect()` hook function that monitors the `book_id` local variable that holds the value of the "id" querystring parameter if it exists. Using this method allows us to directly open the record of a specific book using a bookmarkable URL.

Since the `book_id` variable is now in scope outside of the `setEdit()` function, we no longer need to pass the book ID to the function as an argument, so we removed that.

For the close icon button, instead of setting the value of a state variable to get back to the `landingPage` view, we now just use the `spaRedirect()` function to set the URL to the default route. Then for the add icon button, we created the `handleAdd()` function that calls `spaRedirect()` and adds the "id" querystring parameter with a value of "NEW" to the `bookList` route. As above, this will update the bookModal state variable causing the view to re-render and show the modal bookEdit view with a new book record.

Since we are now using the URL to dictate showing the modal bookEdit view, we no longer need to pass the setEdit() function to the BooksTable component as a prop so it can also be removed. Similarly, we no longer need an onClose() function for the BookEdit component, so that prop can be removed as well.

To edit an existing record using the SPA redirect functionality, we will need to update the **bookListTable.py** module next:

Listing 40-6 File: *bookListTable.py*

```python
from common.pyreact import createElement as el
from common.urlutils import buildParams, spaRedirect
from common.pymui import Box, Link, Tooltip
from common.pymui import TableContainer, Table
from common.pymui import TableHead, TableBody, TableRow, TableCell


def BookRowVu(props):
    book = props['book']

    book_id = book['ID']
    title = book['Title']
    author = book['Author']
    book_type = "Fiction" if book['IsFiction'] else "Non-Fiction"
    category = book['Category']
    book_fmt = book['Format']
    location = book['Location']

    def handleEdit():
        params = buildParams({'id': book_id})
        spaRedirect(f'/books{params}')

    return el(TableRow, {'onClick': handleEdit},
            el(TableCell, None,
                el(Tooltip, {'title': title if title else ''},
                    el(Box, {'width': '10rem',
                             'textOverflow': 'ellipsis',
                             'overflow': 'hidden',
                             'whiteSpace': 'nowrap'}, title),
                )
            ),
            el(TableCell, None,
```

```
                el(Box, {'width': '6rem', 'whiteSpace': 'nowrap'}, author)),
            el(TableCell, None,
                el(Box, {'width': '5rem'}, book_type)),
            el(TableCell, None,
                el(Box, {'width': '8rem'}, category)),
            el(TableCell, None,
                el(Box, {'width': '6rem'}, book_fmt)),
            el(TableCell, None,
                el(Box, {'width': '5rem'}, location)),
        )

def BooksTable(props):
    books = props['books']
    setSortKey = props['setSortKey']

    def bookToRow(book):
        return el(BookRowVu, {'key': book['ID'], 'book': book})

    def BookRows():

...
```

Because it is no longer needed, here we removed the prop for the setEdit() function in both the BooksTable component and the BookRowVu component. The only other change we needed to make in this module was in the handleEdit() function of the BookRowVu component. We replaced the call to setEdit() that was previously there with a call to spaRedirect() instead, where we add the "id" querystring parameter with the ID value of the book we want to edit to the bookList route.

The last module we need to update is **bookEditView.py**, where we just need to modify how we handle closing the modal view:

Listing 40-7 File: *bookEditView.py*

```
from common.jsutils import confirm
from common.pyreact import useState, useEffect, createElement as el, Modal
from common.pymui import Typography, AppBar, Toolbar, Box, useSnackbar
from common.pymui import IconButton, CloseIcon
from common.urlutils import fetch, spaRedirect
from main.appTheme import modalStyles
```

```python
from views.bookEdit.bookEditForm import BookEditForm


book_template = dict(
    ID=None,
    Title="",
    Author=None,
    Publisher=None,
    IsFiction=0,
    Category=None,
    Edition=None,
    DatePublished=None,
    ISBN=None,
    Pages=None,
    DateAcquired=None,
    Condition=None,
    Format=None,
    Location=None,
    Notes=None
)


def BookEdit(props):
    bookId = props['bookId']
    categories = props['categories']
    publishers = props['publishers']
    formats = props['formats']
    conditions = props['conditions']
    getBooks = props['getBooks']

    book, setBook = useState(book_template)
    bookInitial, setBookInitial = useState(book_template)
    modalState = bool(bookId)

    snack = useSnackbar()

...

    def on_update_success():
        getBooks()
        snack.enqueueSnackbar("Book was updated!", {'variant': 'success'})
        spaRedirect('/books')

    def on_update_error():
```

```
    ...
        return el(Modal, {'isOpen': modalState,
                          'style': modalStyles,
                          'ariaHideApp': False,
                         },
              el(AppBar, {'position': 'static',
                          'style': {'marginBottom': '0.5rem'}
                         },
                el(Toolbar, {'variant': 'dense'},
                  el(Box, {'width': '100%'},
                    el(Typography, {'variant': 'h6'}, book.Title)
                  ),
                  el(IconButton, {'edge': 'end',
                                  'color': 'inherit',
                                  'onClick': lambda: spaRedirect('/books')
                                 }, el(CloseIcon, None)
                  ),
                ),
              ),
              el(BookEditForm, {'book': book,
                                'handleInputChange': handleInputChange,
                                'categories': categories,
                                'publishers': publishers,
                                'formats': formats,
                                'conditions': conditions,
                                'isDirty': isDirty,
                                'saveBook': saveBook,
                                'deleteBook': deleteBook
                               }),
        )
```

The only changes we made in this module are related to the onClose() function that we no longer need, which was previously being passed in as a prop. All we had to do was replace the onClose() function with a call to the spaRedirect() function instead, passing it the URL route for the bookList view without any URL query parameters. We made that change both in the on_update_success() function, and for the onClick event of the IconButton used for closing the modal view.

What you will now see when you open up the book list or view an individual book, is that the URL will reflect the state of the specific view. For example, given a specific book ID, you can now jump right to the view for that book without going through the landing page or book list view first:

http://localhost:8080/books?id=3

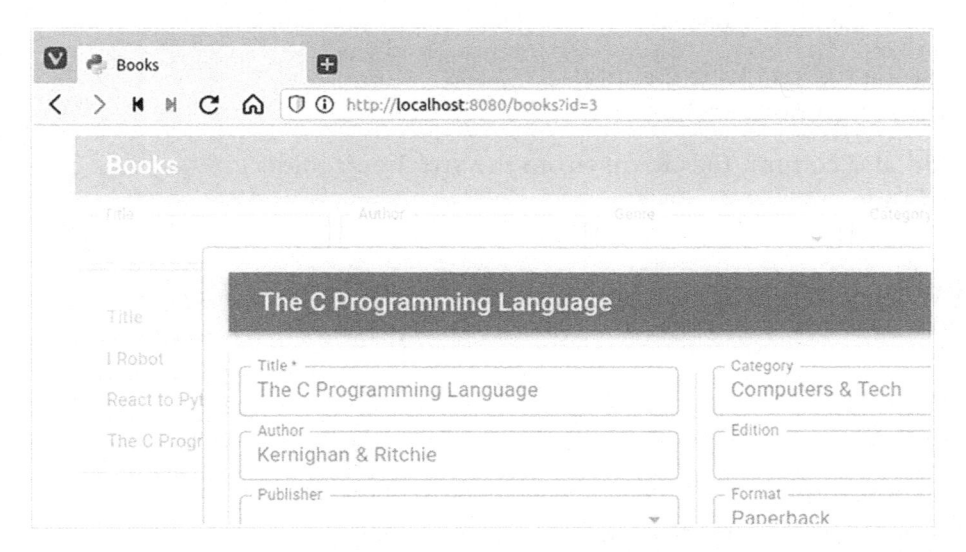

While there were many changes that we made here to achieve the SPA redirect functionality, it is a necessary feature for any single-page application of significant size. But now that the framework is there to utilize, adding new views to the application becomes much more compartmentalized. Using the web browser URL for view navigation is natural for applications running in a web browser environment, and using the SPA redirect framework ultimately helps to reduce complexity in your code.

Chapter Review:

1. Update source files:
   client/src/common/pyreact.py
   client/src/common/urlutils.py
   client/src/app.py
   client/src/views/landingPage/landingPageView.py
   client/src/views/bookList/bookListView.py
   client/src/views/bookList/bookListTable.py
   client/src/views/bookEdit/bookEditView.py

2. Build the application for development with:
   npm run dev

3. Open the application:
   http://localhost:8080

4. Test the redirect functionality:
   http://localhost:8080/books?id=3

5. Add and commit files to git (from the **src/client/** folder):
   git add .
   git commit -m "SPA Redirect"

6. Update version:
   npm version patch

References:

- Chapter code
  https://github.com/rtp-book/project/tree/step13

Chapter 41 – Deploying the Application

Once your application is working in the development environment and you want to deploy it to production, you should run the npm production script:

(venv) $ npm run build

This script transpiles your Python code and then bundles it with a different set of options that make your application optimized for a production environment. The source maps are removed, and the JavaScript is minified to make the bundle as small as possible. The bundled files are saved in the **./dist/prod/** folder of the project. These files can then be copied to wherever they need to be so that the production web server has access to them to serve them up as static files.

There are several ways to deploy applications like the one we've developed here, where you have a Flask back-end server, and also static content that needs to be served up for the front-end application. The basic requirement is that we need a way to serve the dynamic content from Flask using a WSGI container of some sort, and also a way to serve the static content with a web server.

The general server architecture is structured like this:

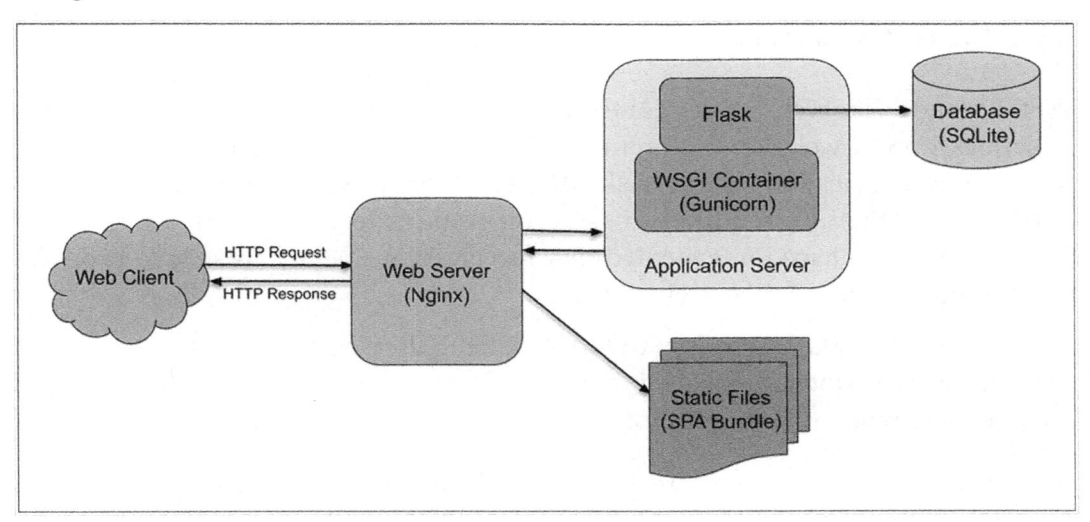

So when an HTTP request comes into the server, the web server will determine if the request is for a static file. If it is, it serves the file back to the client. If the request is for dynamic content, the web server will forward the request to an application server. The application server then processes the request and sends a response back to the web server, which then forwards it on to the client. This configuration is what is known as a reverse-proxy, where the web server is a proxy for the application server. The client making the request never communicates directly with the application server, and instead only communicates with it indirectly via the web server. So even though we are actually running two servers, only one is exposed to the public network.

41.1 Web Server

Most web sites serve up their content using a commercial or open-source web server. The three most popular web servers available today include Apache, NGINX, and Microsoft IIS. They are primarily designed to serve up static web content, but are configurable to forward requests for dynamic content to an application server.

If all you have is static content, such as a bundled single-page-application like the one we have just created, then this is all you need. However, if you also have dynamic content like what is served from a Flask REST server, then we will need to add an application server to serve that content.

41.2 WSGI Container

WSGI stands for Web Server Gateway Interface, which is a specification that describes how a web server communicates with web applications. It helps to separate the application-specific tasks that a web application performs, from more generic tasks that are required to serve up web content. Web frameworks like Flask and Django have implemented this specification, so they are able to properly communicate with popular web servers.

For convenience, Flask comes with the Werkzeug development application server that we might frequently use during the development process. One thing you may have noticed when that development server starts up is a message like this:

```
WARNING: This is a development server. Do not use it in a production
deployment. Use a production WSGI server instead.
```

The development server was not designed to be particularly secure, efficient, or stable and should not be used for production. Instead, we want to use one of the several WSGI containers out there that have actually been designed for production use. Some of the more common ones are:

- Gunicorn
- Phusion Passenger
- uWSGI
- Waitress
- Apache mod_wsgi

What WSGI container you use will be largely dependent on how much configurability you need, and what operating system platform you are running on. Probably the most common pairing of web server and WSGI container used when you have a Flask application, is to use NGINX and Gunicorn. As such, we will demonstrate using those here, but you should know that **these are intended to run in a *Linux* environment**.

On Windows, you have fewer options. The most common seem to be using the Apache web server with mod_wsgi, or possibly using the IIS web server with Waitress as the WSGI container. While the setup for each combination is going to be specific to whatever you decide to use, the basic concept of how it works will be the same as what we will demonstrate here with NGINX and Gunicorn.

41.3 Gunicorn

Gunicorn is a very popular WSGI container for Flask applications. When we run our Flask application using Gunicorn, it performs the role of an application server and responds to requests for dynamic content.

Let's switch back over to our Flask REST application and get Gunicorn set up. Deactivate the client virtual environment if it is currently active, change to the bookapp/server folder, then activate the server virtual environment. If the development Flask server is running, go ahead and stop it.

Conveniently for us, Gunicorn is PIP installable (*note that this is for Linux only*):

```
(venv) $ pip install gunicorn
```

In its simplest form, Gunicorn can start serving our Flask application from the command line with no options. In a terminal window with your virtual environment activated and while in the **bookapp/server/** folder, try this:

```
(venv) $ gunicorn appserver:app
```

This will start the Gunicorn application server, which should now be listening for requests on its default port 8000. If you open your web browser and go to this address:

http://localhost:8000/api/books

you should see a JSON response showing the book records from the *Books* table in SQLite.

The command-line argument that we passed to the Gunicorn server is the Python module that is the entry point for our Flask application, and the module-level variable that holds the main Flask object that we created. The Flask object has the necessary API interface that allows Gunicorn to communicate with our Flask application using WSGI.

Gunicorn has many configuration options that can be used to tune the service, including specifying the number of worker threads used to service requests, timeout options, logging options, and changing the port that it listens on. For the full list of configuration options available and how to use them, documentation is available on the Gunicorn project web site at https://gunicorn.org.

41.4 NGINX

Now that we have the back-end taken care of, we need something that can serve up the static files of the front-end application. NGINX is a highly efficient web server that is both very configurable and easy to implement.

Unlike Gunicorn, NGINX is not PIP installable and needs to be installed as a standalone application on your computer. How you install it will depend on what platform you are running it on and what package manager you use, but for a Linux distribution that uses APT, you can install it with this:

```
sudo apt-get update
sudo apt-get install nginx
```

If your Linux distribution uses Yum for package management, you can similarly use this:

```
sudo yum update
sudo yum install nginx
```

The installation for NGINX will configure it as a system service.

Win32 binaries are also available for NGINX, but I would recommend that you use Apache or IIS instead of NGINX if you want to run a web server on Windows. Additional installation details can be found on the NGINX website at https://www.nginx.com.

Once NGINX is installed, we will need to create a configuration file to tell it how to handle web requests. Configuration files are stored in the **/etc/nginx/sites-available/** folder by default. Here is a sample NGINX configuration file you would put into that folder:

Listing 41-1 File: *bookapp*

```
server {
    listen 80;
    root /home/data/bookapp/client/dist/prod/;
    index index.html;

    location /api {
        proxy_pass http://localhost:8000;
        include proxy_params;
    }

    location / {
        try_files $uri /index.html;
    }

    error_log   /var/log/nginx/api-error.log;
    access_log  /var/log/nginx/api-access.log;
}
```

In the configuration file, the first thing we do is specify the port to listen on with the `listen` option, which we set to port 80, which is the standard HTTP port for most production applications.

The `root` option is set to the file path where the bundled files that parcel produced are located. Here we can point it to where our bundled production JavaScript files are. On some servers, they might be located in a folder called `public` or `static`.

The `index` option tells NGINX what file to serve if none is specified. In this case, we would want to serve our main application **index.html** file.

The `location` entries in the configuration file are like the route entries in Flask. You can handle requests in different ways based on the URL pattern. For our application, we want to send any URLs that start with `/api` to the Flask server. We do this with a `proxy_pass` entry that passes the request through to the specified host. The `include proxy_params` entry adds additional headers so that the forwarded request is handled properly by the Flask server.

The `location` entry for the default URL is set to serve static files from the provided `root` location. The way we specified it here, NGINX will try to serve up any file that was requested, but if the file doesn't exist, it will serve up our **index.html** file instead. This is an important setting that allows us to use internal SPA URLs like `/books`. Without the `/index.html` failover for the default location route, NGINX would respond with a `404 Not Found` error if it received a request for `/books`.

The last part of the configuration specifies just where to keep the error and access logs.

Before NGINX can start using the configuration file we created, we need to enable it by putting a symbolic link or shortcut to the configuration file in the **/etc/nginx/sites-enabled/** folder:

```
sudo ln -s /etc/nginx/sites-available/bookapp /etc/nginx/sites-enabled/bookapp
```

NGINX normally comes with a default site running on port 80 that is enabled. If there is a symbolic link file called `default` in the **/etc/nginx/sites-enabled/** folder, we will need to delete it so that it doesn't interfere with our application that also wants to run on port 80:

```
sudo rm /etc/nginx/sites-enabled/default
```

Once the configuration is enabled, and you have Gunicorn serving up the REST service, you should be able to open the application in a web browser using the standard HTTP port with:

http://127.0.0.1/   or   http://localhost/

NGINX is capable of handling large scale deployments and is highly configurable. While we've barely scratched the surface of what it can do, what we have here should give you a good place to start from.

41.5 Flask for Static Content

While not necessarily recommended for heavily used applications, it *is* possible to forgo the web server for serving static content, and just use the application server to serve the static content along with the dynamic content. The main thing you would lose in this case is scalability and perhaps a bit of performance.

To do this, we will need to slightly modify the routing on our Flask REST server. In the **appserver.py** module for our Flask application, we need to specify the location of the static files that we want to serve, and then also change the way we deal with invalid routes:

Listing 41-2 File: *appserver.py*

```python
from flask import Flask, jsonify, request, Response, session
import flask_login
import logging
import os
from datetime import timedelta

import dbutils as db
from admin_routes import admin_api, User
from db_routes import db_api


fmt = "[%(asctime)s]|%(levelname)s|[%(module)s]:%(funcName)s()|%(message)s"
logging.basicConfig(format=fmt)
log = logging.getLogger()
log.setLevel(logging.INFO)

SERVE_SPA = True
SPA_DIR = '../client/dist/prod'
SESSION_TIMEOUT = 60

app = Flask(__name__, static_folder=SPA_DIR, static_url_path='/')
app.register_blueprint(admin_api)
app.register_blueprint(db_api)
```

```
...
@app.errorhandler(404)
def request_not_found(err):
    if SERVE_SPA:
        return app.send_static_file('index.html')
    else:
        return jsonify({'error': str(err)})

...

@app.route('/api/', methods=['GET'])
def index():
    return Response("OK", 200)


if __name__ == "__main__":
    app.run(debug=True, port=8000)
```

The first change we made was to let Flask know where the static files that we want to serve are stored, and then also specify how the URL is formed. This information is passed on to Flask as keyword arguments when we create the Flask object itself:

```
app = Flask(__name__, static_folder=SPA_DIR, static_url_path='/')
```

We also created a flag variable called SERVE_SPA that we use in the request handler for invalid routes, to determine how to respond in that case. If we are going to be using Flask to serve the static files, then we set that variable to True. If we are using something like NGINX to serve our static files, then we should set it to False instead. Normally the Flask server would just return a 404 response if the route was not valid, but if we are also serving the static files for our front-end application, we want to respond with the main **index.html** file instead. This mimics the behavior of what we did in the NGINX configuration for handling the default route, where it allows our application to properly process internal SPA URLs like /books.

The last minor change we need to make to our Flask application is to change the default route we had from / to /api/. If we leave it the way it was, it will just return an "*OK*" response instead of the **index.html** file from our client application.

To run the Flask application, we still want to use the Gunicorn WSGI container to serve the content, but this time let's bind it to port 8080 instead of its default of 8000:

(venv) $ gunicorn --bind 0.0.0.0:8080 appserver:app

On a side note concerning Linux, regular users can't normally bind to ports below 1024. This means that if you want to bind Gunicorn to port 80, you are likely going to have to do a bit of extra work to allow that to happen. What you need to do will be dependent on what Linux distribution you are using and is outside the scope of this book.

41.6 Security

For brevity, we have ignored the use of SSL for the web server configuration in this book. If you are going to be deploying your application on the internet. You should definitely configure your web server to support HTTPS. Both NGINX and Gunicorn support the use of SSL certificates, and with the availability of free certificates with services like Let's Encrypt, there is no reason not to. Details for how to configure the web server or application server to handle HTTPS requests should be available in the documentation for whichever one you decide to use. Note that only the public-facing interface that is receiving the request from the web client will need to be secured with SSL. So if you have NGINX proxying requests for Gunicorn, you only need to set up SSL for NGINX.

Chapter Review:

1. Build the application for production with:
   npm run build

2. Install Gunicorn:
   pip install gunicorn

3. Run Gunicorn:
   gunicorn appserver:app

4. Test Gunicorn:
   http://localhost:8000/api/books

5. Install NGINX:

```
sudo apt-get update
sudo apt-get install nginx
```

6. Configure NGINX:
   /etc/nginx/sites-available/bookapp

7. Update symbolic links for NGINX:

```
sudo ln -s /etc/nginx/sites-available/bookapp /etc/nginx/sites-enabled/bookapp
sudo rm /etc/nginx/sites-enabled/default
```

8. Test NGINX:
   http://localhost/

9. Update source file:
   server/appserver.py

10. Run Gunicorn:
    ```
    gunicorn --bind 0.0.0.0:8080 appserver:app
    ```

11. Open the application:
    http://localhost:8080

12. Add and commit files to git (from the **src/server/** folder):
    ```
    git add .
    git commit -m "Deployment"
    ```

13. Update version:
    ```
    npm version minor
    ```

References:

- Chapter code
  https://github.com/rtp-book/project/tree/step14

- Apache Web Server
  https://httpd.apache.org

- NGINX Web Server
  https://www.nginx.com

- Microsoft IIS Web Server
  https://www.iis.net

- Gunicorn WSGI Server
  https://gunicorn.org
- Phusion Passenger WSGI Server
  https://www.phusionpassenger.com
- uWSGI Application Server
  https://uwsgi-docs.readthedocs.io/en/latest/
- Waitress WSGI Server
  https://docs.pylonsproject.org/projects/waitress/en/stable/
- Apache mod_wsgi Package
  https://modwsgi.readthedocs.io/en/master/
- Let's Encrypt TLS Certificates
  https://letsencrypt.org

Chapter 42 – Conclusion

Thanks to Transcrypt, it is indeed possible to create a modern, reactive front-end web application using 99% pure Python code. And this is without having to bounce between several languages and config files, or having to spend extra time managing your development toolchain. By combining this approach on the front-end with something like Flask or Django for the back end, it is absolutely possible to create true full-stack Python projects.

While the methodology presented in this book was very specific, the concepts presented here should be adaptable to your own coding style and workflow preferences. Also, keep in mind that there are a myriad of JavaScript libraries available for web development not mentioned here that you can now utilize from your Python code. One bit of advice I will give in that regard is: be selective. While there are many well-written JavaScript libraries out there, many more are, shall we say, of dubious quality.

I look forward to seeing continued development on the Transcrypt project. I believe it has the potential to finally give Python developers a viable door into the world of front-end web development, without having to abandon their favorite programming language in the process. I encourage you to visit their website and GitHub repository for more information about the project. The wider the adoption of Transcrypt is, the more it will continue to improve. There is a wealth of additional information in the Transcrypt documentation covering design philosophy, configuration, use, and compilation options that I would encourage you to look into.

I hope this book has given you a new interest in developing front-end web applications with React using Python. What was presented here was just intended to provide you with a baseline process to start from. You will get the most out of it when you start building your own applications using this approach as a reference point, and then eventually incorporating elements of your own workflow that you may be more comfortable with.

Keep learning and happy coding!

References:

- Finished Project code
  https://github.com/rtp-book/project
- Transcrypt Project Website
  https://www.transcrypt.org/
- Transcrypt GitHub Repository
  https://github.com/QQuick/Transcrypt
- Transcrypt Documentation
  https://www.transcrypt.org/docs/html/index.html

Index

A

Access-Control-Allow-Origin
242
activate
7, 204
addEventListener
26, 209, 352
alert
60, 63-65, 68-70
align
32, 33, 315
alignItems
220, 227
anchorEl
272
Angular
4
annotations (see: types)
anonymous function
99, 105
Apache
374, 375, 377
application server
148, 373-75, 379
apt-get
376
ARIA, Accessible Rich Internet Applications
229
ariaHideApp
229
Array
99

asdict
173
async
162-64
asynchronous
29, 155, 163, 164
autoFocus
138, 159, 338
await
162-64

B

babel (see: polyfill)
backgroundColor
141, 144
Bash
55
bgcolor
142, 145
blueprint
242-44
bootstrap
124, 126, 127
build
2, 5, 52, 54-56, 62, 152, 192, 207, 213
built-ins
173, 174
bin
174
hex
174
oct
174

bundler
    5, 48, 106, 129, 148, 150

C

cache
    151, 252
.cache (folder)
    80, 203, 213
Cache-Control
    242
callback
    73, 155, 161, 162, 255, 258
camelCase
    121
certificates
    381
child
    28, 29, 34, 35, 65, 166
chrome extension
    193-95
class-based component
    4, 35, 95, 97, 98
classes, CSS
    116, 117, 124, 126, 127, 129, 132, 141, 142
className
    116, 141
CLI, Command Line Interface
    8, 15, 42, 376
closure
    24, 82, 262
cmd
    55
color
    115, 121-23
colSpan
    315
compile
    2, 24, 50, 178
compiler directive (see: __pragma__)

component
    4, 28, 29, 34, 35, 72, 78, 89, 96, 97
component lifecycle methods
    97
  componentDidMount
    97
  componentDidUpdate
    97
  componentWillUnmount
    97
component tree
    34, 104, 166, 168, 171, 194
composition
    35, 78, 140, 141
comprehensions
    16, 86, 89, 99, 100, 296
confirm
    209, 211
console
    152, 156, 189, 209
  error
    20, 156, 157, 209
  log
    19, 20, 156, 209
console, developer
    11, 19, 28, 65, 98, 156, 162, 187, 188, 213
constructor
    91, 95, 96, 352
container
    127, 274
container, WSGI
    373-75, 380
Content-Type
    254, 353
context
    29, 166, 168, 169, 171, 172, 304, 307
contrastText
    135, 136, 143, 219
CORS, Cross-Origin Resource Sharing
    27, 38, 148, 154

CPython
  10, 11, 178
createContext
  168, 171
createElement
  28, 30, 32, 33, 39, 40, 63, 72, 73, 78, 104, 105
CRUD
  198
currentTarget
  269, 288

D

dataclasses
  173
deactivate
  7, 204, 235, 252, 375
Debug CSS
  195
decomposition
  86, 270, 297
deepcopy
  103, 176, 189, 207
default
  54, 106, 107, 134, 220, 227
delete
  46, 55
dependency
  3, 39, 42, 48, 65, 150, 174, 193, 204
deploy
  373
destructure
  229, 348
development cycle
  11
dev-server
  151, 152
disabled
  226, 272, 287, 289

dispatchEvent
  209, 354
display
  129, 208, 220, 221
dist (folder)
  53-56, 80
document
  8-10, 15, 16, 24, 27, 97
DOM, Document Object Model
  10, 28, 32, 33, 39, 58, 63, 65, 70-72, 90, 259
DOMContentLoaded
  26, 352
dstat
  178

E

element, HTML
  22, 28, 29, 32-34, 65, 116, 121
  anchor
    222
  button
    8, 22, 24, 64, 69, 81, 115, 122-24, 127
  checkbox
    60
  div
    28, 30, 63, 76, 132, 208, 317, 342
  form
    33, 75-78, 127
  hr
    230, 342
  img
    108, 230
  input
    60, 62-64, 76, 84, 119, 317
  label
    63, 84, 119, 121
  li
    69, 70, 81, 82

ol
69, 85, 127, 334
span
137
ul
127
element tree
33, 34, 121, 124, 222
elevation
138, 220
ellipsis
260, 262
encodeURIComponent
209, 254
enqueueSnackbar
287
errorhandler
242
error object
157
ES5
106, 107
ES6
106, 163
eval
174
event handler
10, 22, 24, 60, 63, 64, 69, 77, 81, 272, 362
event listener
27, 39, 352, 356
event object
64, 77, 231
exception
238, 254, 353, 354
exec
174
exports
107
Express.js
150, 151, 205

F

favicon
208, 211
fetch
155-57, 161, 163, 253, 255, 258
fetchall
238
filter
92, 100, 150, 249
Flask
2, 148, 150, 200, 204, 235, 375, 376, 378-80
flask-login
204, 242
flexbox
220-22, 342
flexDirection
337, 338
flexItem
338
font-family
121
foreign key
236
Fragment
210, 272, 296, 316
full-stack
2, 181, 384
fullWidth
158, 166, 170, 283
functional
2, 4, 5, 35, 63, 89, 101
functional component
4, 28, 33, 35, 71, 78, 95, 97, 99

G

GA4
185

Index | 389

GA Debug
194
gaOptions
187
generator expression
294
getElementById
8, 26, 209
git
55, 180-82, 201, 203
.gitignore
203, 204
Google Analytics
184, 185, 187-91, 194, 196, 225, 255, 264, 359
grid
124, 127
Gunicorn
2, 375, 376, 381

H

hamburger menu
270
hover
141, 142, 193
href
222, 231, 363
HTML5
28, 31
htmlFor
63
http.server
9, 52
http-proxy-middleware
150, 152, 205
HTTP Request
54, 152, 155, 188, 255, 259, 281, 373
  DELETE
    244, 248, 249, 311, 334

  GET
    244, 248, 255, 277, 353
  POST
    244, 248, 249, 277, 286, 311, 334
HTTP Response
156, 157, 163, 164, 242, 259, 287
200 OK
157, 164, 205, 242, 281, 380
401 Unauthorized
242, 281, 287, 355, 362
404 Not Found
378, 380

I

IDE
11, 39, 55, 203, 204
IIS
374, 375, 377
image
108, 193, 201
immutable
29, 69, 73, 89, 123, 172, 175, 176
innerHTML
8, 29, 32, 208
INSERT
239, 240, 245, 247, 248, 311
install
7, 9, 41, 42, 48, 55, 129, 148, 192, 204, 205, 207, 375-77
interpreter (see: CPython)
isDirty
334, 343

J

Java
9
JavaScript object
10, 20, 101, 102, 123, 176, 177, 352

Jinja
 4
jQuery
 3, 22, 24
JSON
 148-50, 157, 164, 248, 249, 376

K

keepMounted
 271, 288
keypress
 318

L

lambda
 81, 82, 85, 89, 97, 99, 100, 105, 232, 299
lifting state
 35
linter
 4, 10, 39, 45, 175, 208
list comprehension
 86, 99, 100, 296
Logger
 49, 206
LoginManager
 241

M

map
 99, 100
margin
 121, 123, 127, 132, 136, 137, 139, 195, 222
material design
 129, 146
Materialize CSS Framework
 129
Material-UI
 2, 3, 107, 129, 130, 132-37, 140, 141, 207
Box
 130, 132, 133, 317
Button
 107, 130, 133, 136, 141, 229
CircularProgress
 218, 258
colors
 134, 135
Container
 134, 139, 255
createMuiTheme
 135, 220
Divider
 218, 230, 342
FormControl
 218
FormLabel
 218
IconButton
 217, 229, 259
 AddIcon
  217, 278, 346
 CloseIcon
  217, 229
Input
 130, 131, 133, 134, 137, 317
InputLabel
 130, 133, 137, 139
Link
 218, 222, 230, 231, 272, 356, 362
makeStyles
 141-44
MenuIcon
 217
MenuItem
 218, 272, 301
Paper
 134, 139
RadioGroup
 218, 331

Index | 391

styled
    122, 123, 140-43, 221, 222
Table
    218, 255, 261
TableBody
    218, 261, 296
TableCell
    218, 262, 297
TableContainer
    218
TableFooter
    218
TableHead
    218
TableRow
    218, 262, 296, 297, 317, 348
TextField
    134, 136, 137, 139, 160, 161, 324
    InputLabelProps
        137
    InputProps
        137
    select
        157, 160, 161, 292, 324
    SelectProps
        160
ThemeProvider
    134, 139, 140, 281
Toolbar
    217
Tooltip
    218, 262, 346
Math
    16
maxHeight
    261
maxSnack
    280, 281
maxWidth
    138, 229

meta
    208
Microsoft IIS (see: IIS)
middleware
    150, 151, 252
minification
    3, 9, 14, 55, 373
minWidth
    141, 142
Modal
    200, 225-29, 232, 283, 287, 294
ModuleNotFoundError
    235
Mui
    130, 133, 136
    MuiButton
        135, 136
    MuiDivider
        219
    MuiPaper
        220
    MuiTable
        220
    MuiTableCell
        220
    MuiTextField
        135-37
    multiline
        341
MuiLink
    352, 355, 356
MVC
    32

N

named
    54, 99, 106, 107, 116
namespace
    10, 22, 27, 45, 46, 106, 108, 209, 227, 356

__new__
  209, 252, 351-54
NGINX
  2, 374-78, 380, 381
no-cache
  52, 207
NODE_ENV
  54, 56
node_modules (folder)
  42-44, 49, 107, 204, 206, 277
Node.js
  41, 42, 51, 55, 106, 150-52, 203, 205
no-hmr
  207, 215
nomin
  9, 14, 49
noscript
  208
no-source-maps
  54, 152, 207
Notistack
  277, 278
npm, Node Package Manager
  2, 5, 41, 42, 48, 55, 58, 180, 181
npm registry
  41, 42
npx
  48, 52
numpy (see: numscrypt)
numscrypt
  16, 173

O

onChange
  60, 63, 64, 317, 324, 334
onClick
  10, 22, 24, 69, 81, 99, 272, 356, 362
onClose
  229, 230, 232, 257, 283, 334, 370

onDoubleClick
  314
onKeyPress
  313
onRequestClose
  229, 232
onSubmit
  75, 76
overflow
  260, 262
overlay
  227, 228
overrides
  135, 136, 220

P

package.json
  42, 48, 49, 54, 108, 152, 180, 181
padding
  132, 195, 222
palette
  135, 137, 220
Parcel
  2, 5, 48, 49, 51-55, 65, 148, 150-52, 205, 206
parcel-bundler
  48, 205
parcel-plugin-bundle-visualiser
  192, 205
parcel-plugin-transcrypt
  48-50, 205, 206
PascalCase
  28, 72, 105
pathRewrite
  151
Phusion Passenger
  375
PIP
  3, 5, 41

plug-ins
  49, 151, 206
polyfill
  163, 207
popstate
  352, 356
PopStateEvent
  209, 354, 356
port
  9, 52, 148, 151-53, 253, 376-78, 381
Postman
  244
__pragma__
  24, 39, 46, 104, 175
  alias
    23, 24
  js
    45, 46
  jsiter
    353
  kwargs
    174, 175
  nokwargs
    175, 254
  noskip
    37, 39, 45, 209, 210
  notconv
    178
  skip
    39, 45, 209, 210
  tconv
    178
  xtrans
    104
preventDefault
  77, 231
primary
  127, 134, 135
print
  11, 19, 20, 255, 301

promise
  155-57, 162-64
  catch
    156, 157, 164
  then
    155-57
Provider
  171, 305
proxy server
  148, 150-52, 207, 252, 253, 265, 374, 378
pseudo-class
  140, 142, 144
PyPI, Python Package Index
  41
pyreact
  35
Python
  1-5, 7-11, 16
Python package
  208, 212, 219, 330

Q

querystring
  352, 355, 356, 359, 366, 368

R

radix
  174
raise
  254, 353-55
random
  14-16
React
  2, 4, 26, 32, 33, 35
React Developer Tools
  194
ReactDOM
  27, 28, 32, 33, 42, 43, 45, 46

ReactGA
   184-90, 207
   event
      186, 188, 189, 253
   modalview
      188
   pageview
      358
   timing
      189, 190, 255
react-modal
   226
ready
   24, 152
render
   26-28, 32, 33, 39, 95, 98, 351, 352, 356
require
   49, 51, 106-8, 225, 227, 278
REST
   2, 150, 199, 235, 240, 242, 244, 248, 249, 253, 281, 287, 311, 334, 343
RESTful
   150, 200
reverse-proxy (see: proxy server)
route
   152, 242, 244, 274, 281, 286, 358, 378, 380
router
   274, 358
routing
   151, 200, 273, 274, 351, 356
run
   55, 152, 162, 192

S

save
   277
save-dev
   48, 150, 192, 205

scope
   10, 46, 86, 106, 366
script (npm)
   54, 55, 151, 152, 181, 182, 252, 373
script-shell (see: Bash)
script tag
   5, 10, 24, 53, 65
secondary
   134, 135
selector
   116, 135
semver
   180, 181
session
   199, 242, 244, 277, 278, 280, 281, 362
setAttribute
   32
Single Page Application
   200, 374, 378, 380
sites-available
   377, 378
sites-enabled
   378
siteSpeedSampleRate
   187
sleep
   173, 258
snackbar
   200, 277, 281, 286, 287, 294, 311, 334, 355
SnackbarProvider
   278, 281, 286
sourcemap
   3, 14, 18, 20, 54, 55
SPA (see: Single Page Application)
spaRedirect
   351, 355, 356, 359, 362, 366, 368, 370
Spread
   102, 103
SQL
   235, 239, 240, 248

SQLite
199, 200, 235, 244, 292
sqlite3 (see: SQLite)
SSL
381
standard library
173, 174, 178, 200, 235
   cmath
173
   datetime
173, 241
   itertools
173
   logging
173
   math
173
   random
173
   re
173
   time
173, 189
   turtle
173
   warnings
173
state
4, 29, 32, 35, 60, 127, 175, 283, 342, 370
stickyHeader
220, 296
stringify
209, 254
stub
39, 45, 208-10
style
28, 116, 119, 121-24, 126, 129, 132, 136, 139-42
stylesheet
115, 116, 119, 121, 124, 136

submit
60, 64, 76, 77, 84
synchronous
155, 163, 164

T

table
236, 238, 244, 248, 249
tag
28, 105
target
64
__target__ (folder)
8, 15, 16, 80, 89, 213
ternary expression
84, 85, 89, 101, 119, 160, 258, 262
textContent
270, 288
textOverflow
260, 262
timedelta
241, 379
title
93, 96, 97, 112
TLS (see: SSL)
Transcrypt
2-4, 7-11, 48, 49, 173-75
transcrypt plug-in (see: parcel-plugin-transcrypt)
transformOrigin
271, 272
transpile
3-5, 8, 11, 39, 48, 104, 174, 177
truthiness
85, 177, 178
types
178
Typography
130, 132, 139, 222

U

update
101, 103
UPDATE
237, 245, 247, 248
URLSearchParams
209, 351, 352
useContext
168, 171, 307, 308
useEffect
97, 98, 112, 161, 162, 258, 259, 287, 328, 334, 362, 366
UserMixin
243
useSnackbar
278
useState
29, 39, 69, 96
useStyle
141, 142, 144
useTheme
134, 139
uwsgi
375

V

venv (see: virtual environment)
version
180-82, 201
  major
  42, 180
  minor
  180
  patch
  180, 223, 233
virtual environment
7, 8, 14, 49, 204, 205, 235

W

W3C
28
Waitress
375
web browser console (see: console, developer)
Webpack
5, 48
web server
9, 54, 148, 150-52, 373, 375-77, 379, 381
werkzeug
243, 374
wget
211, 225
whiteSpace
260, 262
worker
376
WSGI
373-76, 380

X

XHR
162
XML
103, 200

Y

yum
376, 377

Z

Zen of Python
5

Made in the USA
Las Vegas, NV
06 November 2021